D1021928

Culture and Customs
of Uganda

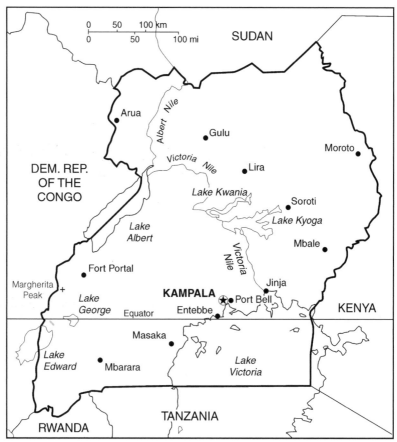

Uganda's international boundaries and major towns. Cartography by Book-comp, Inc.

Culture and Customs of Uganda

✎∘✎

KEFA M. OTISO

Culture and Customs of Africa
Toyin Falola, Series Editor

GREENWOOD PRESS
Westport, Connecticut • London

Library of Congress Cataloging-in-Publication Data

Otiso, Kefa M.
   Culture and customs of Uganda / Kefa M. Otiso.
      p. cm. — (Culture and customs of Africa, ISSN 1530–8367)
   Includes bibliographical references and index.
   ISBN 0–313–33148–0
   1. Uganda—Civilization. 2. Uganda—Social life and customs. I. Title. II. Series.
   DT433.24.C85 2006
   967.61—dc22   2006001177

British Library Cataloguing in Publication Data is available.

Copyright © 2006 by Kefa M. Otiso

All rights reserved. No portion of this book may be
reproduced, by any process or technique, without the
express written consent of the publisher.

Library of Congress Catalog Card Number: 2006001177
ISBN: 0–313–33148–0
ISSN: 1530–8367

First published in 2006

Greenwood Press, 88 Post Road West, Westport, CT 06881
An imprint of Greenwood Publishing Group, Inc.
www.greenwood.com

Printed in the United States of America

The paper used in this book complies with the
Permanent Paper Standard issued by the National
Information Standards Organization (Z39.48–1984).

10 9 8 7 6 5 4 3 2 1

To all who have given up their utmost for Uganda;
your sacrifice is not in vain.

Contents

Series Foreword

Africa is a vast continent, the second largest, after Asia. It is four times the size of the United States, excluding Alaska. It is the cradle of human civilization. A diverse continent, Africa has more than fifty countries with a population of over 700 million people who speak over 1,000 languages. Ecological and cultural differences vary from one region to another. As an old continent, Africa is one of the richest in culture and customs, and its contributions to world civilization are impressive indeed.

Africans regard culture as essential to their lives and future development. Culture embodies their philosophy, worldview, behavior patterns, arts, and institutions. The books in this series intend to capture the comprehensiveness of African culture and customs, dwelling on such important aspects as religion, worldview, literature, media, art, housing, architecture, cuisine, traditional dress, gender, marriage, family, lifestyles, social customs, music, and dance.

The uses and definitions of "culture" vary, reflecting its prestigious association with civilization and social status, its restriction to attitude and behavior, its globalization, and the debates surrounding issues of tradition, modernity, and postmodernity. The participating authors have chosen a comprehensive meaning of culture while not ignoring the alternative uses of the term.

Each volume in the series focuses on a single country, and the format is uniform. The first chapter presents a historical overview, in addition to information on geography, economy, and politics. Each volume then proceeds to examine the various aspects of culture and customs. The series highlights the mechanisms for the transmission of tradition and culture across generations: the significance of orality, traditions, kinship rites, and family property distribution; the rise of print culture; and the impact of educational institutions. The series also explores the intersections between local, regional, national, and global bases for identity and social relations. While the volumes are organized nationally, they pay attention to ethnicity and language groups and the links between Africa and the wider world.

The books in the series capture the elements of continuity and change in culture and customs. Custom is not represented as static or as a museum artifact, but as a dynamic phenomenon. Furthermore, the authors recognize the current challenges to traditional wisdom, which include gender relations; the negotiation of local identities in relation to the state; the significance of struggles for power at national and local levels and their impact on cultural traditions and community-based forms of authority; and the tensions between agrarian and industrial/manufacturing/oil-based economic modes of production.

Africa is a continent of great changes, instigated mainly by Africans but also through influences from other continents. The rise of youth culture, the penetration of the global media, and the challenges to generational stability are some of the components of modern changes explored in the series. The ways in which traditional (non-Western and nonimitative) African cultural forms continue to survive and thrive, that is, how they have taken advantage of the market system to enhance their influence and reproductions also receive attention.

Through the books in this series, readers can see their own cultures in a different perspective, understand the habits of Africans, and educate themselves about the customs and cultures of other countries and people. The hope is that the readers will come to respect the cultures of others and see them not as inferior or superior to theirs, but merely as different. Africa has always been important to Europe and the United States, essentially as a source of labor, raw materials, and markets. Blacks are in Europe and the Americas as part of the African diaspora, a migration that took place primarily due to the slave trade. Recent African migrants increasingly swell their number and visibility. It is important to understand the history of the diaspora and the newer migrants, as well as the roots of the culture and customs of the places from where they come. It is equally important to understand others in order to be able to interact successfully in a world that keeps shrinking. The accessible nature of the books in this series will contribute to this understanding and enhance the quality of human interaction in a new millennium.

Toyin Falola
Frances Higginbothom, Nalle Centennial Professor in History
The University of Texas at Austin

Preface

Uganda is in East Africa and has a diverse cultural base of 19 major indigenous groups and a scattering of nonnative people groups from Europe and Asia. The country is named after the Baganda people who have dominated its cultural, political, social, and economic life since the days of the powerful eighteenth-century Buganda Kingdom. Because of kingdom's influence, British colonialists focused on the kingdom from the outset and eventually ruled the country through it, to the vexation of the other native kingdoms and people groups. Thus, the seeds of Uganda's postcolonial political instability in the first quarter-century of independence were sown.

As my objective is to introduce Uganda to new readers, I focus on the main features of its geography, culture, politics, and economy with the help of a few illustrative examples. Because of my own travel and familiarity with southern Uganda and the dearth of literature on most Ugandan communities (largely caused by the country's tragic political history in the 1960–86 period), I mostly use illustrative material from the south and from the few people groups (e.g., the Baganda and Banyoro) whose socioeconomic and cultural life is well documented. I hope, however, that others will use the return of relative political order to most of Uganda to help enrich our knowledge of the country.

Acknowledgments

As with a child, it takes a village to produce a book. It began when Toyin Falola insisted that I write the book, despite my attempts to disqualify myself because of other commitments. Having agreed to write it, I soon understood the gravity of the challenge when confronted with the serious shortage of reference material on Uganda in the United States. Thanks to Rose Bosire and Martin Ongeri, I was able to secure a reasonable reference library straight from East Africa. I also gained additional critical insight about various aspects of Ugandan culture and socioeconomic conditions from my interviews with Mr. and Mrs. Emmanuel Twesigye and Jotham Nyamari.

I am indebted to Emmanuel Twesigye (Ohio Wesleyan University) and Toyin Falola (University of Texas at Austin) for invaluable feedback on the initial draft of this book. Ken Goyer (AidUganda), Earl Scott (University of Minnesota), and Emmanuel Twesigye provided me with most of the pictures that appear in this volume.

Wendi Schnaufer, my editor at Greenwood Press, provided priceless expert guidance and follow-up along the way. Without her and the production staff at Apex Publishing, the book would simply not have been possible.

My family, Jackline and Jojo, graciously let me have uninterrupted writing forays at the office and at home and somehow found it in them to encourage me. The eternal faith of my parents, Hezron and Priscilla Otiso, in me has been a source of great encouragement in times of need. My Cornerstone spiritual family provided me with invaluable support, but only God could have made the entire project possible. I am also very appreciative of Bowling Green State University's congenial work base and material support.

To the great multitude of helpers that I am unaware of and unable to acknowledge, especially the pen warriors who have gone before me, thanks.

To the people of the great and beautiful country of Uganda, you really are the "Pearl of Africa."

Chronology

1500s	Nilotic migrants from contemporary southeastern Sudan establish the Bito dynasties of Buganda, Bunyoro, and Ankole.
1700s	Buganda starts to gain territory from Bunyoro.
1800	Buganda's territory around Lake Victoria stretches from the Nile to the Kagera River.
1840	Buganda initiates trade with Muslim traders from the Indian Ocean island of Zanzibar, exchanging its ivory and slaves for firearms, cloth, and beads.
1840–60	Egyptian government officials and European missionaries and explorers advance toward Uganda, reaching present-day West Nile area of Uganda between 1841 and 1842. This area, later nicknamed the "Lado Enclave" becomes a slave-trading center between 1842 and 1882.
1852	Kabaka (King) Mutesa I ascends to the throne of Buganda. He reigns until 1884.
1862	Beginning of British influence in Buganda as British explorer John Hanning Speke (1827–1864) becomes the first European to reach the source of

the Nile at Jinja. Speke and James Augustus Grant (1827–1892) become the first Europeans to reach Buganda.

1864   Sir Samuel Baker (1821–1893) and his wife Florence become the first Europeans to reach Lake Albert (Bunyoro area), having followed the Nile upstream from Egypt. Suspecting the Bakers to be Egyptian spies, the Kabarega of Bunyoro does not receive them well.

1870   Omukama Kabarega ascends to the throne of Bunyoro.

1872   Baker annexes Bunyoro for the Egyptian Sudan government. In subsequent years, Baker and Emin Pasha (1840–1892) try to use Sudanese Nubian soldiers to annex the whole of present-day Uganda, but this attempt is aborted in the 1880s because of the Mahdist revolt in Sudan and the British decision to use their Zanzibar envoy's contacts with Kabaka Mutesa I to open the area from the east. But the Sudanese Nubian soldiers are retained in Uganda.

1875   King Mutesa I invites Irish American explorer Sir Henry Morton Stanley (1841–1904) to send British Anglican missionaries to Buganda. By this time, Zanzibar Muslims are actively trying to Islamize Buganda.

1877   British missionaries from the Church Missionary Society arrive in Buganda and Emin Pasha starts to govern the Lado Enclave.

1879   French Roman Catholics initiate the White Fathers of Algeria mission in Buganda. Tripartite religious rivalry between the Protestants, Catholics, and Muslims commences. Meanwhile, traditional Ganda religious practices are also common in the court.

1884   Kabaka Mutesa I dies and is succeeded by his son Mwanga (reigned 1884–86, 1889–97). Religious disputes between Protestants, Catholics, and Muslims break out.

1885	Kabaka Mwanga orders the torture and murder of Bishop James Hannington (1847–1885) and many local Christians (since known as the Uganda martyrs). This creates a window for a period of concerted Islamization that includes forced circumcision. The crisis engulfs diverse German, French, and British interests. The Mahdi capture Khartoum and kill General Charles Gordon (1833–1885).
1886	Kabaka Mwanga attempts to end growing influence of foreign religions in Buganda. But a Protestant, Catholic, and Muslim alliance forces him out of power, and a new Kabaka is installed. However, when the new Kabaka turns on the Christians, they rally behind their former enemy Mwanga and help him recover the throne in 1889. From then on, he is a pawn in the hands of the Christians.
1889	Stanley and Emin Pasha leave the Lado Enclave on their way to the East African coast. The enclave goes without government for the next decade until Britain grants it to King Leopold II of Belgium in 1894 for life, and he administers it as part of the Congo Free State (present-day Democratic Republic of the Congo) from 1897.
1890	Britain and Germany sign a treaty giving Britain rights to what is to become Uganda. Captain Frederick Lugard (1858–1945), representative of the Imperial British East Africa Company (IBEA), arrives to secure British interests. He becomes "Uganda's" first colonial military administrator.
1891	Lugard inherits about 8,000 of Samuel Baker's and Emin Pasha's Sudanese Nubian soldiers, women, children, and slaves. He defeats some Muslim factions, and establishes a unified army in barracks throughout contemporary central Uganda. Sporadic religious and civil wars continue.
1892	Lugard recruits 400 more Sudanese Nubian soldiers to help maintain stability and extends IBEA's control to southern Uganda. Catholic-Protestant war

erupts, and Lugard helps the Protestants to defeat their French Catholic competitors in Buganda.

1893	British replace the IBEA with a protectorate administration and Sir Gerald Herbert Portal (1858–1945) becomes the first colonial commissioner of the Buganda (Uganda) Protectorate. Colonel Henry Edward Colvile (1852–1907) declares war on Bunyoro and its Kabarega.
1894	Buganda (Uganda) is formally declared a British Protectorate, and this is ratified in the Buganda Agreement of 1900.
1895	British establish a separate protectorate over contemporary Kenya. Colonel Colvile initiates the Uganda Rifles.
1896	British expand the Uganda Protectorate to include Busoga, Bunyoro, Toro, and Ankole; minor extensions take place between 1899 and 1901.
1897	Kabaka Mwanga of Buganda escapes from the capital to avoid imminent British capture; his son, Daudi Chwa, aged 4 years, becomes Kabaka and rules with the aid of regents until 1914. He then reigns on his own until 1942. Uganda mutiny (revolt of Sudanese soldiers) commences and is eventually ended in 1898, with aid of Indian troops. Ongoing revolt in various parts of the country.
1899	Kabaka Mwanga of Buganda and Kabarega of Bunyoro are captured and sent into exile in the Indian Ocean islands of Seychelles. Because the Kabarega had caused the British the most trouble, Bunyoro's territories are ceded to Buganda, becoming the controversial "Lost Counties" of the 1960s. Sir Harry Hamilton Johnston (1858–1927) becomes Commissioner of the Uganda Protectorate.
1900	Buganda-British agreement (commonly known as the Uganda Agreement) signed, making Buganda an autonomous constitutional monarchy controlled primarily by Protestant chiefs.

1901	Construction of the Uganda railway starts in the Indian Ocean coastal town of Mombasa.
1902	Railway reaches Lake Victoria town of Kisumu. Subsequent extensions in 1912, 1928, 1949, 1957, and even 1960s enable railway to reach the center, north, and west of Uganda. The eastern province of Uganda (now the territory consisting of the Mau Plateau, the Rift Valley, and the Eastern escarpment) is transferred to Kenya (in the 1970s, Idi Amin (1928–2003) attempts to regain this territory, nearly sparking a war with Kenya). Uganda Rifles unites with the King's African Rifles; together they later become the Uganda army.
1904	Commercial cotton cultivation is initiated and significantly expanded until the 1930s.
1905	British Colonial Office takes over administration of Uganda from the Foreign Office.
1909	King Leopold II of Belgium dies and in 1910, the "Lado Enclave" is transferred to the Sudanese government.
1914	Lado Enclave (West Nile District) reverts to Uganda in exchange for Gondokoro and Nimule districts, effectively establishing Uganda's boundaries, save for the 1926 transfer of Rudolph Province to Kenya and some land to the Sudan.
1914–18	World War I breaks out. A total of 30,000 Ugandans in the King's African Rifles (KAR) and 178,000 carriers are involved, substantially slowing down economic growth for the next few decades.
1920	Coffee and sugar are introduced as alternative cash crops. First sugar refinery in Uganda opens in 1924.
1921	Uganda gains an executive council (cabinet) and a legislative council (parliament) to help the governor run the country. No Africans are admitted to the legislative council until 1945. Makerere technical college opens.

1939–45	World War II involves 77,000 Ugandan soldiers.
1945–53	High world demand, and prices, for coffee and cotton enable colonial administration to embark on major economic rehabilitation of country; expanded local government prepares many Ugandans for postcolonial government management.
1947	East African High Commission is initiated.
1950	Makerere College becomes the Makerere University College of East Africa, offering University of London degrees. It becomes a constituent college of the University of East Africa in 1963 and an independent university in 1970.
1952–59	Kenya's Mau Mau rebellion breaks out, and the Uganda Rifles is deployed in Kenya against the Mau Mau. Idi Amin's mettle becomes evident. He acquires his nickname "Dada" for cunningly telling a senior British officer, on being confronted about his amorous escapades, that the woman he is caught with is his elder "sister" or *dada*.
1953	Legislative council is made more representative. Political parties emerge. Kabaka Mutesa II (1924–1969) is deported for opposing integration of Buganda into Uganda and the imminent East African Federation. Instead, the Kabaka demands Buganda's independence and Governor Andrew Benjamin Cohen (1909–1968) deports him to Britain for two years, triggering a state of emergency in Buganda.
1955	Kabaka Mutesa II returns from exile under a compromise agreement. Southern Sudanese Nubian soldiers mutiny.
1957	East Africa High Commission assumes defense responsibility for East Africa.
1958	Legislative elections take place throughout Uganda, but Buganda is not represented in the legislative council because it declines to participate in the elections. Uganda is given internal self-government.

1959	National census reveals a population of 6.5 million. Influx of Rwandan refugees after intertribal clashes.
1960	Legislative council expands to make it more representative; executive council becomes council of ministers; Belgian refugees flow in from the Democratic Republic of the Congo after independence.
1961	Predominantly Catholic Democratic Party wins national elections, and Benedicto Kiwanuka becomes Uganda's first chief minister (prime minister); Buganda successfully presses for federal status at London constitutional conference.
1962	Uganda gains independence with Milton Obote as prime minister; Buganda retains substantial autonomy.
1963	Kabaka Mutesa II becomes president of Uganda (a titular head of state, and commander in chief of the armed forces).
1964	African troops at Jinja mutiny over poor working conditions; British troops are used to crush the mutiny but rapid promotion of African officers ensues (notably that of Idi Amin who becomes deputy army commander and Brigadier Shaban Opolot who becomes army commander); Milton Obote's ruling alliance of the Uganda People's Party and Kabaka Yekka splinters; referendum in Bunyoro over the "Lost Counties."
1966	Buganda attempts to secede from Uganda; Milton Obote (the Prime Minister) suspends 1962 constitution, ends Buganda's autonomy, and orders army to invade Kabaka's palace. Kabaka Mutesa II goes into exile in London for the second time. Idi Amin replaces Brigadier Shaban Opolot as army commander.
1967	New republican constitution gives Milton Obote wide-ranging executive powers, ends traditional monarchies, and breaks Buganda into four smaller administrative districts.

1968	Idi Amin promoted to major general.
1969	Obote publishes his socialist manifesto, *The Common Man's Charter*. Kabaka Mutesa II dies in exile.
1970	Amin suspected in the murder of his deputy Brigadier Pierino Okoya (second highest-ranking army officer) and Okoya's wife, Anna; Obote strips Amin of most of his powers.
1971	Amin leads a coup d'etat that topples Milton Obote while he is attending a commonwealth conference of heads of state. Kabaka Mutesa II's remains are buried near Kampala. Civilians and Ugandan officials begin to disappear on Amin's orders. Army terrorizes country.
1972	Amin orders nearly 60,000 Asian non-Ugandan citizens out of the country in order to wrestle control of the economy from them and bestow it on locals. Fifty-eight European missionaries are expelled. Ugandan exile forces in Tanzania unsuccessfully invade Uganda in an attempt to dislodge Amin from power. Amin cuts diplomatic relations with Israel and aligns himself with Palestinians and other anti-Israeli groups.
1972–73	Drastic decline in Uganda's agricultural production. Border clashes with Tanzania.
1976	Amin claims parts of Kenya that were once part of Uganda until the early 1900s and declares himself life president of Uganda. He allows hijacked Air France jet full of Israelis to land at Entebbe; Israelis storm the airport and rescue all but one of the hostages.
1978	Amin's Uganda invades Tanzania and occupies Kagera region.
1979	Tanzania counterinvades Uganda with the help of the Uganda National Liberation Front (UNLF)—an umbrella organization of Ugandan exile anti-Amin forces, including Yoweri Museveni. Amin is defeated and flees into exile in Saudi Arabia. Yusufu

Lule becomes president but is soon replaced by Godfrey Binaisa.

1980   Army overthrows Binaisa, and Milton Obote becomes president for a second time after controversial elections.

1981   Yoweri Museveni launches guerilla war against Obote.

1985   Tito Okello replaces Obote after he is overthrown by the military. Peace talks between Museveni's National Resistance Army (NRA) and Military Council are held in Nairobi and a peace accord is signed in December.

1986   Yoweri Museveni's National Resistance Army overthrows Military Council. Museveni becomes president.

1993   Museveni reinstates traditional kingdoms but denies them political power.

1995   New constitution that allows for the formation of political parties but bans their political activity is enacted.

1996   Museveni wins Uganda's first direct presidential election.

1997–98   Ugandan troops help install Laurent Kabila after helping to depose Mobutu Sese Seko of the Democratic Republic of the Congo (formerly Zaire). Later, Ugandan troops try to overthrow Kabila.

2000   Nationwide referendum favors Museveni's no-party political system over multiparty politics.

2001   Ugandan and Rwandese troops oppose each other in the Democratic Republic of the Congo civil war and the two former allies become enemies; Museveni wins another presidential term in office by a wide margin; Dr. Kizza Besigye, his main challenger, flees into exile.

2003   Idi Amin dies in exile in Saudi Arabia and is buried there.

2005

Milton Obote dies in exile and is buried in Uganda. Dr. Kizza Besigye, leader of an opposition political party and losing contender in the 2001 presidential elections, returns to Uganda from exile to run against Museveni in the February 2006 parliamentary and presidential elections. Soon after, he is arrested and charged with rape and treason. There is a riot in Kampala in which one person is killed and a lot of property damaged. President Museveni seeks a third term in office amidst international protest.

2006

The first multiparty parliamentary and presidential elections in Uganda in a quarter-century are held with Museveni and Besigye as the main presidential contenders. Museveni wins by a large margin.

1

Introduction

Since Uganda's independence from Great Britain in 1962, the East African country has been ravaged by political turmoil and wars that, combined with the HIV/AIDS epidemic, have significantly decreased its population and severely disrupted its socioeconomic life. Many factors have contributed to the country's sociopolitical instability, including its cultural diversity, successive military regimes, and mismanagement of its internal affairs. Since current President Yoweri Museveni came to power in 1986, the country has experienced relative social and political stability and is in the process of rebuilding and democratizing its socioeconomic institutions. However, open hostilities remain in the northern part of the country. Uganda's political and commercial center is the city of Kampala and its second most important commercial center is the city of Jinja, located on the shores of Lake Victoria at the source of the River Nile.[1]

LAND

Uganda's 236,040-square-kilometer territory consists of 36,330 square kilometers of water and 199,710 square kilometers of land. Its north-south and east-west expanses are approximately 550 kilometers (330 miles) and 480 kilometers (300 miles), respectively. Uganda is bordered by five countries: Kenya, Sudan, the Democratic Republic of the Congo (formerly Zaire), Rwanda, and Tanzania.

Uganda's territory is divided by the Equator into two unequal parts: a much larger northern part and a smaller southern half. The country extends from 4° north to 1° south and from 29° east to 35° east. Much of the country consists of a high plateau that varies in elevation between 1,067 and 1,372 meters (3,500 and 4,500 feet) above sea level and is flanked by major mountains. On the east is Mount Elgon (4,321 meters or 14,178 feet), and to the southwest are the volcanic Ruwenzori Mountains that straddle the border with the Democratic Republic of the Congo. At an elevation of 5,113 meters (16,774 feet), Mount Stanley's Margherita Peak, which is part of the Ruwenzori mountain range, is Uganda's highest point. Conversely, Lake Albert, which lies at 621 meters (2,037 feet) above sea level, is the lowest point in the country.

The country's equatorial location and high average elevation give Uganda a pleasant tropical climate with moderate temperatures and ample rainfall throughout the year. Annual rainfall varies between 500 millimeters (19.7 inches) in the northeast and 2,100 millimeters (82.7 inches) in the southeast region near Lake Victoria. Rainfall patterns vary from north to south Uganda. The drier northern region's rainy season lasts from April to October while the dry season stretches from November to March. The wet south has two rainy seasons, April to May and October to November, with the other months being relatively dry. Daily temperatures usually vary between 85°F

Because of ample rainfall, southern Uganda is characterized by lush vegetation. Bricks, such as these that are being dried before being kilned, are a common housing construction material in the country. Courtesy of Earl P. Scott.

(29.4°C) during the day to 55°F (12.7°C) at night. In the hot and dry June to August months, temperatures vary from 88°F to 95°F. Because altitude significantly influences Uganda's temperatures, it is generally cooler in the higher and wetter south and warmer in the low-lying and drier northeast.[2]

Uganda is one of the best-watered countries in the world, as 16 percent (or 36,330 square kilometers) of its total land area of 236,040 square kilometers consists of freshwater sources, including several large lakes (Albert, Edward, George, Kwania, Kyoga, and Victoria) and the Victoria/Albert Nile, the larger of the two major tributaries of the River Nile. It is contemporary Uganda's possession of the source of the Nile that led to Uganda's colonization by the British.

The country's vegetation patterns vary by climate from tropical forest in the more moist south and southwest to savanna grasslands in the drier northeast. Agriculture is closely associated with rainfall patterns and local soil conditions. Crop agriculture is mainly concentrated in the wetter south and western parts of the country, while animal husbandry is practiced in the drier north and northeastern parts of the country. Agricultural patterns are also determined by the cultural and nutritional preferences of local people groups.

PEOPLES

Uganda has a population of 24,699,073 people and is increasing at an annual rate of 3.3 percent—a growth rate that could double the country's population in 21 years. Its infant mortality rate stands at 68 deaths per thousand live births, while its average lifespan is 52 years. Both of these adverse conditions are the result of poverty, civil wars, and the ravages of the HIV/ AIDS epidemic.

There are 19 major ethnic groups in Uganda. In order of national population size, these are Baganda (17%); Banyankole (8%); Basoga (8%); Iteso (8%); Bakiga (7%); Langi (6%); Banyarwanda (6%); Bagisu (5%); Acholi (4%); Lugbara (4%); Batoro (3%); Banyoro (3%); Alur (2%); Bagwere (2%); Bakonjo (2%); Jopadhola (2%); Karamojong (2%); Rundi (2%); nonnative groups, for example, European, Asian, and Arab (1%); and others (8%). The native ethnic groups fall into four major categories: the Bantu (e.g., Baganda, Banyankole, Basoga, Bakiga, Banyarwanda, Bagisu, Batoro, Banyoro, Bagwere, and Bakonjo); the Nilotes (e.g., Langi, Alur, Acholi, and Jopadhola); the Nilo-Hamites (e.g., Karimojong and Iteso); and the Sudanic (e.g., Lugbara and Kakwa). In general, these groups live in mutually exclusive parts of the country: most of the Bantu groups in the south, the Nilotes in north central, the Nilo-Hamites in the northeast, and the Sudanic in the northwest. Moreover, these groups have significant cultural differences. For instance, although most Bantus tend to be sedentary agriculturists, Nilo-Hamitic groups, especially the Karimojong, are nomadic pastoralists that subsist on cattle and goats. Approximately 85 percent of Ugandans live in rural areas.[3]

LANGUAGES

English is the official national language of Uganda. As such, it dominates the media, the judiciary, and the school system and a good working knowledge of the language is a prerequisite for employment in the formal business and public sector. The rise of English to Uganda's official and national language began in the colonial period. Unable to find a widespread local language that could serve their national political and economic integration

Major language and ethnic groups. Bantu is the major language group. Courtesy of the author.

objectives, the British colonial authorities set out to promote English through the school system and massive adult literacy programs. These programs were fully supported and often initiated by the Christian church in order to make the Bible more widely accessible to locals. For these programs to succeed, literacy in local languages was seldom promoted. The growth of English has also benefited from Uganda's traditional ethnic rivalry and postcolonial political and economic reality. Although there were attempts in the 1970s to declare either Kiswahili or Luganda as the national or official language, these efforts failed because each of the country's many ethnic groups supported its own language. This situation, which resulted from precolonial ethnic rivalry and the colonial policy of "divide and rule" which actively discouraged cooperation among the locals lest they undermine the colonial government, caused many Ugandans to view the possible elevation of any one local language as politically threatening and tantamount to devaluation of their own language. Under these circumstances, English came to be seen by many as a safe neutral language.

Moreover, because Uganda's postcolonial elites share the colonial view of national political and economic unity and integration, they continue to support English as the country's official and national language despite its elitism and "undemocratic" nature as most Ugandans have a low English proficiency. As a result, many Ugandan elites are multi-lingual speakers who use English in official or public circles and their native languages in private.

The prominent role of English in contemporary Uganda has equally benefited from its perception as a better medium for teaching science and technology in the country's school system and for promoting Uganda's integration into the global society. Additionally, many urban mixed couples (that is, those consisting of partners from different ethnic/racial groups) in the country use English to communicate among themselves and with their children, thereby promoting the language.[4]

Next to English, Uganda's other most important languages are Luganda, Kiswahili (Swahili), Luo, and Arabic. Of these four, only Luganda and Kiswahili are likely candidates for national language because of their relatively large number of speakers in the country. Although Luganda, the language of the country's most populous Ganda people, is Uganda's lingua franca, its elevation to a national language is undermined by many non-Bagandas' resentment of the Baganda for their dominance of national affairs since the colonial era. Nevertheless, Luganda has a lot of literature, newspapers, and other media that continue to aid its growth.

Although Idi Amin declared Kiswahili as Uganda's national language in the 1970s, this did not substantially change the place of the language in the country because the policy was never implemented nor reversed by subsequent governments. Kiswahili's current uncertain position in the country is because: it is not indigenous enough; it has fewer speakers than Luganda; it has limited indigenous literature that can be used to promote it; there are many varieties of the language to choose from, for example, those spoken in neighboring Kenya and Tanzania (although Tanzanian Kiswahili is widely considered standard) and Uganda itself; it would require a lot of resources to switch from English to Kiswahili; it is not one of the official languages of major international fora such as the UN; and it is not seen as a good medium for teaching science and technology, although neighboring Tanzania has tried it.

Nevertheless, Kiswahili's future prospects in Uganda are good because it is the lingua franca of Kenya and Tanzania, which are not only Uganda's partners in the recently revived East African Community, but are also the country's neighbors and major trading partners. Because of the language's rapid spread in East and Central Africa it has become one of the major broadcast languages of various international media houses such as the BBC (UK), Radio Cairo (Egypt), the Voice of America (U.S.A), Radio Deutsche Welle (Germany), Radio Moscow International (Russia), Radio Japan International, Radio China International, and Radio South Africa. Since the colonial era, Kiswahili has also been widely used by members of Uganda's armed forces, who would help to spread the language in the country but have been unable to do so because of their tarnished image after decades of brutal military rule. Thus, for many Ugandans, especially the dominant Baganda who lost power soon after independence and bore the brunt of the country's military rule (especially under dictator Idi Amin), shunning Kiswahili is a means of political resistance—moreover, most Baganda would rather see their own language, Luganda, become the national language. But as the military's discipline, civility, human rights record, level of education, and reputation have improved since Yoweri Museveni's ascent to power in the mid-1980s, Kiswahili's fortunes in Uganda have also improved significantly.[5]

In addition to English, Luganda, Kiswahili, Luo, and Arabic, there are the 35 or more languages spoken by the country's various native ethnic groups and the numerous minor languages spoken by the country's nonnative population, especially the diverse Asian community.

EDUCATION

Uganda's educational system is patterned after that of Britain, the former colonial power. The system consists of seven years of primary education, four years of secondary education, two years of advanced secondary school, and three to five years of college or university education, depending on the course of study. Currently, 67 percent of Ugandan adults are literate. The country has been providing full universal but noncompulsory primary education (UPE) to its children since 1997. Initially, UPE covered four children per family but has recently been expanded to cover all children, increasing the enrollment rate in primary schools to 98 percent. Although Uganda spends 70 percent of its education budget on UPE, parents still shoulder a significant portion of the cost of educating their children.[6]

The government is the leading provider of education in Uganda. In 2002, for instance, the ownership of the country's 13,332 primary schools was as follows: the government,10,420 (more than 78%); the private sector, 1,884 (14%); the community, 994 (8%); and others/unreported, 34 (0.3%). In that year, there were 7,354,153 pupils in the country's primary schools, 50.1 percent of whom were males and 49.7 percent female. Similarly, there were 2,198 secondary schools in Uganda in 2002 with a total enrollment of 655,951 students; 359,494 (54.8%) of whom were males and 296,457 (45.2%) females. Forty-eight percent of these students were enrolled in 711 government secondary schools, while 31 percent were in 799 private secondary schools and 21 percent in 688 community secondary schools. Because most of the country's education budget is spent on primary education, secondary and tertiary education is not only less accessible to most Ugandans, it is also starved for resources.

Uganda has 52 tertiary education institutions: 17 universities, 10 teachers' colleges, 5 technical colleges, 5 commercial colleges, 5 agricultural/animal husbandry colleges, 1 forestry college, 2 co-operative colleges, 1 hotel and tourism college, 4 health and medical colleges, and 2 vocational institutes. Most students in tertiary institutions are males (60 percent) and are enrolled in university and teacher training colleges. Although Uganda has only two public universities (Makerere and Mbarara), these two institutions enroll nearly half of all university students in Uganda.[7]

Except for Makerere, which was founded in 1922 and is the oldest university in East Africa, the country's other universities have come into being since the late 1980s. With the exception of the government's Mbarara University of Science and Technology, most of the newly established universities have a religious affiliation, a curriculum emphasis on marketable courses such as business, computer technology, and theology. Most of their instructors are moonlighting lecturers and professors from public universities, especially Makerere.

Makerere continues to solidify its position as Uganda's most prestigious and largest university and has an estimated current enrollment of 40,000 students. In the colonial and immediate postcolonial period, Makerere was a constituent college of the University of London serving the then–British East Africa region that now consists of Uganda, Kenya, and Tanzania. Between 1963 and 1970,

Makerere was a leading component of the University of East Africa. Afterward, it became an independent university of the Republic of Uganda. During Idi Amin's 1971–79 military dictatorship, the institution nearly collapsed but has since been rebuilding and regaining its prestige.

The explosive growth of tertiary education in Uganda is in response to the rapid expansion of primary and secondary school enrollment since the country's adoption of UPE in 1997. However, the rapidly rising demand for tertiary education in Uganda is stretching its universities and colleges to the limit. Thus, the system is characterized by problems such as congestion; poor student supervision; inadequate funding for classrooms, dorms, sewerage and other infrastructure, equipment, and libraries; and increased competition for limited numbers of qualified instructors and professors. The high cost and shortage of science instructors and facilities has also led to the overproduction of theology, social science, and humanities graduates, many of whom are unemployed. Moreover, because the system is not streamlined, it is difficult for students to transfer from technical colleges to universities without loss of credit.[8]

In addition, Uganda's tertiary education system is faced with the challenge of closing its gender enrollment gap in the face of lower female students' achievement and high drop-out rates at the primary and secondary school level. This situation is caused by many factors, including the country's high poverty levels that tempt many teenage girls to earn income from sex, the disproportionate burden Uganda's high incidence of HIV/AIDS places on girls as surrogate caregivers, government policies that bar pregnant girls and teenage mothers from completing their primary and secondary education despite the country's high teen pregnancy, and girls' fear of sexual harassment in schools. Moreover, factors such as parental education and income level; the widespread cultural preference for educating boys rather than girls; and political instability, especially in the north, contribute to gender disparities in access to education in Uganda.[9]

CITIES

Uganda's urbanization level or proportion of the population living in urban areas is only 12 percent. This is the result of the country's overwhelming rural existence and the many ungazetted urban areas whose population is reckoned as rural in the official census. Nevertheless, between 1969 and 2002, the number of urban areas grew from 58 to 74; the urban population increased from 634,952 to 2,999,387; the country's annual urban growth rate declined from 8.2 to 3.73 percent; the proportion of the urban population in the capital city of Kampala decreased from 54 to 40 percent; and the proportion of the urban population in the 20 largest towns decreased from 87 to 77 percent despite the fact that these towns have experienced explosive growth in that period, implying that the country's secondary towns have significantly grown over time. Forty-one percent (i.e., 1,189,142) of the country's urban population lives in the major city of Kampala.[10]

The 20 largest urban areas in Uganda are shown in Table 1.1. Many of these cities are in the more densely populated southern and western parts of the country. Nevertheless, the population of northern Ugandan cities such as Gulu, Kitgum, Lira, and Kasese has in recent decades grown significantly because of the influx of people displaced by the region's ongoing civil war.

Urban life in Uganda mirrors that in many other African countries. Generally, the country's urban population is growing faster than the cities' ability to provide basic urban services such as sewerage, electricity, and housing. As a result,

Table 1.1
Population of the 20 Largest Urban Centers, 1969–2002

2002 Rank	Name	1969	1980	1991	2002	% Growth 1969/2002
1	Kampala	330,700	458,503	774,241	1,189,142	260
2	Gulu	18,170	14,958	38,297	119,430	557
3	Lira	7,340	9,122	27,568	80,879	1,002
4	Jinja	47,872	45,060	65,169	71,213	49
5	Mbale	23,544	28,039	53,987	71,130	202
6	Mbarara	16,078	23,255	41,031	69,363	331
7	Masaka	12,987	29,123	49,585	67,768	422
8	Entebbe	21,096	21,289	42,763	55,086	161
9	Kasese	7,213	9,917	18,750	53,907	647
10	Njeru	4,637	3,880	36,731	51,236	1,005
11	Mukono	3,565	5,783	7,406	46,506	1,205
12	Arua	10,837	9,663	22,217	43,929	305
13	Kitgum	3,242	4,961	12,978	41,821	1,190
14	Soroti	12,398	15,048	40,970	41,711	236
15	Kabale	8,234	21,469	29,246	41,344	402
16	Fort Portal	7,947	26,806	32,789	40,993	416
17	Iganga	5,958	9,899	19,740	39,472	563
18	Busia	1,146	8,663	27,967	36,630	3,096
19	Tororo	15,977	16,707	26,783	34,810	118
20	Mityana	2,263	2,547	22,579	34,116	1,407

Source: Thomas Brinkhoff, "Uganda—City Population," http://www.citypopulation.de/Uganda.html, 2005. The percent growth in 1969–2002 was generated by the author.

The quality of slum housing in Kampala varies tremendously based on size and the materials used for construction. But in most cases, slum settlements are unhealthy because of the lack basic urban services such as garbage collection and sewerage. Courtesy of Earl P. Scott.

Because many urban Ugandans are unemployed, they make a living in the informal sector. For instance, these urban caterers prepare food and sell it to other urban workers, for a small profit. Because of low pay, many Ugandan urban workers cannot afford expensive restaurant food. Courtesy of Earl P. Scott.

a significant portion of Uganda's urban population lives in slums that are characterized by substandard housing, overcrowding, and a generally unhealthy living environment devoid of basic services such as safe drinking water. Consequently, people living in such settlements are frequently ill and unable to lead decent lives.

Because of the country's rapid urban population growth and poor economy, most Ugandans, even those who are educated, lack decent employment opportunities. Although the general unemployment rate for Ugandans has hovered around 7.4 percent in recent years, the urban unemployment rate is much higher at an estimated 22 percent. Unemployment in the city of Kampala is even higher (31 percent) because the city contains most of the country's modern economy which attracts excessive numbers of rural jobseekers only to have their hopes dashed. High urban unemployment is a reality that also confronts many people in other large East African cities such as Nairobi, Kenya, and Dar es Salaam, Tanzania.

RESOURCES, OCCUPATIONS, AND ECONOMY

About 75 percent of Uganda's land area is arable. However, only 10 percent of this land area falls in the high productive category, with the rest considered to be of moderate productivity. Nevertheless, Uganda has some of the most productive farmland in Africa, producing a wide variety of agricultural products that are the basis of its economy. Its main cash crops include coffee, tea, cotton, tobacco, and sugar cane. It also produces a wide variety of fruits (e.g., bananas, plantains, pineapples, avocados, passion fruits, mangoes, jack fruits, and papaws); vegetables such as okra, dudhi, onion, mushrooms, French beans, eggplant, tomatoes, asparagus, and potatoes; spices (e.g., chilies, vanilla, ginger, and papain); cereals and pulses (e.g., beans, maize, rice, and wheat); and essential oils such as citronella, eucalyptus, ginger, peppermint, and geranium. Its animal products include sheep, goats, chicken, honey, silk cocoons, and various cattle byproducts. The country also exports a significant quantity of fish and fish products.[11]

Because of Uganda's dependence on agriculture and its increasing population, competition for good farmland has been intensifying. As a result, agricultural land uses are beginning to encroach on the country's sensitive ecological zones. Thus, the country is faced with environmental challenges such as the loss of wetlands to expanding agricultural land uses, deforestation from the clearing of forests for agricultural land and overexploitation of forest resources for timber and fuel wood, overgrazing caused by livestock overpopulation, soil erosion from overuse and misuse of farm land, and loss of wildlife from poaching and loss of habitat. Moreover, Lake Victoria has recently been invaded by water hyacinth (lake weed), thereby threatening the country's vibrant fishing and water transport industry.

Although Uganda's mineral resources are modest, it has commercially viable mineral deposits of tungsten, wolfram ores, tantalite, vermiculite, gold, cobalt cathode (metal), nickel, salt, and copper hydroxide. Much of the country's industry consists of agricultural processing, textiles, clothing and footwear, leather, paper products, chemicals, pharmaceuticals, building materials, wood, timber, and assorted metal products.[12]

International tourism, production of various handicrafts and jewelry items, and electricity exports to Kenya are other key aspects of Uganda's economy. The country's main imports are petroleum and related products, electrical machinery, transport equipment, nonelectrical machinery, iron, steel, and manufactured goods. Besides Kenya, Uganda's most important trading partners include the United Kingdom, India, Japan, Germany, France, South Africa, Hong Kong, Italy, and the United States.

Uganda's labor force distribution by economic sector is agriculture (82%), industry (5%), and services (13%). This distribution is indicative of the country's dependency on agriculture and its predominantly poor and rural population. Per capita gross domestic product (GDP) based on the purchasing power parity is about $1,200, meaning that on average each Ugandan consumes $1,200 worth of goods and services in a year. The distribution of household income in the country is relatively iniquitous with the lowest 10 percent of the population having 4 percent of national income and the highest 10 percent having 21 percent of national income. Thirty-five percent of the country's population is below the national poverty line.[13]

Uganda's GDP based on purchasing power parity is estimated at $39 billion. The GDP composition by sector is agriculture (44%), industry (18%,) and services (38%). Between 1990 and 2001, Uganda's economic growth was impressive as the country rebuilt most of its key infrastructure following decades of civil war. By 2001, Uganda's real GDP growth was estimated at an annual 5.1 percent. In 2000, the country's economy got a big boost when it obtained $2 billion worth of debt relief from Western donors and lenders. The country's current external debt of approximately $4.5 billion represents 11.4 percent of the country's GDP and ranks it 104th (out of 202 countries) in global external debt rankings. However, Uganda's total public debt stands at 63 percent of GDP, making this one of the most indebted countries.

Although the size of Uganda's formal (monetarized) economy is modest, a larger portion of the country's economy is informal, that is, consisting of barter and unregulated petty trade and production of various household products. This condition makes it difficult for official statistics to capture fully the size of Uganda's economy. This situation pertains to many other African countries.

GOVERNMENT

Uganda's government consists of three branches: the executive, the judiciary, and the legislature. The president heads the executive branch, and other principal officials are the vice president, the prime minister, and cabinet ministers. However, much of the country's executive powers are vested in the president, who has the power to appoint or remove the vice-president, the prime minister, and cabinet ministers.

The judiciary, which is headed by the chief justice, is responsible for the administration and delivery of justice in the country and is critical in the promotion of law and order, human rights, social justice, morality, and good governance. Moreover, it interprets and enforces the constitution of the country. Uganda's judiciary is relatively independent, being constitutionally protected from interference from the legislature and executive. The judiciary consists of the Supreme Court, the Court of Appeal, the High Court, the Commercial Court, and the magistrate courts.

Uganda's legislature or parliament is unicameral, that is, it consists of one chamber, and is headed by the speaker with the assistance of five other members, namely, the leader of government business (represented by the minister for parliamentary affairs); the minister of finance, planning and economic development; and three commissioners elected from among the members of parliament.

Besides these national level government organs, there are various units of local government at the district and subcounty level. Urban local governments are organized according to urban rank, that is, city, municipality, and town. Cities are governed by city councils whose constituent parts are the city division councils. Municipal councils and municipal division councils govern municipalities while town councils are responsible for towns. In rural areas, local government consists of the county, parish, and village.[14]

HISTORY

Early History

Uganda has been populated since the fourth century B.C. This long history of human occupation is partly the result of its abundant rainfall, fertile soils, moderate temperatures, and lush forests and grasslands that supported large herds of edible wildlife. Although hunter-gatherer people groups were the first to settle in Uganda, they were later displaced by agriculturalists and pastoralists drawn to the area by its good farming and grazing conditions. Gradually, the agriculturalists and pastoralists grew in number and strength and dislodged the hunter-gatherers, forcing them to occupy the less hospitable mountainous terrain to the west and southwestern part of the country.[15]

British Colonialism

Contemporary Uganda first came under formal British influence in 1890 when the Imperial British East Africa Company (IBEA), under Captain Frederick Lugard, gained control of its territory. When the company left Uganda in March 1893, at the expiry of its charter, the British government declared the country a protectorate in 1894, because of its strategic importance to British economic interests given the country's rich ivory, coffee, rubber, wheat, cotton, and gum products. However the presence of powerful indigenous kingdoms such as Buganda and Bunyoro compelled the British to use military force to successfully colonize contemporary Uganda.[16]

Uganda's formal colonization by the British was also the culmination of a long series of events and engagements with the region following John Hanning Speke's discovery of the source of the Nile at Rippon Falls near Jinja, Uganda, on July 28, 1862. The British were keen to control the entire length of the river for several reasons. First, they wanted to secure their North African colony of Egypt, which they had seized from the waning Ottoman Empire to ensure unfettered access to the Suez Canal (built by the French between 1859 and 1869)—the lifeline of British-Indian trade. Controlling the source of the Nile had been a high priority even for the Ottoman Empire; hence, the empire's southward expansion into the Sudan and contemporary northwest Uganda by the time of British colonialism. Second, the British saw the Nile as a potential water route to the interior of Africa; control of the river could aid their imperial interests in the continent. But the Nile proved to be impassable because of waterfalls and rapids. Third, the British were keen to preempt the control of the Nile headwaters by other foreign powers (especially Germany, whose sphere of influence included contemporary Tanzania, Uganda's southern neighbor), as this would strangle Egypt. Thus, after John Speke's discovery of the source of the Nile, Captain Frederick Lugard came to Uganda in December 1890 to protect British interests including the Nile. Although he came as a representative of the newly founded Imperial British East Africa Company (IBEA), at the time, IBEA's interests were synonymous with those of the British state. Therefore, Lugard's arrival not only helped the British gain control of the Nile, but also set the stage for the country's subsequent colonization in 1894.

The early days of British colonial rule in Uganda were difficult because the British faced substantial opposition from the country's powerful indigenous kingdoms and had to use military force to subdue them. For instance, in 1897, the kingdoms of Buganda (under *Kabaka* [King] Mwanga), and Bunyoro (led by *Omukama* [King] Kabarega) revolted against British colonial rule. At the same time, the Sudanese army that the British had used to conquer and maintain control of the Uganda protectorate mutinied over poor pay and underappreciation, necessitating the use of Indian and other foreign troops to restore order.

Colonial military rule in Uganda lasted a period of three years, from 1897 to 1899, and was replaced by a civilian administration after major resistance had been suppressed. The civilian administration, led by Sir Harry Johnston, consolidated its control of Uganda by signing treaties favorable to the British with Uganda's many indigenous kingdoms. The first was in March 1900, with the influential kingdom of Buganda, which was the first kingdom to be subdued by British military power and whose leader *Kabaka* Mwanga was captured and exiled in 1899, and replaced by his 4-year-old son Daudi Chwa. The three regents appointed to govern the kingdom in Daudi Chwa's juvenile years signed the agreement with the British. By this time the Baganda were "allied" to the British colonialists, and the cooperation pact that they signed with the British, later dubbed the Uganda agreement, was the most mutually beneficial. Moreover, it privileged Baganda interests and made them dominant over other native ethnic groups in the country. As a result, subsequent British treaties with the kingdoms of Toro (June 29, 1900), Ankole (August 7, 1901), and Bunyoro (October 23, 1933) were not as beneficial to these kingdoms. Although the defective treaties secured Uganda for the British, who subsequently sought to develop the country as part of their expansive colonial empire, they were to help fuel Uganda's political instability in the immediate postcolonial period.

The Independence Era

Uganda attained its independence in 1963 with the late Apolo Milton Obote as prime minister and the late Sir Edward Mutesa, the *Kabaka* of Buganda, as president. Unlike the bloodshed that characterized Kenya's independence struggle, Uganda had a peaceful political transition that gave many hope that the country was destined for rapid socioeconomic development, given the limited disruptions to its civil service and socioeconomic infrastructure during the transition to independence. Instead, the political blunders of the colonial and immediate postcolonial governments doomed the country.[17]

To begin with, Uganda emerged from colonialism with significant religious, economic, and ethnic divisions. These had worked to the colonial administration's advantage, but they were to prove fatal in the postindependence period, especially in Obote's hands. In the colonial era, the country's southern Bantu tribes, especially the Baganda, had been favored at the expense of the Nilotic (e.g., the Acholi and Langi) and Nilo-Hamitic groups (e.g., the

Iteso and Karimojong) in the northern part of the country. For instance, because the Uganda agreement of 1900 had given the Baganda substantial political power and influence in the colony, they, unlike any other native ethnic group in the country, got more access to education and soon controlled the colonial administrative and civil service. Many Baganda became part of the country's colonial middle class. Moreover, as they and other southern Bantu groups became increasingly Christianized and Westernized, their economic and political power became more entrenched, as the British used Baganda administrators in other parts of Uganda, thereby creating substantial anti-Baganda sentiment in the country—which was to backfire against the Baganda at independence. The favorable environmental conditions in the south also enabled the area's agricultural Bantu groups to play a central role in the country's emerging modern economy.

Conversely, the harsh northern environment, the nomadic lifestyle of some northerners, for example, the Karimojong, the long distances from the colonial capital of Entebbe (1893–1958), colonial designation of the region as a labor reserve in contrast to the cash crop economy promoted in the south, and the dominance of Islam in the region (more so in the northwest) made it less amenable to colonial needs and investments. Thus, opportunities for socioeconomic growth were much fewer in the north than in the south, partly because of the concentration of the country's European population in the south, a factor which further helped to advance the south's economy relative to other regions of the country. Overall, by independence, the north was much less developed compared with the south, though it was disproportionately represented in the military.

This is the socioeconomic environment under which Obote, a Langi from the north, became prime minister of Uganda in 1962 and immediately began to contend with the political and socioeconomic power of the Baganda, whose native territory included Uganda's postcolonial capital of Kampala. Obote's administration was handicapped from the beginning by three factors: a federalist independence constitution that granted substantial autonomy to the country's indigenous kingdoms especially Buganda; an awkward political alliance between his populist Uganda People's Congress party and the Baganda nationalist party, *Kabaka* Yekka (i.e., *Kabaka* Only), that made it difficult for him to legislate or implement many of his policy initiatives; and the alliance's shared authority clause that forced him to share power with Sir Edward Mutesa (*Kabaka* Mutesa II of Buganda), Uganda's titular head of state, president, and commander-in-chief of the armed forces.

When the political alliance between the Uganda People's Congress party and *Kabaka* Yekka partly collapsed in 1964, a period of political uncertainty and conflict between Obote and *Kabaka* Mutesa II ensued. This led to Obote's abolition of the country's federalist independence constitution in 1966; his elimination of the prime minister's office and assumption of full executive authority of Uganda as president; and his termination of the traditional kingdoms' federal status. In the ensuing *Kabaka* and Baganda protest and power struggle with Obote, the *Kabaka*'s Palace at Mango Hill was attacked by the army (now under the command of Colonel Idi Amin who Obote had hastily elevated to army and air force chief of staff in place of the *Kabaka* loyalist, Brigadier Shaban Opolot) and the *Kabaka* was forced into exile in Britain.[18] This created major animosity between the Baganda and Obote and Amin (in spite of these leaders' Ganda wives) which, together with Obote's politicization of the armed forces, set the stage for Uganda's political implosion and bloodshed in the 1971–86 period.

After Obote's overthrow of the *Kabaka*, he continued to encounter mild political opposition from the fractious coalition of regional parties in his ruling Uganda People's Congress until Idi Amin became too powerful for Obote's liking and Obote stripped him of most of his powers in 1970. In 1971, while on a trip to Singapore, Obote gave secret orders to his army supporters to arrest Amin. But things failed to go as planned, and Amin staged a military coup against Obote and declared himself president of Uganda, thereby marking the beginning of his brutal nine-year rule.

Soon after taking power, Amin declared war on the country's Asian community in an attempt to take away their economic power and transfer it to native Ugandans. He simultaneously started to purge the political opposition, which in the latter days came to include some of his wives, cabinet ministers, members of the clergy, and intellectuals. In sum, during Amin's reign from January 25, 1971, to April 11, 1979, more than 300,000 Ugandans were killed and the economy ruined. His tyranny spared no part of the country and alienated Ugandans of all social, economic, and religious stripes, including fellow Muslims.

In September 1972, Ugandan exiles in Tanzania unsuccessfully tried to overthrow Amin, thereby initiating the tense relationship between Uganda and Tanzania throughout Amin's rule. This situation was to help bring about Amin's exit from power. In October 1978, Amin invaded Tanzania and occupied and brutalized the Kagera region for two months. Soon after, the Tanzanian army repulsed the attack, counterinvaded Uganda, and, with the aid of Ugandan exile forces, especially the Ugandan National Liberation Front (UNLF), drove Amin's army back to Kampala, finally overthrowing him in April 1979. Amin fled to exile in Saudi Arabia (via Libya), where he died in August 2003. After Amin's overthrow, the fractured UNLF transitional government came to power but lasted less than two years, even though it managed to field two different presidents, Yusufu Lule, a Muslim (April 13–June 20,

1979) and Godfrey Binaisa (June 20, 1979–May 11, 1980), in that time. Binaisa was succeeded by Paul Muwanga (May 12–May 22, 1980), who in turn was succeeded by the presidential commission (May 22–December 15, 1980).

In December 1980, a general election monitored by a commonwealth team saw Obote regain the presidency, even though his United People's Congress Party (UPC) was accused of electoral fraud. But Obote's second regime was no better than the first, though it lasted nearly five years, from December 17, 1980, to July 27, 1985. On regaining power, Obote quickly fell out with some in the UNLF movement, notably Yoweri Museveni, who soon launched the National Resistance Army (NRA) to end Obote's rule.

Meanwhile, soldiers led by Bazilio Olara Okello overthrew Obote's second government on July 27, 1985, and formed a military council that included

President Yoweri Museveni is credited with restoring order in Uganda since coming to power in 1986. Courtesy of Ken Goyer.

many groups except Museveni's NRA. Okello became chairman of the council, hence president of the country but lasted only three days, paving the way for the next chairman, Tito Okello (July 29, 1985–January 26, 1986). In December 1985, the NRA and the military council signed a peace treaty in Nairobi, Kenya, but the NRA promptly broke the accord and overthrew the military council on January 25, 1986, propelling Yoweri Museveni to Uganda's presidency. Although Museveni seized power in 1986, he was first popularly elected in 1996, and has become Uganda's longest-serving president.

Museveni's administration has managed to return Uganda to normalcy despite continuing hostility in the West Nile and northern regions that border Sudan. Under his rule, the country has rebuilt most of its basic socioeconomic institutions. However, continuing political challenges keep Uganda from being the "pearl of Africa" that former British Prime Minister Winston Churchill envisioned it to be in 1943.

CULTURE

Uganda's culture is characterized by significant ethnic, religious, and linguistic pluralism. Most of the country's population consists of black Africans with a scattering of non-Africans, especially Europeans, Asians, and Arabs. Nevertheless, the small non-African population plays a critical role in the country's economy—an anomalous reality that former dictator Idi Amin sought to change by expelling the country's Asian community in the early 1970s, only to have the country's economy collapse. Beyond the obvious black skin color, Uganda's African population is quite diverse, composed of as many as 40 different ethnic groups that fall into four major classes: the Bantu, the Nilotes, the Nilo-Hamites, and the Sudanic. Bantu groups constitute nearly 60 percent of the country's population. The Baganda, who account for 17 percent of Uganda's population, are the country's largest Bantu and ethnic group.[19]

Because the Bantu groups dominate Uganda's population, the country's culture is also overwhelmingly Bantu in nature. The Bantu groups are largely sedentary agriculturalists, and they speak languages that are mutually intelligible to varying degrees. Many Nilotic, Nilo-Hamitic, and Sudanic groups are also agriculturalists. But the Karimojong, a Nilo-Hamitic group in northeast Uganda, consists of nomadic pastoralists that predominantly keep cattle. There is also a small population of nomadic hunter-gatherer Batwa and Bambuti pygmoid (or pygmies) peoples in the country's southwestern forest regions adjoining the Democratic Republic of the Congo.

As Uganda is still an agrarian society, much of the population has close ties to the land. They practice farming, herding, and hunting and have a communal social outlook. Like many of their counterparts in Sub-Saharan Africa, they are an oral society that transmits folk knowledge through storytelling, music, and dance. However, many of these aspects are being modified through interactions with the outside world, the media, and the educational system.

Uganda's ethnic diversity is matched by linguistic diversity because each ethnic group has its own language. Thus, the languages of the dominant groups, for example, Luganda, the native/mother tongue of the Baganda, are widely spoken as are many other minor languages. Although most Ugandans are multilingual, the languages that unite the country are all foreign. English, the official language, was introduced in Uganda by British colonialists. Kiswahili (Swahili), a language that evolved in coastal Kenya and Tanzania and has since spread to Uganda and Central Africa and is even one of the broadcast languages of international media houses such as the Voice of America and BBC, is officially Uganda's national language. But it has yet to achieve the same level of use in Uganda as in Kenya and Tanzania. Nevertheless, it has been designated the national language because of its anticipated growth. Uganda's linguistic divisions and the lack of a unifying local language have been significant factors in the country's political instability since the 1960s.

2

Religion and Worldview

WORLDVIEW

Like many other African societies, Ugandans are generally very religious. They believe in a higher being or beings and follow the teachings of various religions, especially African Traditional Religions (ATRs), Christianity and Islam, or combinations of these.[1] Unlike Westerners, most Ugandans see physical and spiritual life as a continuum, where spiritual and material reality blends so seamlessly that the two are inseparable. Thus, Ugandans attribute most life events, both good and evil, to unseen spiritual forces. Whenever two Ugandans are engaged in conversation, God and gods are readily invoked, especially among the more traditional ones. Participation in religious events is widespread.

Also unlike in the West, religion features prominently in all aspects of Ugandan life, both private and public. Thus, social events, such as funerals, weddings, graduations, and public events, such as independence celebrations, incorporate religious performances, such as prayers, musicals, songs, and dances. These religious performances are usually presided over by religious leaders such as priests and pastors (in Christianity), imams (in Islam), and shamans or medicine men (in traditional religious settings). Because of the centrality of religion in Ugandan society and worldview, religious leaders are revered throughout the country and are a powerful counterforce to state power. Very few social initiatives can succeed in Uganda and Africa in general without the participation of religious leaders.

Uganda's religious landscape consists of three main players: (1) African Traditional/Indigenous Religions (ATRs), (2) world religions (e.g., Christianity,

Islam, Hinduism, Judaism, Baha'i, and Sikhism), and (3) new religious traditions (e.g., African Independent Churches).[2] In many instances, Ugandans readily create their own unique belief systems by blending various elements from these religions.

Although ATRs, Christianity, and Islam have coexisted in Uganda for more than a century, ATRs have lost much ground to Christianity and Islam. Currently, 85 percent of Ugandans are Christians, 12 percent are Muslims, and 3 percent are practitioners of ATRs, Hinduism, Baha'i, and Judaism, or are irreligious or secular. The overwhelming majority of Ugandan Christians are either Roman Catholics (42%) or Anglicans (36%). The remaining 7 percent of Ugandan Christians are Pentecostals (4.6%), Seventh-Day Adventists (1.5%), and Mormons, Jehovah's Witnesses, Baptists, or adherents of African Independent Churches (AICs).[3] The AICs, which are often viewed as cults by mainstream Christian churches, are a protest against dominant European control of the Christian church throughout Uganda (and much of Africa), especially in the colonial and immediate postcolonial period. As in many parts of Africa, especially where Christianity is dominant, the liberal mixing of Christian and traditional indigenous beliefs is widespread.[4]

Although most of the Muslims in Uganda are Sunnis, there are some Shi'a followers among the Asian (Aga Khan) community. Worldwide, the Sunni branch of Islam accounts for the majority (85%) of Muslims, and the Shi'a and other minor branches account for the rest. These branches of Islam arose in 661 A.D., following disagreements on who should succeed the religion's founder, Mohammed. The Sunnis wanted the Caliph (successor to Mohammed or a person acting in his place) to come from Mohammed's tribe, the Qurayah, and that he should be chosen by consensus. The first four caliphs that were so chosen (i.e., Abu Bakr 632–34, Umar 634–44, Uthman 644–56, and Ali 656–61) are revered by Sunni Muslims because their conduct and practice (or *sunna* from which Sunnis derive their name) are considered to be closest to that of Mohammed, and, therefore, binding on Muslims.

Conversely, the Shi'a wanted to retain the leadership of Mohammed's household through Shi'a Ali. Shi'ites (or followers of Shi'a Islam) adore Muhammed's family and have rituals and shrines for them; they have religious leaders known as imams or ayatollahs (sign of Allah); they expect the return of the last imam (Mahdi) to establish the Shi'ite Islamic faith before Judgment Day; they consider as sacred the cities of Karbala and Najaf (Iraq) and Meshed (Iran); and they hold the annual Karbala Festival in remembrance of Husayn ibn Ali, who was killed at Karbala in 680 A.D., while fighting with Yazid for the caliphate. Because the 680 A.D. war marked the final separation between Sunni and Shi'a Islam, Husayn ibn Ali is regarded as the founder of Shia Islam.

Most in Uganda's Asian/Indian community are followers of the various branches of Hinduism; others are Muslims. There are few atheists in Uganda.

INDIGENOUS RELIGIONS

Before colonialism and the advent of Christianity and Islam, Ugandans were followers of African Traditional Religions (ATRs). Nowadays, few Ugandans are true followers of ATRs, thanks to the strong push for converts by Christianity, and, to a smaller extent, Islam, over the last near century and a half. Moreover, Christian, and, to some extent, Muslim, organizations have in that period played a critical role in the provision of modern social services such as education and hospitals, all of which have helped to weaken ATRs, especially among the young who are increasingly disconnected from traditional society and its institutions.

In traditional society, religious training was central to the socialization process, that is, training children and outsiders how to become part of society. But most children are now growing up or being socialized in the modern school system, so opportunities for learning indigenous religious practices have declined significantly. Moreover, many modern young people despise traditional religious practices even as they embrace the modern religions of their educational institutions. The decline of traditional religions in Uganda has also been accelerated by many people's exposure to the outside world through travel and the mass media.

Although Uganda's traditional religious beliefs and practices vary widely among the country's ethnic groups, there are many common characteristics. First is the belief in a remote everlasting and all powerful creator who must be approached through intermediaries (such as fetish priests) and is evident in awesome natural forces such as the sun, moon, thunder and lighting, stars, rain, rainbows, unusual rock formations, and giant trees that serve as serve as places of worship and sacrifice.

Second, unlike most major world religions, ATRs lack sacred texts, owing to the absence of the written script in most traditional African societies. Thus, core teachings are handed down orally from generation to generation—their oral transmission permitting them to more easily evolve with the times.[5]

Third, ATRs seldom have an organized hierarchy and preeminent leaders beyond the local fetish priest, thus they tend to be very democratic. Fourth, ATR adherents can approach the gods through a chain of command that begins with living fetish priests, diviners or fortune-tellers, then proceeds to dead ancestors (spirits) and culminates in the gods. Fifth, ATRs involve regular prayer, pouring of libations (liquid religious offerings), and animal sacrifices to exorcise evil spirits and appease the gods—not to be confused with the evil spirits that operate through witches and often require human sacrifices. Sixth, the will of God is sought in every major step in life by consulting diviners and fortune-tellers.

Seventh, ATRs have a firm sense of good and evil and that recompense for either behavior is immediate. This belief stems from the understanding that spiritual forces are involved in people's daily lives. Thus, good behavior in this life pleases the ancestral spirits and gods, brings success or good fortune, and ensures that at death one becomes an ancestral spirit that mediates between the living and the gods. Conversely, bad or evil behavior in this life displeases the spirits and the gods, brings curses, and causes one to become an evil spirit at death. Moreover, a person's evil behavior results in the person being haunted by the ghosts of those he or she has wronged, especially when one commits capital offenses such as murder or practices witchcraft or sorcery. In ATRs, ghosts are ancestral spirits who exact revenge on the living.

The belief in immediate recompense has contributed to the decline of ATRs because many of their teachings have proven doubtful or ineffective in rapidly modernizing and Christianizing Uganda. To illustrate, in many Ugandans' eyes, the gods of ATRs suffered irreparable loss of credibility when they failed to stop European conquest of the country. More than anything else, this failure appears to have signaled the superiority of the European Christian God over his traditional African equivalents, setting the stage for massive conversion to Christianity, and ,to a lesser extent, Islam, especially in the postcolonial period.

Eight, ATRs have no clear concept of heaven and hell, although the transformation to good or evil spirit based on one's behavior in life closely resembles the idea of heaven and hell in monotheistic religions such as Christianity and Islam. Last, there is widespread belief in the power of witchcraft and sorcery even among many Ugandan Christians and Muslims. This is, perhaps, the most persistent aspect of ATRs, as it is prevalent even among many urban elites who consult witch doctors to protect themselves from the harmful effects of witchcraft and sorcery. Such protection usually involves specially prepared trinkets, necklaces, wristbands, waistbands, and other charms.[6]

Although there are many varieties of ATR practices in Uganda, they tend to follow the general patterns outlined in the following discussion of traditional Baganda or Ganda religion.

Traditional Ganda Religion

Like other ATRs, indigenous Ganda religion flourished during the precolonial period.[7] The Ganda believed in the existence of a spiritual hierarchy that consists of the Supreme Being (*Katonda*), creator and father of all gods, guardian saints (*Balubaale*), and numerous lesser spirits of departed ancestors (*Mizimu*). *Katonda* was believed to be a distant god who did not routinely intervene in human affairs. *Katonda*'s priests (*Mandwa*) were drawn from the elephant (*Njovu*) clan. *Katonda* has been worshipped at the *Namakwa, Buzu,* and *Bukule* shrines in Kyaggwe.

Under *Katonda* are the more than two dozen guardian saints (*Balubaale*) who are more active in human society, the most powerful of whom is *Muwanga. Balubaale* are thought to have been erstwhile ancestors who possessed magical powers even when they were alive. Each *Lubaale* presides over the area that he or she excelled in when alive. Thus, there is a *Lubaale* for earthquakes, physical handicaps, good health, marriage and fertility, wealth, war, long life, sickness and death, game hunting, rain and harvest, smallpox, plague, and obstetrics. These *Balubaale,* who represent community attempts to cope with particular good or bad social, economic, or environmental experiences, have shrines in various parts of Buganda.[8]

Next in rank to *Balubaale* have been the numerous benevolent but lesser spirits of departed ancestors (*Mizimu*), who were kept appeased by regular offerings. Every Ganda household had a shrine for the departed ancestors, where regular token offerings were made to maintain the help of the "gods." Major personal or communal problems such as the start of war required supplications to the appropriate *Lubaale.* During the reign of *Kabaka* Mutesa I (1856–84), the advent of Christianity and Islam began to erode the influence of the *Balubaale* in the palace and in the kingdom and had virtually eclipsed them by the early 1900s.

There was another class of malevolent spirits believed to occupy parts of local landscapes such as gigantic rocks, forests, unusual trees, streams, or even dangerous animals such as pythons. These were mainly dealt with through avoidance and by keeping certain taboos, for example, avoidance of certain places and not doing certain things at certain times. Many of these taboos were also instituted to engender good moral behavior in society and were seldom challenged. On the rare occasion when taboos were violated, severe community sanctions were used to minimize such behavior.

Ganda religion provided the foundation for individual and communal social behavior and ensured the well-being of society, especially in precolonial times. As with other ATRs, the advent of Christianity and Islam ushered in an era of rapid decline of traditional Ganda religion, especially because these external religions derided Ganda traditional religious teachings and practices. Moreover, colonial state power was used to aid the spread of Christianity. As traditional Ganda religion and society were intricately entangled, the decline of traditional Ganda religion resulted in a precipitous moral and social decline that the foreign religions were immediately unable to deal with because their value systems were frequently at odds with those of Ganda traditional religion. Thus, although Christianity and Islam are now dominant, they have not quite managed to create an equally coherent social system. As a result, there are some ongoing attempts to renew and revive indigenous Ganda religious practices.

Other Indigenous Religions in Uganda

Besides the Baganda, each of Uganda's indigenous people groups has had its religion. But because the country is dominated by Bantu groups such as the Baganda and Banyoro, there are many similarities between indigenous Ganda religion and those of other ethnic groups. These similarities even transcend Bantu-Nilo Hamitic boundaries because indigenous religion is often an expression of these groups' responses to similar or near similar environmental conditions.[9] In sum, most Ugandans have believed in an omniscient, omnipresent, and omnipotent Supreme Creator God who greatly predates and exceeds creation, just as the sky is far above the earth.[10]

INDIGENOUS RELIGIONS AND CHANGE

Indigenous religions are inseparable from their respective societies and local environment, so any changes in the societies and environment are bound to trigger change in the religions. If a religion keeps pace with societal and environmental change, then it will survive and prosper. But if a religion fails to keep pace with social and environmental change, then it is unlikely to thrive. Thus, the relative decline of ATRs in Uganda is evidence of their failure to adapt to rapid changes in Ugandan society, culture, and physical environment, especially since the arrival of Europeans in the mid-1800s.

As in many other African countries, European colonialism led to the introduction of new social, religious, political, and economic systems that began to undermine their traditional Ugandan equivalents. In time, ATRs lost their vitality and began to decline. Consequently, the younger generations, schooled in the colonial social, political, and economic systems, slowly lost touch with indigenous religions and soon abandoned them while simultaneously embracing their foreign European equivalents.

ISLAM AND ITS IMPACT

Islam was the first nonindigenous religion to reach Uganda. Unlike in neighboring Kenya and Tanzania where Islam was introduced only from the

Indian Ocean coast, in Uganda the religion was introduced from the east and from the north.[11] Islam first reached the *Kabaka's* court with the arrival of Arabs from the slave market at Zanzibar in about 1848. In the early part of the reign of *Kabaka* Mutesa I (1856–84), the Arabs managed to "convert" Mutesa, and although he never got circumcised according to the tenets of Islam, he helped to build mosques, kept Ramadan (Islam's holy month), and often taught the Qur'an (Islam's holy book).[12] With Mutesa's so-called conversion, Buganda had two state religions—traditional Ganda religion and Islam—for almost two decades prior to the introduction of Christianity to the *Kabaka's* court in the 1870s.

Although *Kabaka* Mutesa I never took Islam seriously, some of his courtiers did and became true Muslims, an act that eventually led to their martyrdom when they committed treason by refusing to eat the *Kabaka's* meat which they considered ritually unclean. When *Kabaka* Mutesa's successor, Mwanga, tried to follow Mutesa in playing Christians against the Muslims and began to persecute Christians, the more organized and well-supplied Muslims took advantage of the situation and overthrew him, expelled the weakened Christians, and enthroned a new *Kabaka* who soon became a true Muslim and took the name *Kabaka* Nuhu Kalema—Nuhu being the Islamic equivalent of the Judaic or Christian name Noah. During Kalema's short-lived rule (1884–89), Islam prospered in Buganda and its followers even tried unsuccessfully to forcefully convert many Baganda into Muslims. In the meantime, the Christians regrouped, cut-off Muslim supply routes from the coast, rallied behind the deposed *Kabaka* Mwanga, returned him to power in 1889, and consigned the Muslims to a small section of Buganda. When the Muslims unsuccessfully tried to regain the throne in a failed countercoup in 1893, the Christians completely marginalized them socioeconomically and politically until Amin assumed Uganda's presidency in 1971. Nevertheless, *Kabaka* Kalema's short rule helped to solidify an Islamic presence (of the Shafi'te school) in Buganda and the descendants of these early Muslim converts can still be found in Buganda, Busoga, and Ankole and around the capital city Kampala.

From the north, Islam reached the Alur and Kakwa communities of northwest Uganda through the influence of the Malikite Muslims from North Africa. They also converted the Nubians of Sudan whose members later joined the British army and helped to colonize Uganda in the 1870s.[13] When Britain later annexed Uganda and made it a protectorate in 1894, these soldiers were used to suppress local resistance and protect vital trade routes to the East African coast.[14] Although these Nubian soldiers proved to be ineffective proselytizers for Islam because of their aloofness, and ethnic and linguistic isolation from the locals, their descendants are an important component of contemporary Ugandan Muslims. The impact of these soldiers on Uganda's religious landscape continued throughout the colonial period and extended into the postcolonial era when Idi Amin (a Kakwa Muslim) used them and other West Nile-region Muslims to undergird his administration in the 1970s.

Because of their long period of political and socioeconomic marginalization, many Ugandan Muslims initially welcomed Amin's rise to power in 1971. However, his rule turned out to be a mixed blessing for them and Islam in many ways. First, his presidency came at a time when Uganda's Muslim population was much smaller and divided (as it still is, along the lines of the Malikite tradition in the northwest and the Shafi'te tradition in the south) and, therefore, unable to quickly capitalize on his presidency. Second, even though he elevated many Muslims into important positions in government and industry, his 1972 expulsion of Asians in an attempt to bestow control of the country's economy on locals did not spare Asian Muslims. Third, unlike the nineteenth century *Kabaka* Kalema, Amin proved to be a poor Muslim role model who drunk freely and married many wives outside the mosque; wantonly dismissed Muslim bureaucrats and religious leaders from their positions; profaned Islamic holidays by, for instance, conducting public executions during the month of Ramadan; and misused funds meant for mosque construction and other Islamic institutions. Fourth, his brutal regime persecuted many Muslims and non-Muslims alike and led to an anti-Muslim backlash that victimized many more Muslims after his fall from power in 1979. Last, his departure forced many of his Muslim supporters, especially the Nubians soldiers, into exile thereby further reducing Uganda's small Muslim population.[15] Nevertheless, Muslims now constitute 12 percent of Uganda's population and their influence in the country could yet grow if they take steps to elevate their social and economic standing.

CHRISTIANITY AND ITS IMPACT

Henry Morton Stanley, the *New York Times* journalist sent to Africa in search of the famous British explorer and missionary David Livingstone, is credited with the introduction of Christianity in Uganda. Stanley, who had set off from Bagamoyo in the coastal region of modern-day Tanzania in 1869, found Livingstone at Ujiji by the shores of Lake Tanganyika, Tanzania, in 1871.[16] He stayed with Livingstone until 1872 and decided to help Livingstone find the source of the Nile. However, leaving Livingtone behind, he traveled to Boma in the present-day Democratic Republic of the Congo (formerly Zaire) between 1874 and 1877 via the kingdom of Buganda and the *Kabaka*'s court. Among others, he was accompanied by an African Christian called Dallington Scopian Maftaa. While in Uganda, Stanley, with the help of a Muslim scribe, prepared a condensed Swahili Bible and left Maftaa behind as a missionary to the Ganda people.[17] Soon after, the Church Missionary Society's (CMS) Buganda mission was established, following Stanley's appeal for missionaries in the *Daily Telegraph* on November 15, 1875.[18]

Because the *Kabaka*'s office was not tied to the indigenous religious structure, it was easy for *Kabaka* Mutesa I to entertain any religion he desired. Thus, the arrival of Stanley in Mutesa's court gave him three religions to choose from—traditional Ganda religion, Islam, and Christianity—depending on his immediate political, economic, and military needs. As one source has aptly put it:

> for at one time he [Mutesa] had commanded his subjects to embrace Islam; at another he was almost a protestant; and again the [French] "White [Roman Catholic] Fathers" imagined they had secured him. At heart he was a pagan, and a cruel and licentious ruler, and his death on the 10th October, 1884, was not a matter of regret to Christians, Mohammedans [Muslims], or heathens [African Traditional Religionists].[19]

Mutesa's shifting religious allegiance soon led to conflict as the three religions began to jostle for dominance of his court. On realizing this, Mutesa began to use the religious rivalry to his advantage. For instance, aware of the intrinsic danger in Ottoman Egypt's advance into modern-day northern

Kampala's St. Paul's Cathedral, Namirembe, is the center of Anglican Christianity in Uganda. Courtesy of the author.

Uganda, he welcomed European Christianity as a political counterweight to this Muslim incursion and as a source of technical aid.[20] Moreover, the *Kabaka* welcomed Christians, despite their warring factions, because he reasoned that their technological superiority pointed to the superiority of their religion over Islam and indigenous traditional religions. But because neither *Kabaka* Mutesa nor his son Mwanga fully supported any one of the external religions, conditions that allowed for open political and religious competition and conflict were created, hence the prolonged period of civil war and political instability between 1875 and 1892.[21]

Although some of this conflict was caused by Muslim assaults on Buganda, most of it was caused by rivalry between French Roman Catholicism and British Protestant Christianity. Had these two branches of Christianity originated in one country, say Great Britain, much of this warfare would have perhaps been avoided and the cause of Christianity in Uganda would have been much better served. But the open hostilities continued until the 1890 arrival of Captain Frederick Lugard, the Imperial British East Africa Company representative in Buganda, and the subsequent formal initiation of British colonialism of the country.[22] Besides ending open religious hostilities in Uganda, British colonialism dashed any Muslim hopes of controlling the country while ushering in the beginning of rapid expansion of Christianity (both Protestantism and Roman Catholicism).[23] The growth of Christianity was so rapid that by 1901, Protestants had established more than 200 churches with more than 20,000 members, 50 European staff, 20 mission stations, and more than 2,400 native teachers. They had also distributed thousands of copies of Bible translations by that year. Similarly, Roman Catholics had created 17 stations in various districts, built a stone cathedral in the capital, and built about 450 places of worship elsewhere in the country.[24] The rapid growth of Christianity in this period set the stage for its current dominance of Uganda's religious and national life.

These historical events underlie the current religious landscape, in which 85 percent of Ugandans are Christian, 12 percent are Muslim, and 3 percent practice either traditional indigenous religions, Hinduism, Baha'i, Judaism, or are irreligious or secular. And although Ugandan Christians are nearly equally divided between Protestants (especially Anglicans) and Roman Catholics, many other smaller denominations are represented in the country.[25]

OTHER RELIGIOUS MOVEMENTS

Besides Christianity, Islam, and ATRs, there are other, smaller religions practiced in Uganda, for example, Hinduism and Buddhism. Moreover, there is a new breed of blended religious movements that often combine elements of Christianity and traditional religions. Examples of these movements that are often considered cults by mainstream churches include the Holy Spirit Movement, Millenarian Religion, Yakan, and the Movement for the Restoration of the Ten Commandments of God.

The Holy Spirit Movement arose in the 1980s in the Acholi district of Uganda led by the Prophetess Alice Lakwena. The movement was a response to the extreme social upheaval and suffering that local people had experienced in the previous two decades under the Obote and Amin regimes. Born out of desperation, the movement taught its followers that cooking oil can protect them from bullets and that their stones and bottles will turn into grenades when hurled at government soldiers. As would be expected, many of Lakwena's followers died in skirmishes with government troops. Eventually, Lakwena fled to Kenya and was jailed and succeeded by her cousin Joseph Kony.

A similarly conceived but older movement is Yakan, which originated in northwest Uganda in the late 1890s. At the time, local Kakwa tribesmen, having been decimated by epidemics and Arab slave traders, were beginning to be affected by expanding European colonial interests. Overpowered by these external forces, the Kakwa resorted to Yakan, a cult that promised restored health, eternal life, and the return of the ancestors and dead cattle of all those who drunk sacred Yakan water. Moreover, Yakan religious leaders promised adherents protection from European bullets and the eventual overthrow of European colonizers. When the British later outlawed the cult but were unable to enforce the ban and were forced to lift it, Yakan was vindicated and begun to grow.

Although Yakan did not live up to its promises, it brought welcome psychological relief to a people under siege from disease, famine, slavery, and foreign occupation. In the early twentieth century, the religion flourished, and its leaders acquired political power and caused a rebellion that was quelled by the colonial army. Subsequently, Yakan declined, then reappeared in the war-torn Uganda of the 1980s, but with a millennialist aspect.[26]

RELIGION AND POLITICS

Since the 1870s three-way fight for control of *Kabaka* Mutesa's court by African Traditional Religions, Christianity, and Islam, religion and politics in Uganda have been inseparable. In fact, the early religious conflicts were largely political because each religious faction knew that control of the *Kabaka* would benefit its cause. Thus, from the founding of modern Uganda, religious factionalism was political factionalism.[27] And although none of the religions immediately got control of the *Kabaka's* court, Christianity and Islam gained converts among some of the court's chiefs, and these became instrumental in the expansion of the religions.

Ultimately, the religious rivalry was won by the Protestants after their British countrymen colonized Uganda and helped to neutralize the political influence of Roman Catholicism and Islam for much of the colonial period. Thus, even though the colonial authorities were secular and were in theory supportive of all religions, in reality, a religious and political hierarchy consisting of Protestants, Roman Catholics, and Muslims existed in the country throughout the colonial period. As a result, Roman Catholicism and Islam suffered because the colonial government mainly recruited Protestant chiefs at the county and subcounty level, thereby entrenching Protestant control of the country. In 1920, for instance, 40 of the 46 chiefs in Busoga were Protestants, while 4 were Catholics and 2 were Muslims.[28] Moreover, to ensure continued availability of chiefs predisposed to the colonial order, young chiefs, and, later, their sons, were sent to Protestant schools within and outside the country.

Although Catholics and Muslims were aware of this iniquitous political situation, they did not have enough political elites and the clout to challenge it. But when Catholics started to acquire their own elites in the 1920s, pressure mounted on the Protestant-dominated government, eventually yielding more Catholic chiefs by the 1940s. Muslims were not as fortunate.

Protestant dominance of Ugandan politics continued into the eve of independence with the formation of the powerful Uganda National (later People's) Congress (UNC) under Obote. Not to be outdone, Catholics formed the Democratic Party. But the UNC, which by the early 1960s had a less obvious Protestant identity because it had become leftist and had embraced non-Protestants, overcame the opposition and formed the first independence government. As the party became more inclusive, it began to lose its base support and was forced to modify but not completely abandon its leftist ideology—which was later to inform Obote's unsuccessful attempt to create a secular creed around which to mobilize the country in the early independence period.[29]

When Idi Amin overthrew President Obote on January 25, 1971, many Muslims were elated that one of their own had risen to the country's presidency. Initially, Amin helped the Muslim minority to gain disproportionate access to national resources, despite his promise of wanting to create a religiously neutral state. This made many Muslims hopeful that Amin could help to Islamize Uganda, just as Christian leaders before him had helped Christianize the country. But their joy and hopes for the Amin presidency did not last long, as Amin, with the aid of fellow Muslim Kakwa and allied Sudanese Nubian soldiers, soon unleashed a reign of terror that killed an estimated 300,000–500,000 Ugandans, to the horror of Muslims and non-Muslims alike.[30] Moreover, he persecuted Christians, especially Catholics, whom his Nubian Muslim soldiers considered the major obstacle to Uganda's Islamization.[31] His 1979 overthrow and exile was a welcome relief to Ugandans of all religious persuasions.

In the 1979–86 period, Uganda had a quick succession of Muslim and Christian leaders that culminated in Yoweri Museveni's presidency. Soon after gaining the presidency by overthrowing the military council headed by Tito Okello, Museveni sought to neutralize the political power of religion and ethnic-based political parties. He therefore banned all political parties in the country and transformed his rebel National Resistance Army into the governing National Resistance Movement. For the 10 years ending in 1996, Museveni governed by decree and was first popularly elected in that year with little political opposition. In 2002, his government passed the Political Organizations Act that, among other things, restricts the formation of religious political parties, thereby reducing the role of religion in politics.[32] To further divorce politics and religion in Uganda, the Museveni government has also created a secular constitution for the country and has tried to remain religiously neutral. Only time will tell whether the country's damaging religious rivalry has ended and whether it has been replaced by positive political involvement by the country's various religious entities..

3

Literature, Film, and Media

ORAL LITERATURE

As elsewhere in Africa, oral literature is a central aspect of Ugandan culture because written communication in the country dates back only to the colonial era. Even with growing access to formal education, it is unlikely that written communication will become dominant in Uganda because universal literacy is still many years away. Moreover, Uganda's long turbulent history has undermined the development of print communication and deprived many people of an opportunity to go to school. Thus, oral literature continues to be an important mode of cultural transmission in Uganda.

Oral literature takes many forms, including song, poems, proverbs or wise sayings, taboos, riddles, tales, stories or legends (fiction), and drama and is a major method of education, instruction, and socialization in Ugandan society, especially in rural areas. Oral literature is continuously being updated in response to current needs.[1] Although the written word is becoming commonplace, oral literature is so paramount in Ugandan society that "whenever, an elder dies, a library dies" because much of the knowledge is not being preserved in print or other more durable forms.[2]

INDIGENOUS LANGUAGE LITERATURE

Uganda has limited written literature in indigenous languages because "politics and economics of publishing" work against it.[3] This is because the market for such material is too small to sustain profitable publishing, and the colonial and postcolonial governments have worked against the development of local language literature because they either see it as contrary to the development of a multicultural and modern national culture or as a vehicle for potential political rebellion. Moreover, there is widespread belief among many Ugandans that indigenous language publications and media are for the uneducated and uninformed masses and that well-educated people read English-language materials. Thus, the existing collection of indigenous language literature is very small. It includes *Lak Tar, Song of Lawino,* and *Song of Ocol* by the late Okot p' Bitek. *Song of Lawino* and *Song of Ocol* were both written and published in Dholuo before their subsequent translation into English. However, if all of Uganda's oral literature was published in local languages, it would create a library that would dwarf the country's English-language literature.

LITERATURE IN ENGLISH

The vast majority of Uganda's published literary work is in English. It is explored here under the broad categories of female and male authors and poetry.

Female Authors

As with the rest of East Africa, Uganda has few women writers, given their limited access to education in the colonial and postcolonial period and their heavy social responsibilities as mothers and caregivers. Nevertheless, Uganda has managed to produce some notable women authors such as Barbara Kimenye (1930–), Goretti Kyomuhendo, Mary Karooro Okurut, Rose Rwakasisi, Lillian Tindyebwa, Hope Keshubi, Regina Amollo, Christine Oryema-Lalobo, Violet Barungi, Jane Kaberuka, Ayeta Anne Wangusa, Susan Kiguli, Mildred Kiconco Barya, and Jane Okot p'Bitek.[4,5] With the exception of Barbara Kimenye and Jane Okot p'Bitek, the other female authors have published their works since the 1990s, following the formation of Femrite (the association of Ugandan women writers) in 1996 to promote female authors in Uganda and to challenge the country's male literary dominance. If the recent increase in the number of female authors is any indication, then Femrite may be well on its way to achieving its goals. A brief examination of some of these authors' works follows.

Barbara Kimenye is by far the most prolific and best-known female writer in Uganda. She primarily writes for children and teenagers. She was born in England in 1930 and joined a convent in Yorkshire before training as a nurse in London. She then went to East Africa and became a journalist before finding her true calling as a children's fiction writer.[6] She has written more than 25 short story books for schoolchildren, for example, the Moses series that contains more than 10 titles describing the adventures of a Kenyan schoolboy named Moses. Books in this series include *Moses and Mildred* (1967), *Moses and the Kidnappers* (1968), *Moses in Trouble* (1968), and *Moses* (1969). Some of her other popular books are *The Smugglers* (1966), *The Gemstone Affair* (1978), and *The Scoop* (1978). Although these books are fiction, many are based on socioeconomic events in East Africa. One of her short stories, "The Battle of the Sacred Tree," has been made into a feature film. Although Kimenye has sometimes been criticized for imposing a European imagination on African village stories, her books are popular among schoolchildren in East Africa.

The children's literature genre that Kimenye pioneered has recently drawn contributions from many new Ugandan female authors, for example, Rose Rwakasisi, who has written several children's and young adult books, including *The Old Woman and the Shell* (1994), *How Friends Became Enemies* (1993), *How Goats Lost Their Beautiful Tails* (2004), and *Sunshine after Rain* (2002). *The Old Woman and the Shell* tells the story of an old woman who finds a magic shell that provides for her as long as she keeps her word. The book teaches children to be trustworthy. *How Friends Became Enemies* is a rendition of popular folktales from Uganda's various communities. *How Goats Lost Their Beautiful Tails* is an allegory of the rivalry between goats and sheep and is designed to convey to children the destructive power of jealousy. *Sunshine after Rain* delves into Uganda's HIV/AIDS crisis and advises young people to learn from the mistakes of those who have contracted the disease, lest they be victimized by it. Many of Rwakasisi's books are designed to pass on Uganda's rich cultural treasure to its children.

Recent women authors are also tackling issues in contemporary Ugandan society. Goretti Kyomuhendo's novel, *The First Daughter* (1996), uses the story of a girl named Kasemiire to address the challenges of female education in Uganda. In the story, Kasemiire goes to school to the scorn of her father's friends who see his investment in her as a waste—most Ugandan communities devalue female education because of the cultural thinking that a girl's education mostly benefits her family of marriage. In due course, Kasemiire shames and infuriates her father when she becomes pregnant before taking her exams—a very common occurrence in Uganda. But she persists against all odds and succeeds.[7] In her other novel, *Secrets No More* (1999), Kyomuhendo exposes the suffering of children in Uganda's civil wars as well as those that have engulfed neighboring countries. In the novel, a Rwandese child loses her parents in a recent war and is forced into an orphanage, where she becomes pregnant and decides to run away to the city to start a new life.

Violet Barungi, in her novel *Cassandra* (1999), seeks to challenge the constraints placed on women by traditional Ugandan society. Set in the tumultuous 1980s, *Cassandra* is a story of a self-assured and determined Ugandan girl who hopes to break the mold of traditional female roles and excel in other areas of society without the help of men. But her plans become immensely complicated when she falls in love.

Jane Kaberuka's work *Silent Patience* (1999) explores the issues of gender discrimination and sectarianism in East Africa. Set in Rwanda, the novel is the multigenerational story of Stella, a young girl who is forced by tradition to abandon school and enter into an arranged marriage with an older Tutsi man whom she has never met. Over time, however, her society comes to terms with the negative effects of its discriminatory gender relations, traditions, and social divisions.

The late Hope Keshubi's novel *Going Solo* (1997) is a tale of Doreen, a modern Ugandan woman who seeks to make it on her own after her husband is kidnapped by armed men. Penniless and beleaguered by her brothers-in-law, she becomes a teacher but has to contend with the mistreatment of two corrupt headmasters. But she persists despite these and other challenges.

Mary Karooro Okurut has published two recent books, *The Invisible Weevil* (1998) and *The Official Wife* (2003). Whereas *The Invisible Weevil* explores Uganda's dreadful political experience since independence, *The Official Wife* returns to the theme that unites many contemporary Ugandan female authors, that is, the many challenges of the modern Ugandan woman, in this case, polygamy. Following the lines of Okot p'Bitek's *Song of Lawino,* Okurut challenges such marriages as well as her country's naive reception of Western cultural ways.

There are many other notable Ugandan female authors who deal with various themes of interest to Ugandans. Among these are women and the dangers of materialism (e.g., Lillian Tindyebwa, *Recipe for Disaster,* 2000); the challenges of everyday Ugandan life (e.g., Jane Okot p'Bitek, *Song of Farewell,* 1994, and Susan Kiguli, *The African Saga,* 1998); the victimization of children by war (e.g., Christine Oryema-Lalobo, *No Hearts at Home,* 1999); romance and masculinity (e.g., Mildred Kiconco Barya, *Men Love Chocolates but They Don't Say,* 2000); and male chauvinism and women's oppression (e.g., Regina Amollo, *A Season of Mirth,* 1999, and Ayeta Wangusa, *Memoirs of a Mother,* 1998).[8]

Male Authors

Some of Uganda's leading male authors are Austin Bukenya (1944–), Okot p' Bitek (1931–82), Taban lo Liyong (1939–), John Ruganda (1941–),

Bonnie Lubega (1929–), Cliff Lubwa p'Chong (1946–), John Nagenda (1938–), Peter Nazareth (1940–), Richard Carl Ntiru (1946–), Okello Oculi (1942–), George Seremba (1957–), Eneriko Seruma (Henry S. Kimbugwe, 1944–), Robert Serumaga (1939–80), Bahadur Tejani (1942–), and Timothy Wangusa (1942–). Most of these authors' works focus on contemporary social, political, and economic issues and are meant for mature audiences. Many others lament the decline of African culture from Western influence since the colonial period. Okot p' Bitek, Taban lo Liyong, John Ruganda, Austin Bukenya, and Bonnie Lubega are Uganda's better-known male authors and are, therefore, discussed in greater detail here.

Okot p'Bitek is, perhaps, Uganda's most well-known literary figure. He was born in Gulu in 1931 and was schooled at Gulu High School, King's College, Budo, and Government Teacher Training College, Mbarara. After graduation, he taught English and religion at Sir Samuel Baker School near Gulu and was a member of a local Christian community. A man of diverse talents, he was a teacher, a choirmaster, an opera composer and producer, an actor, a politician, a professional soccer player, a playwright, and a community organizer. His professional soccer career enabled him to tour Britain in 1958, where he stayed and studied education at Bristol University, law at Aberystwyth, Wales (where he lost his Christian commitment), and anthropology at Oxford University.

While at Oxford, he wrote a thesis on Acoli and Lango traditional songs. Upon completion of his studies, he returned to Uganda and initiated an arts festival in Gulu, before moving to Kampala in 1966. Afterward, he became the director of the Ugandan Cultural Center. In the early 1970s, he was fired from his position for criticizing Idi Amin's government and was forced into exile in Kenya, where he taught literature at the University of Nairobi. His exile turned out to be a blessing, as many of his contemporaries lost their lives during Amin's 1970–79 regime. After Amin's overthrow in 1979, p'Bitek returned from exile and taught creative writing at Makerere University until his death in 1982. p'Bitek's literary works include the novel *White Teeth* (1989, originally written in Acholi/Acoli in 1953 under the title *Lak Tar*) and the following works of poetry: *Song of Lawino* (1956, published in English in 1966), *Song of Ocol* (1970), *Two Songs: Song of a Prisoner* and *Song of Malaya* (1971), and *The Horn of My Love* (1974).[9] Although the *Two Songs* critique the exploitation of the weak by the rich, the *Song of a Prisoner* is specifically dedicated to the memory of Patrick Lumumba, the late prime minister of the Democratic Republic of the Congo (formerly Zaire) who was killed in 1961. The novel *White Teeth* is a story about the struggles of a young Acoli man who goes to Kampala to work to raise bride wealth or dowry so he can marry. Though first written in the 1950s, the novel foresaw the impending doom of dowry in Uganda's rapidly modernizing society. Because of the unbearable burden of bride price, the Ugandan government has recently sought to outlaw it.

p'Bitek's most well-known works are *Song of Lawino,* which is the longest and most influential African poem in English, and *Song of Ocol.* In *Song of Lawino,* p'Bitek uses the story of an Acholi/Acoli couple, Lawino and her husband Ocol, to explore the negative consequences of Western colonialism and culture on Africa. Lawino, a jilted traditional Acoli wife, criticizes her husband for abandoning her in favor of the modern (Westernized) Clementine, who is educated, speaks English, and acts like a white lady. As Lawino describes her family life, before and after Clementine, the social, cultural, and economic changes that Europeans have imposed on her traditional African society become clear. For instance, the social and cultural skills that served her well in traditional Acoli society are being used against her or made irrelevant by the country's rapid modernization. She laments the fact that even though she supported her husband Ocol's schooling, he abandons her after graduation because she is illiterate and "backward" and marries the educated and "cultured" Clementine.

In *Song of Ocol,* Ocol responds to the criticisms leveled against him in *Song of Lawino* 14 years earlier. But instead of addressing Lawino's questions, Ocol chides her for her "backwardness," that is, non-Western ways. He also uses the occasion to belittle African culture and tradition and expresses his admiration for Western culture, which he notes will eventually overrun Africa. In the end, Ocol's prophesied defeat of African culture fails to materialize because he overestimates the power of Western culture. Moreover, because *Song of Ocol* was published 14 years after *Song of Lawino,* many of the issues it deals with in response to *Song of Lawino* had been overtaken by history. For instance, by the time *Song of Ocol* was written in 1970, Uganda had been an independent country for eight years and was beginning to undo the cultural damage of colonialism. Despite p'Bitek's missteps in *Song of Ocol,* he is nevertheless one of the most important Ugandan writers, as his influence goes far beyond Uganda's borders. He also inspired many younger authors and succeeded in sensitizing them to the need to use their gifts to convey and preserve beneficial aspects of African culture.

Taban lo Liyong was born in Sudan of Ugandan parents and raised in Uganda. He has published more than 14 literary works: novels, plays, and social commentaries. His main objectives are to preserve African culture and to encourage Africans to write their own history rather than letting foreigners do so. Some of his works are *The Last Word* (1969), *Fixions & Other Stories—A Compilation of Luo Mythologies and Folktales* (1969), *Frantz Fanon's Uneven Ribs* (1971), *Another Nigger Dead* (1972), *Thirteen*

Offensives against Our Enemies (1973), *Ballads of Underdevelopment* (1976), *Another Last Word* (1990), *Culture Is Rustan* (1991), and *The Cows of Shambat: Sudanese Poems* (1992). Seen as the greatest contemporary literary figure in Uganda, Liyong offers a complex and diverse array of themes and writing styles in his works.

John Ruganda has written two novels, *Black Mamba* (1973) and *Covenant with Death* (1973), the renowned play *The Burdens* (1972), and other plays such as *The Floods* (1980), *Music without Tears* (1982), and *Echoes of Silence* (1986). *Black Mamba* (literally "crocodile") satirizes the oppression of African people by leaders who look like them but are every bit as vicious as the white rulers (*mamba*) they replaced at independence. *Covenant with Death* looks into the social and psychological alienation of Africans during and after colonialism, especially the elite. *The Burdens* examines everyday social problems in contemporary Africa, while *The Floods, Music without Tears,* and *Echoes of Silence* deplore the suffering of the African masses at the hands of corrupt and incompetent governments while the elites do nothing.

Bonnie Lubega's works include *The Burning Bush* (1970), *The Outcasts* (1971), *The Great Animal Land* (1971), *Cry, Jungle Children* (1974), and *Olulimi Oluganda Amakula* (1995). Whereas *The Burning Bush* chronicles the tension between the traditional and modern material aspects of the village, *The Outcasts* deals with the plight of nonnative migrant workers in colonial and early postcolonial Buganda. His *Olulimi Oluganda Amakula* is a Luganda semantic dictionary, while *The Great Animal Land* and *Cry, Jungle Children* highlight the dangers of environmental destruction in Africa. The latter is a theme that few Ugandan literary figures have addressed.

Austin Bukenya's major works are *The Bride* (1984) and *The People's Bachelor* (1972). *The Bride* is a critique of many African societies' adherence to outdated traditions and taboos; *The People's Bachelor* criticizes the pompous behavior of African elites and their inability to deal with their societies' problems. His most recent book, *Understanding Oral Literature* (1994), is an edited volume that seeks to promote Africa's oral culture by teaching it to contemporary literate African societies. This may be his most lasting contribution to African literature.

Poetry

A fair amount of Uganda's published literature consists of poetry by writers such as Okot p' Bitek, Jane Okot p' Bitek, Taban lo Liyong, Mildred Kiconco Barya, Christine Oryema-Lalobo, and Susan N. Kiguli. The poems deal with a host of social problems and issues, including war, love, hatred, and the pressures of everyday living.

Okot p' Bitek's poems *Song of Lawino* and *Song of Ocol* are Uganda's most popular poetry works and are concerned with the challenges of cultural change in Uganda in the colonial and early postcolonial period. Jane Okot p'Bitek's *Song of Farewell* (1994), though a farewell memoriam to her father, Okot p'Bitek, is an examination of an array of social issues, including war and love. Mildred Kiconco Barya's *Men Love Chocolates but They Don't Say* (2003) deals with many issues, including the contradictory nature of masculinity, for example, its exemplification of both strength and gentleness. Christine Oryema-Lalobo's *No Hearts at Home* (1999) deals exclusively with war, especially its effect on children and its ability to engulf any society quickly. Susan Kiguli's *The African Saga* (1998) is an examination of a wide variety of societal problems.

Taban lo Liyong is, perhaps, the only other Ugandan poet whose acclaim rivals that of Okot p'Bitek. He has published more than seven poetic works, as previously mentioned. His prolific writing benefited immensely from growing up listening to traditional fireside stories. His poems deal with a wide variety of cultural, political, and social issues. His long writing career has enabled him to explore these issues over time. His *Words That Melt a Mountain* reflects on his two-year stay in Japan.[10]

MEDIA

Because of Uganda's relative freedom of the press, the country has many newspapers and magazines, especially in major urban areas such as Kampala. Uganda's major newspapers are the *Daily Monitor* and the Uganda government's *New Vision* and *Sunday Vision*. *New Vision* also publishes vernacular newspapers such as *Bukedde* (in Luganda), *Orumuri* (in Runyankole), *Rupiny* (in Dholuo or Luo), and *Etop* (in Ateso).[11] Kenya's Nation Media Group owns the *Daily Monitor* and the regional weekly newspaper, *The East African,* which is also sold in Uganda. To compete with the *New Vision*'s vernacular newspapers, the *Daily Monitor* has also recently launched *Ngoma* (in Luganda). In the past, Uganda has had other newspapers (e.g., the *Star, Financial Times, Munno,* and *People*) that have all ceased publication for various reasons.

Uganda is also witnessing the emergence of the tabloid press, and the 2002 launch of the *Red Pepper* has generated a lot of controversy and led to calls for such papers to be banned for promoting pornography and corrupting the morals of Ugandan society.[12] The country's vernacular-language papers are also considered by some Ugandans to be significant pornographic outlets.[13] Although Uganda inherited British laws that ban trafficking in pornographic material, these are considered inadequate. The country is in the process of

preparing a media bill that would, among other things, define what consti-
tutes pornography in Uganda.

There are also a number of magazines such as the *Citizen* (weekly), *Heritage Magazine* (quarterly), *Munnansi* (weekly), *Success* (quarterly), *New Era*
(quarterly), *Woman's Dawn* (monthly), *Educator* (monthly), *Uganda Journal*
(semiannual), and the Catholic Church's monthly magazine *Musizi.*

The overwhelming majority of these newspapers and magazines are published in English, the country's main literary medium, in the metropolitan
center of Kampala. Outside of the main urban areas, newspaper circulation is
poor because of low literacy levels and incomes and poor transport systems,
especially in rural areas.[14] Together, these factors have produced some of the
lowest newspaper and magazine circulation figures anywhere. For instance, in
1994, there were two daily newspapers for every 1,000 people in Uganda. By
comparison, there were 228 newspapers per 1,000 people (or 1 newspaper for
every 4 people) in the United States in the same year.[15] Although Uganda is
a communal society where newspapers, magazines, and other resources are
routinely shared by many people, the country's low level of newspaper and
magazine availability undermines meaningful sharing or access to these
resources, making them a minor source of news and information.

Like many other sectors of Ugandan society, the poor state of its newspaper
and magazine industry can be attributed to the country's turbulent social and
political history. For example, in the 1970s, Amin's regime either killed or
forced many Ugandan journalists, writers, and publishers into exile. His economic policies not only ruined the country's economy, but they also made
newspapers and magazines a luxury for many Ugandans.[16]

ONLINE NEWS

Uganda has one of the most open Internet access environments in Africa.
As of 2004, the country had 2,692 Internet hosts and about 125,000 Internet
users.[17] As a result, online publishing in the country is growing. Its online
news sources include Africa Online Uganda (http://www.africaonline.co.ug),
which has news and information on business, computing, travel, sports, education, and health; afrol News Uganda (http://www.afrol.com/countries/
uganda), with regularly updated independent news and analyses on Uganda;
allAfrica.com: Uganda (http://allafrica.com/uganda), with summary news
reports and headlines from the Ugandan press; Kampala1 Netcom (http://
www.kampala1.com), with news and information about Uganda and the
capital Kampala, academic resources for Ugandan students, free e-mail, and
classified advertisements; Uganda News—Topix.net (http://www.topix.net/
world/uganda), with continually updated news on Uganda from Internet

sources and the web portals of the country's major daily newspapers, the *Daily Monitor* (http://www.monitor.co.ug), *New Vision* (http://www.newvision.co.ug), and *Sunday Vision* (http://www.sundayvision.co.ug).

The country's Internet boom also means that Ugandans are beginning to access online pornography through the country's many Internet cafes. Although some cafes use varying levels of software filters to prevent their clients' access to such sites, many others do not, considering this to be a violation of their clients' rights. Nevertheless, the advent of published and online pornography in Uganda is worrisome to many Ugandans and religious organizations.[18]

RADIO AND TELEVISION

There are several radio and television stations in Uganda, thanks to recent liberalization of the airwaves, that is, the government's opening of the broadcast media sector to local and foreign private investment by individuals and corporations. As of 2001, the country had 42 radio stations (the most in East Africa): 7 AM, 33 FM, 2 shortwave, and 8 television stations. Another 100 broadcast licenses have been issued but are yet to be put to use.[19]

Specific examples of Uganda's radio stations include Sanyu FM 2000 (Kampala); Monitor FM (Kampala); RFI 1 Afrique/RFI 2 (Kampala); Radio Simba FM (Kampala); BBC World Service (Kampala, Mbarara, and Mbale); Radio Maria Uganda (Kampala); Impact FM (Kampala, Mbale, and Masaka region); Radio Maria Uganda (Mbarara); Radio Apac (Apac); and Mama FM.

Television stations include LTV-Lighthouse TV/TBN Uganda (Kampala); International Television Network, International TV Network Uganda, TV Africa 28, and WBS-Wavah Broadcasting Services (Kampala).[20] Because the cost of setting up radio stations is miniscule compared with television stations, the ratio of radio to television stations in the country is 5 to 1.

Uganda's radio and television broadcasting stations offer a variety of programming, including music, news, or a combination of both. Radio Maria Uganda and LTV-Lighthouse TV/TBN Uganda offer religious broadcasts. Although many of the country's radio and television stations are local, others such as the British Broadcasting Corporation's (BBC) World Service are owned by international news organizations. Many of Uganda's radio and television broadcasts focus on the major urban markets, especially Kampala, with many rural areas poorly served.

The abundance of radio stations in Uganda is indicative of the fact that radio is the country's main form of mass communication. Radios are widespread in the country because they are cheap to buy and operate and are easily portable. In 1996, for instance, there were 123 radios per 1,000 people (roughly 1 radio for every 8 Ugandans) or nearly 2,460,000 radios for the country's then nearly 20 million people. In 2002, half of the country's households owned a radio.[21] Aside from the total number of radios, their distribution differs widely among the nation's regions because of variations in wealth levels and political stability. Thus, southern Uganda, with its higher level of political stability, wealth, and more literate population, has more radios than the northern half of the country that lacks these advantages. Moreover, there are large gaps in access to radios between rural and urban areas, with most of the country's radios being found in urban areas, especially the more prosperous ones in the south. The distribution of radio stations and signal strength are also in favor of the southern half of the country.

These distribution patterns are also applicable to television access. In 1996, for instance, Uganda had 26 television sets per 1,000 people or 1 television set for every 38 Ugandans. This means that Uganda had approximately 520,000 television sets for its then nearly 20 million people in that year, and most of these were in urban areas. In comparison, there were 806 television sets per 1,000 people (or nearly 1 television set per person) in the United States in that year. In 2002, only 4.5 percent of Uganda's households owned a television set.[22] The lower number of televisions in Uganda is attributable to the relatively high cost of purchasing them, the lack of electric power in many rural and urban neighborhoods, the limited availability of relevant television material, and the limited number of television stations in the country, especially in rural areas, owing to the high cost of owning and operating them. The lack of electric power in many rural areas also forces many rural television owners to operate them with costly solar energy systems or car batteries that require regular and tedious transportation to power-supplied areas for charging.

Although radio is relatively widespread, its contribution to Ugandan society is somewhat limited because of poor reception in much of the country, low radio ownership by women and poor programming and timing for women listeners, the frequent use of inaccessible broadcast languages such as English, and the common broadcast of culturally irrelevant and distasteful material and the occasional use of offensive language. Male journalists' dominance of the media (by a 6 to 1 ratio) contributes to the production of programming that is irrelevant to the needs of women. Limited radio ownership by women also denies them a chance to decide what programs to listen to.[23] This situation needs to change to enable these media to have a more beneficial role in society. Moreover, the country might benefit from the widespread availability of more affordable radio sets.

Nevertheless, there are examples of relevant and effective radio broadcasting in Uganda, for example, Radio Freedom in Gulu district and 101.7 Mama FM. Located in Gulu in the northern rural war-torn part of Uganda, Radio Freedom involves local people in its program production, broadcasts relevant programs in the local language, and is reputed to have contributed to reduction of hostilities in the region.[24]

The only women's radio station in Africa, and one of three in the world, is Uganda's 101.7 Mama FM. With a coverage of 65 percent of south, west, east, and central Uganda, the station was set up in 1997 to counteract the shortage of radio programming for least-heard women and other minorities (children, people with disabilities, and youth) in Uganda—a situation that made them lag behind other groups in access to information. Specifically, the station seeks to broadcast gender-sensitive programs, offer training and practical experience opportunities to female journalists, meet minorities' daily information needs (unlike other radio stations' tendency to focus on them only during disasters and other unusual events), provide a forum for exchange of ideas among minorities, champion minority issues and put them on the national agenda, promote good governance in order to minimize minority suffering from bad governance, reawaken the sense of duty and responsibility, lobby for gender balance in the community, and promote responsible environmental use.

To accomplish these objectives, Mama FM focuses on issues pertaining to health, law, land, economic development, education, human rights, politics, leadership, religion, agriculture, and environment. To reach the widest possible audience, it broadcasts in English, Kiswahili, and many other local languages, such as Luganda, Lusoga, Runyoro, Rutooro, Runyankole, Rukiga, Ateso, Luo, and Lumasaaba. Like Radio Freedom, Mama FM promotes community involvement in its programming and production by encouraging the formation of women radio listener clubs, working with community groups and nongovernmental organizations (NGOs), and by encouraging listener call/phone-ins, e-mail, and mail.[25] If more broadcasters followed Radio Freedom and Mama FM's lead, radio could have an enormous beneficial impact on Uganda.

FILM

Uganda's film industry is poorly developed because the country has no filmmaking tradition; there is a shortage of technical and financial resources; the country's low incomes provide a limited market for movies; and many Ugandans are unfamiliar with the medium. Nevertheless, films that have featured Uganda include Barbet Schroeder's *General Idi Amin Dada: A Self-Portrait*

(1974), a chronicle of Amin's rule of the country; *The Rise and Fall of Idi Amin* (1980), starring Joseph Olita and Dennis Hill and directed by Sharad Patel, which shows how Amin came to power and how he managed to continue his atrocities in Uganda for so long; and Mira Nair's *Mississippi Masala* (1992), which stars Denzel Washington and Sarita Choudhury, and is about a young Ugandan Indian woman who moves to the United States when Idi Amin expels her family and other Asians in 1971 and falls in love with a black man, forcing families on either side to confront that reality.

First-generation Ugandan-American Ntare Guma Mbaho Mwine has also recently produced *Beware of Time,* a documentary on the lives Uganda's HIV-positive people and the armed conflict in northern Uganda. It also contains a conversation with Amule Amin, Idi Amin's brother.[26]

The country's film industry has a bright future following the recent inauguration of the Great Lakes Film Production Company in Kampala and the Amakula Film Festival that seeks to promote movie production and entertainment in the country.[27]

4

Art and Architecture/Housing

Ugandan society has its own unique brand of art, architecture, and housing. The country's art, architecture, and housing have functional, aesthetic, and entertainment roles. Moreover, an analysis of Uganda's art, architecture, and housing reveals much about this society.

ART

Like language, Ugandan art plays a central role in the country's cultural transmission, expression, and preservation. It transmits knowledge and values that are central to the country's culture and history, promotes the sharing of social aspirations and goals, and helps foster agreement on current issues and ideals.[1] Artistic expression is, therefore, a central and universal element of Ugandan society and is a powerful transmitter of culture. Because the medium is accessible to virtually every member of society regardless of literacy or social status, it plays an important role in all levels of Ugandan society. As Ugandan sculptor Lilian Nabulime has noted, art can overcome the limits of language and speech and communicate to an ethnically, culturally, and linguistically diverse audience.[2] This is unlike the written word that is accessible to the small, literate segment of Ugandan society.

Ugandan culture and art are intertwined. Because Ugandan society is communal, its artistic expression and enjoyment also places emphasis on the communal rather than the individual, as is the case in Western society.[3]

The modern history of Ugandan art begins in the colonial period when formal art education was introduced into the school curriculum in the early 1900s, after the British colonial authorities realized that Uganda was of less long-term strategic importance to them than neighboring Kenya. As a result, the colonial authorities did not control the development of the Ugandan school system as closely as they did in Kenya, where art education was limited to white-only schools. In Uganda, art education was even taught at Makerere University College, thereby making Uganda the center of formal art education in East Africa from the colonial period to the onset of Idi Amin's regime (1971–79), which eliminated many prominent artists, forced others into exile, and generally made it difficult for those that survived to work.[4]

Formal art education in the country also owes its origin to Christian missionaries and the work of Margaret Trowell, who established the Fine Art School in 1937 at Makerere University (now known as the Margaret Trowell School of Industrial and Fine Arts). Colonial art education was meant to help improve the lives of native Ugandans by transforming art into a vocation. Some of those who received art education in the colonial period were teachers who introduced art education in Ugandan schools. Initially, art education trainees earned teacher certificates, but later on, these were upgraded to diplomas. By the attainment of independence in 1962, the Trowell School had become a leading center of art and design education in eastern and southern Africa. At one time, the school also served as the national museum, with its principal also serving as the museum's director. This dual role further added to the school's prominence; early students include the renowned sculptor Francis Nnaggenda and the Tanzanian painter Sam Ntiro. In the preindependence period, artistic expression in Uganda mainly focused on magical, religious, and political motifs or subjects, these being considered to be appropriate to Uganda at the time.[5]

Uganda's colonial and early postcolonial fame as the art center of eastern and southern Africa began to decline in the early 1970s with Idi Amin's ascendancy to power. Although by then the Margaret Trowell School had many African lecturers, many were killed and others were forced into exile as Amin's regime limited freedom of expression. Yet the school remained open with a skeletal staff throughout the Amin years, although its contribution to the development of art in Uganda in this period was minimal. The situation began to improve again after Amin's departure, and currently, the school has a sizable number of notable resident artists and lecturers, including the sculptors Lilian Nabulime and Rose Kirumira and painters Godfrey Banadda and Paul Lubowa. Many of these artists' works are featured in major international exhibitions and in Sidney Littlefield Kasfir's 1999 book, *Contemporary African Art.*[6]

Although art is once again blossoming in Uganda, its development faces many significant challenges. First, although art and design education is taught at all educational levels in Uganda, it is not considered a core part of the curriculum or as a practical or vocational subject because of the relatively high costs of teaching art; the shortage of well-trained art teachers, especially at the primary school level; and the limited knowledge of and market for Ugandan art in major world art markets. The latter is partly the result of poor marketing and the country's history of civil strife that has inhibited art production and marketing. Nevertheless, Ugandan art has slowly begun to make its way to world markets.[7]

Second, the poor living conditions of Ugandan artists are forcing them to compromise their integrity by engaging in the production of Western-oriented or tourist art, which, although profitable, undermines the preservation, development, and production of genuine Ugandan art that serves local cultural needs.[8]

Third is the limited preservation of Ugandan art in the country because of the shortage of galleries and the general underfunding of those that exist and the underpayment of staff. As a result, Uganda's most prized art has been lost to international art syndicates, foreign art museums and galleries, and private collections that are inaccessible to the average Ugandan.

Fourth is that formal Ugandan art and design education is still anchored in its colonial roots and has a Western bent. To restore its rightful place in society, the country's formal art education program must adopt a local outlook, approach, and design that would enable it to foster Uganda's social, cultural, and economic development.[9] Such a change may also help to soften criticism of local artists for working with some of the country's dictatorial regimes (e.g., Amin's), possibly against their wish, and for failing to use their talents to help restore the country's social order—this despite their success in documenting the country's social strife and injustices.[10]

Fifth is that Ugandan artists are facing considerable market pressure to internationalize their work. If this happens, it might undermine local art knowledge systems and help disconnect Ugandan art from its roots, thereby limiting the medium's ability to contribute to the preservation of Ugandan culture.[11] Although it is not possible to completely insulate Ugandan art from external influences, this exposure can be managed to protect local art culture.

The major repositories of art in Uganda are museums (e.g., Uganda National Museum); universities and colleges (e.g., Makerere University; Institute for Teacher Education at Kyambogo (ITEK); King's College Buddo); public art commissions or art works commissioned by the government (e.g., Independence Monument, Kampala City Center); galleries (e.g., Nommo National Gallery, painting and sculpture; Tuli Fanya Gallery, painting and sculpture; Nnyanzi Art Studio, painting, sculpture, and printmaking); and hotels (e.g., Nile Hotel, Speke Hotel, Hotel Africana).

TRADITIONAL ART

Artistic expression in Uganda predates the arrival of the written word following European exploration and conquest of Uganda. Hence, unlike literacy that often requires formal schooling, art is readily accessible to all members of society, including those who have not been to school. Art is, therefore, the most authentic form of individual and social expression in Uganda. Ironically, it is no accident that many of the world's major alphabet systems are derived from ancient art symbols. Although traditional Ugandan art did not rise to the level of a written alphabet, it served as a powerful tool for communication.

In precolonial times, Uganda was ruled by a diverse set of feudal states and other political units that were governed by kings and chiefs and were always competing for supremacy. As a result, artistic expression in this period was used as a symbol of prestige and power. Each political unit created an array of symbols of office and ceremonial objects, for example, figures, staffs, jewelry, and clothing in accordance with its level of influence.[12]

Traditional art also took the form of mats, baskets, earthen pots, bark cloth, wooden and stone sculpture, and cave paintings. These works of art, both functional and culturally valuable, were made using designs, skills, materials, and tools that were available locally.[13] Traditional Ugandan societies also had foundries that made functional artistic items such as knives, swords, and spears.

CONTEMPORARY ART FORMS

Uganda (along with Kenya, Zimbabwe, and South Africa) is one of the locales of new genres of African art that are distinct from traditional art.[14] Many of these new art genres can be traced to the introduction of Western education in the country, growing commercialization of Ugandan art, growing exposure of Ugandan artists to art forms from other parts of the world, and the increasing availability of modern art materials and techniques in the country.

Contemporary Ugandan artists of all genres fall into two classes: those who are formally trained and those who use art for commercial gain. Formally trained artists work in formal settings such as universities; view their work as a form of self-expression; produce relatively few signed artworks; and exhibit their work in galleries, museums, and cultural centers. Conversely, commercial artists work in informal settings and see themselves as artist-entrepreneurs mass-producing a commodity for the street or open market. Because of market forces, artist-entrepreneurs dominate the contemporary Ugandan art scene.[15] Examples of Uganda's contemporary art forms include sculpture, ceramics, drawings, paintings, textiles and fashion, and various household items.

Sculpture

Ugandan sculpture artists use materials such as wood, ceramics, and metal. Although sculpture has been part of the Uganda art scene from precolonial times, it has especially flourished in the postindependence period because of commercialization. Whereas precolonial sculpture was mainly used for cultural and spiritual rituals and for representing traditional political power, contemporary sculpture is primarily produced for sale. Although this trend worries some because it is seen as compromising the development of genuine art, many contemporary Ugandan artists produce commercial art. As a result, new sculpture that is made to suit the tastes of tourists (souvenirs) and the urban elite is on the increase in Uganda. Examples of this sculpture include Mushaba Isa's chair carvings for the export market.[16]

Other contemporary Ugandan sculptors include Gregory Maloba, George Kyeyune, Lilian Nabulime, Bruno Sserunkuuma, Robert Ssempagala, Francis Nnaggenda, John Mugisha, and Philip Kwesiga.[17] Nnaggenda specializes in extensive wooden and metal sculptures that, among other subjects, examine how humans cope with war and violence, for example, that visited on Ugandans by Idi Amin and Milton Obote.[18] Nnaggenda's focus on war and violence derives, perhaps, from his narrow evasion of detention and possible death at Idi Amin's hands.

George Kyeyune produces medium- to monumental-sized sculptures. One of his most outstanding works, *Reaching Out,* which symbolizes students striving for knowledge, is on display at the Institute for Teacher Education at Kyambogo (ITEK), Kampala.[19] Kyeyune is also a painter and ceramic artist. Gregory Maloba, one of the earliest graduates of the Margaret Trowell School, is noted for works such as the *Independence Monument* at the Kampala City Center.

One of Uganda's prominent female sculptors is Lilian Nabulime. She makes monumental sculptures from a combination of wood and sheet metal. Her trademark is the tree stump sculptures that mostly depict women and have a "dynamic, organic rhythm that follows the grain and growth pattern of the tree and often produces a sensation of spiral movement."[20] She hopes to use art to liberate Ugandan women, many of whom are illiterate. As appreciation of art requires no special skills or training, it can be used as a medium

Urban sculpture in Kampala.
Courtesy of Earl P. Scott.

of educating women to take charge of their lives. She hopes that more women artists will use the medium for this purpose.[21]

Ceramics

Uganda has many accomplished potters such as Bruno Sserunkuuma and George Kyeyune. Sserunkuuma has produced some of the most spectacular ceramic artifacts in contemporary Uganda. His work mostly depicts Ganda, Ankole, and Nyoro sociocultural activities such as religion, weddings, schooling, gender roles, cattle herding, family, and fashion. Examples of his indigenous traditional Ugandan pottery are uniquely imprinted with batik drawings of various sociocultural activities.[22]

Drawing

Although drawing is a common art form in Uganda, its most visible forms are the cartoons carried by major newspapers, especially *New Vision* and the *Daily Monitor*. Both of these papers have accomplished cartoonists who offer a humorous commentary on social and news events and have a widespread following. The cartoons, along with photographs, are an indispensable aspect of Ugandan newspapers.

Painting

With the exception of rock art, pictorial art was not well developed in Uganda before the arrival of Europeans. However, this art form has since become, perhaps, the most popular in Uganda because it requires relatively cheap materials and can be done in a relatively short period of time.

Margaret Trowell, in particular, is credited with the introduction and development of painting as an art form in contemporary Uganda. Trowell introduced her African students to easel painting and silkscreen printing, insisting on the need for them to remain true to their African roots instead of aping Western culture. As a result of Trowell's work, paintings that extol Uganda's traditional and mythological past, for example, Peter Mulindwa's *The Owl Drums Death,* are common in Uganda.[23]

The commercialization of art in Uganda has also led to the production of paintings (commonly known as batiks) for popular local and foreign market consumption. For instance, Jak Katarikwe's *People Happy at Christmas* uses animals with smiley faces to parody the excessive merriment that accompanies Christmas in East Africa.[24] Nuwa Nnyanzi's colorful batik artwork is another popular example of this genre. Nnyanzi is one of Uganda's most accomplished batik and mural artists. He has produced commissioned work for international agencies such as UNICEF and United Nations Population Fund (UNFPA) and has been featured in international media such as the BBC.[25] Uganda has also produced other renowned painters, including Mathias Muwonge, Ifee Francis, George Kyeyune, Henry Lumu, Maria Kizito Kasule, Pilkington Ssengendo, and Robert Ssempagala. Mathias Muwonge and Ifee Francis have murals at Kampala's Makerere Art Gallery and the United Nations Development Program (UNDP) offices.[26]

Pilkington Ssengendo is an impressionistic landscape painter. He stresses the need for African artists to embrace, understand, and be grounded in their roots before launching into abstract art. Some of his memorable works include *Landscape in Peace* (1995), *Helene* (1995), and *The Beast* (1991).[27]

The late Henry Lumu (1939–89) was perhaps Uganda's foremost contemporary painter. Lumu, who studied under Margaret Trowell, is credited with inspiring many of the current generation of painters through his art classes on Uganda national television beginning in 1968. Although his training emphasized abstract art, he discouraged it among his students, preferring that they become skilled at drawing before entering the arena of abstract art. Moreover, he favored objective art over the abstract. Some of his works graced corporate calendars by diverse companies, including petroleum giant Esso. Some of his most famous pencil drawings include *Untitled* (first-prize Esso Calendar Competition, 1963) and *Market Scene, Thorns* (acrylics on paper). He also produced many other untitled watercolors.[28]

Textiles and Fashion

As in other East African countries, textiles and clothing are also a major forum for artist expression in Uganda. Tablecloths and seat covers are often made of decorative textile material and so are most women's clothes and handbags that come in a wide variety of colors and feature various artistic patterns such as flowers and African wildlife (e.g., elephants). Some men's clothes, such as the *boubou,* a long embroidered man's shirt, can also be artistically decorated. As in other African countries, hairstyles are an important fashion accessory and art form and are continually evolving. Braided hairstyles are especially popular among Ugandan women, and they vary from simple corn-row braids to more complex flower patterns.

Other Functional and Aesthetic Crafts

Ugandans make extensive use of functional and aesthetic art and crafts for the home. Besides their utility, many of the country's household items (e.g., mats, pots, baskets, bark cloth, stools, and various containers) have an obvious aesthetic appeal. Although modern industrial household items are now widely available in Uganda, the production of traditional variants persists, especially in rural areas, because of their cultural value, affordability, and provision of livelihood to many rural dwellers.

Famous examples of this art form are the traditional ceramic or earthen pots that have been used for cooking and decoration since the precolonial era. The Gisu community of the Mount Elgon (Masaba) region has been one of the largest and most celebrated sources of these pots in the country. The community uses local materials, tools, and designs to produce pots and other items for sale locally and nationally. Some of the pots are for water storage, brewing and serving beer, cooking and serving food, and for ceremonial or sacred use in traditional rituals. The Gisu also make trays, teapots, flat irons, flower vases, and flat-bottomed pots that are recent innovations designed to meet the needs of contemporary users. The decorations found on these items vary by artisan and are used to showcase workmanship, establish local trademark, and to attract customers.[29]

ARCHITECTURE

Ugandan architecture can be classified as either traditional or foreign. Traditional architecture is embraced by most Ugandans, especially in the rural areas. Although traditional Ugandan architecture varies from place to place and from culture to culture, many traditional Ugandan houses are bare because, traditionally, this society has venerated spiritual over temporal or material life.[30] Moreover, the country's tropical climate that supports much outdoor activity has traditionally undermined the development of elaborate architecture. Most rural Ugandan housing consists of simple round wattle-and-daub grass-thatched huts. A modern variation of this traditional architecture is the square hut with mud walls and iron roofs.

Foreign (or the so-called modern) architecture is predominant in urban areas. This architecture features European, Middle Eastern, and American designs that were first brought to Uganda during the colonial period. Although many of these designs worked well for people from these respective regions, their place in modern Uganda has been criticized for failing to meet local housing needs and promote the use of local materials and forms. Because Uganda's social and economic elite prefer modern architecture, the country's architectural identity remains to be defined and is one aspect of the country's search for its soul following decades of colonial rule and internal civil conflict.[31]

Rural Settlements

Ugandans have traditionally lived in rural villages whose size varies by region, ethnicity, occupation, and land availability. The sedentary agricultural groups (e.g., Baganda) in the south have larger populations and more permanent villages relative to their nomadic counterparts in the north. The population of southern Uganda is larger because it subsists on farming, which provides a more stable source of food compared with nomadic pastoralism. Traditional Ugandan village life is exemplified here by the renowned Baganda settlements.

In the precolonial era, Ganda villages often consisted of about 50 homesteads that were governed by chiefs answerable to the *Kabaka* or king of Buganda. Because of the hilly Ganda landscape, their villages were perched on hilltops to avoid flood damage from the area's frequent heavy rains caused by its humid tropical climate. Conversely, the farms were located on the hillsides and moist lowlands.[32]

Although most Ganda villages initially consisted of close relatives, the expansion of Buganda kingdom into adjacent communities led to the incorporation of foreigners into the villages in the immediate precolonial period. Moreover, the kingdom's highly centralized political and economic power over time created an environment that fostered significant internal migration and intermixing of people from various families and clans. Additionally, feudal capitalism developed in the kingdom, resulting in the emergence of landlords and peasants who worked the land for tribute.[33] This system not only benefited popular landlords and penalized the unpopular ones by costing them peasants but it also promoted migration and intermixing of diverse peoples.[34] Moreover, because some landlords owned large tracts of land outside the villages and frequently needed more labor than was readily available, they frequently used slave labor from conquered people groups. Yet because of the Ganda region's abundance of well-watered fertile land, everyone from the slave/peasant to the *Kabaka* had plenty of food to eat. This settlement system began to weaken in the late 1800s with the advent of colonialism and the attendant disruption of the traditional political order, heightened population migration, and the occasional revolt of the suppressed peoples.[35]

Village houses were usually of the round grass-walled and thatched-hut variety. The houses also consisted of earthen floors that were daubed with a consistent mixture of cow dung and clay. There were drains around the houses to keep them dry and safe from the surface runoff caused by regular afternoon downpours. The structures usually had one entrance, and smoke from the heating and cooking fires usually escaped by permeating through the grass-thatched roofs. Besides promoting a host of respiratory diseases owing to their poor ventilation, the structures were a constant fire hazard. The settlement patterns of the other Bantu or agricultural groups of Uganda (e.g., the Basoga, Bagisu, Banyoro, and Batoro) have not been that much different from those of the Baganda, although adjustments have been made in view of local environmental and security conditions.

Currently, most houses in the expansive and influential southern Bantu region of Uganda are of the round wattle-and-daub grass-thatched hut variety, with a sprinkling of the modern square huts with iron sheet roofs and cement walls and floors. For the country as a whole, 10 percent of the rural houses are made of permanent materials, 55 percent have mud and pole walls, 50 percent have iron sheet roofs, 50 percent have thatch roofs, and 85 percent have rammed earth floors. The use of more durable building materials is concentrated in the relatively modern and affluent southern parts of the country that were also the focus of missionary and colonial activity. House size varies

Northern Uganda rural homestead. Courtesy of Ken Goyer.

Southern Uganda rural settlement. Courtesy of Emmanuel Twesigye.

with individual family space needs and income. These changes in building techniques have been brought about by the introduction of modern construction materials and the advent of the modern economy.

Among the Nilo-Hamitic groups such as the pastoral Karimojong, circular homestead clusters enclosing cattle pens (kraals) are common. This settlement pattern possibly grew out of the need to protect livestock (their main source of livelihood) from raiders and wild animals, especially at night.

In nearly all Ugandan ethnic groups, settlement patterns are organized according to clan. Because these clans are mostly patrilineal, that is, male-dominated, resources such as land are usually passed on along the male line.

An important factor in the current state of Uganda's rural settlements is the country's long history of social strife that has led to untold loss of human life and property. In the north, active hostilities and settlement disruptions are still ongoing. It is equally noteworthy that Amin's 1975 Land Decree that nationalized all land in Uganda, and the National Resistance Movement's (NRM) 1998 Land Act that tried to reverse it, have substantially disrupted land tenure in Uganda, resulting in significant changes to the country's rural settlement system.[36] Since the 1998 Land Act is still being implemented, even as large sections of Uganda continue to recover from years of internal strife, it is safe to say that Uganda's rural settlement system is still evolving.

Urban Settlements

The best example of precolonial urbanization in Uganda was the *kibuga* or capital city of the Buganda Kingdom at Mengo Hill. According to early European travelers' accounts, the *kibuga* was clean and well laid-out and had a road network and residential neighborhoods for the representatives of the districts in the kingdom. At one time, the capital was home to more than 3,000 people and had separate quarters for the king and queen and a regiment of workers to maintain it. Supplemental food supplies were brought in as tribute from the surrounding countryside to complement the supplies produced within the capital.[37]

The *kibuga* arose because Buganda's fertile land and commercial agricultural system produced a food surplus that fed the capital and allowed for the development of urban occupations. Moreover, Buganda's relatively open society that encouraged cultural mixing produced a sophisticated political and economic system that did not materialize elsewhere in Uganda. As a result, the British co-opted Buganda into a partnership that governed Uganda until independence. This arrangement effectively extended the *Kabaka's* (king) rule over the rest of Uganda, with the backing of the British.[38]

Another example of precolonial urbanization were the slave and ivory trading posts that the Arabs created in the modern-day Acholi region of Uganda. Established in the 1850s, these posts were the first nonindigenous urban areas in the country; they were occupied by coastal Arabs and their slave cargo and were supported by taxes collected from the local Acholi people. The Arabs fomented intra-Acholi animosities to facilitate the plunder of the community and the capture of slaves.[39]

Outside Buganda's precolonial urban capital and the Arab settlements in Acholiland, widespread urbanization in Uganda commenced with colonialism. Although Buganda's capital survived until the early 1960s, it was destroyed by Obote's regime, and along with it, Uganda's best chance of continuing the development of an indigenous city. Nevertheless, it is noteworthy that the cities of Kampala and Entebbe, the current and former Ugandan capital, respectively, are built on or near traditional kingdom capitals.

Because of limited colonial European settlement in Uganda, the country's major urban areas do not have as strong a European imprint as, say, neighboring Kenyan cities where European settlement was more pronounced. As a result, Ugandan cities have a strong African imprint that varies by social and economic class. Hence, consumer habits in the elite or upper-class neighborhoods of Kampala are comparable to those of middle- and upper-income classes in many Western societies. Overall, Uganda's urban middle class is relatively small because of the country's low level of development. Most urban Ugandans are poor and have strong links to their rural areas of origin, hence their dual rural-urban identity.

Currently, only 15 percent of Ugandans live in urban areas. Most of this population lives in major urban areas such as Kampala. Uganda's 10 largest cities and populations are Kampala (1,189,142), Gulu (119,430), Lira (80,879), Jinja (71,213), Mbale (71,130), Mbarara (69,363), Masaka (67,768), Entebbe (55,086), Kasese (53,907), and Njeru (51,236).[40] The population of these cities varies widely between day and night, with substantial increases occurring during the day when people from surrounding regions come to town for various reasons. Kampala, Entebbe, and Jinja, the most important urban settlements in Uganda, are briefly examined here.

Kampala is Uganda's capital and largest commercial center. The city's name is derived from the Kiganda (the language of the Baganda people) phrase *kasozi k' mpala* (or "hill of impala," initially pronounced *ka Impala* and eventually, *ka mpala*), an obvious indication of the abundant impala and other wildlife that once roamed the area.[41] The city came into existence in 1890 when Frederick Lugard built a fort for the Imperial British East Africa Company near Mengo Hill, the original headquarters of the traditional kingdom of Buganda, which together with the kingdoms of Bunyoro-Kitara, Ankole,

Busoga, and Toro constituted much of the British Colonial Protectorate of Uganda and the current Republic of Uganda.[42]

As the country's primary or dominant city, Kampala is the country's commercial, political, administrative, industrial, cultural, and educational center. Its current population is estimated at 1,189,142 people—representing nearly 40 percent of Uganda's urban population. The city occupies the Greater Kampala administrative district that has a land area of about 190 square kilometers. The city lies 8 kilometers north of Lake Victoria at an altitude of 1,300 meters (or 4,265 feet) above sea level. It sits on 46 low flat-topped hills, including Mengo Hill, whose recent inclusion in the Greater Kampala administrative district makes it unlikely that the site will once again become the headquarters of the restored but greatly weakened Buganda Kingdom.

The Greater Kampala area's topography has led to very distinct land uses. The flat hilltops are occupied by prestigious church, state, and private institutions; the valleys contain the central business district, the industrial areas, and poor residential areas; and the slopes are used for an assortment of residential, commercial, and state buildings.[43]

Nearly 75 percent of Kampala residents have a low quality of life because of poverty, lack of affordable land, outdated land tenure systems, unemployment,

Downtown Kampala. Courtesy of Emmanuel Twesigye.

underemployment (i.e., employment in poorly paid positions and petty businesses), and residence in shanties. As a result, nearly 70 percent of Kampala's residents live below the poverty line, which in the 1990s was $171 per person per year.[44] Many do not have access to enough food and have to practice urban agriculture to supplement their food and income needs.[45] Poor-quality housing and a lack of basic urban infrastructure such as roads, sewers, sanitation, and potable piped water characterize Kampala's shanty settlements such as Kawempe and Makindye. The lifestyle in Kampala's shanties, where most of the population lives, is remarkably similar to that in rural areas. In fact, outside of the central business district, Kampala is essentially a rural city and many of its shanty settlements resemble rural villages and are mostly occupied by recent rural-urban migrants who have yet to establish themselves in the city.[46] Despite the poverty of the residents, Kampala's shanties are bustling with life.

The state of Kampala's physical infrastructure is poor. This is the result of the political turmoil that engulfed Uganda in the 1970s and 1980s; high urban population growth (currently estimated at 5 percent per year) caused by rural-urban migration and natural increase; and the local municipal government's inability to meet the city's growing social, physical, and infrastructural needs. For instance, only 20 percent of the total waste generated by Kampala residents in a month is collected and disposed off properly by the city government.[47]

Although most Kampala residents are poor, there is a small but thriving middle and upper class that collectively amounts to about 30 percent of the population. Despite these classes' small share of the city's population, they control the lion's share of Kampala's, and indeed Uganda's, wealth, and its best jobs, neighborhoods, and productive resources. With these assets, Kampala's affluent and upper-middle-class people are able to live very well. Although the city's middle and upper classes were nearly wiped out by the civil wars of the 1970s and early 1980s, they have recovered nicely since the mid-1980s and are now at the forefront of Kampala's reconstruction. The city's economy is once again booming as demonstrated by the many high-quality residences that are under construction around the city.[48]

A significant component of Kampala's wealthy business class consists of Ugandans of Asian extraction. Amin expelled virtually all of them in the early 1970s and turned over their wealth to his military cronies and supporters, in an attempt to Africanize control of the economy. However, many of those who acquired these assets were inept business managers who quickly ruined them along with the country's economy. To hasten the country's economic reconstruction, Museveni's government recently allowed the expelled Asians to return from exile and reclaim their property, and many have returned.

The quality of residential housing in Kampala increases towards the hilltop where other prestigious buildings such as cathedrals and government buildings are also located. Poor people occupy the lowlands that are prone to flooding. Urban agriculture (e.g., the banana crop in the foreground) is an important source of food for many urban Ugandans. Courtesy of Earl P. Scott.

Their business expertise, combined with the ongoing reconstruction of Uganda's social, economic, and political institutions, and the emerging middle class have given Uganda a new economic foundation and has produced rapid economic growth over the last decade.

Entebbe has a population of 55,086 people. It lies astride the Equator at approximately 3,782 feet (1,152 meters) above sea level, near the shores of Lake Victoria, about 40 kilometers southwest of Kampala.[49] The city is named Entebbe (which means "seat" in the local Luganda language) because a precolonial chief used to hold court there. The city was founded in 1893, when it became a British colonial administrative and commercial center after Sir Gerald Portal used it as a base. It served as the capital of the British Protectorate of Uganda from 1894 until independence in 1962, when the capital was transferred to Kampala. But the city retains the official residence of the Ugandan president where cabinet meetings are also held. Because of its status as the colonial capital, Entebbe has a good mix of both old (colonial) and new (postcolonial) buildings that add to the city's beauty. Moreover, Entebbe has become a popular local and international tourist resort because of its beautiful beaches.[50]

Entebbe has been the location for Uganda's only international airport since 1951. Construction of the airport in or near the capital, Kampala, was precluded by its rough topography. In 1976, former Ugandan dictator Idi Amin allowed a hijacked Israeli airliner to land at Entebbe airport, thereby triggering a series of events that culminated in the Entebbe raid in which Israeli commandos stormed the airport and freed nearly all hostages, extensively damaging the Israeli-built airport in the process.

Jinja is located on the shores of Lake Victoria at the mouth of the White Nile, 80 kilometers east of Kampala. The city's population is 71,213 people. The population is growing at 3 percent per year, has an HIV/AIDS prevalence rate of 10 percent, an unemployment rate of 38 percent, and a poverty rate of 45 percent. Because of its proximity to the Owens Falls Dam and its large hydroelectric power plant, the city has become a major industrial center with major concerns in coffee, fish, oil, grain, tobacco, plastic, wood, and leather processing as well as paper and steel production.[51] The city's high unemployment and poverty level is caused by its rapid population growth (mostly through excessive rural-to-urban migration), which results in an overwhelming number of job seekers for the available industrial, commercial, and civil service jobs.

As in Kampala and Entebbe, Jinja's living environment, infrastructure, and economy is recovering from the devastation of the 1970s and 1980s. As a result, many of its residents are not adequately supplied with housing, jobs, and other basic urban necessities. Moreover, the topography of the Jinja area includes many wide valleys and swamps that are good breeding grounds for mosquitoes that spread the deadly malaria disease.[52] Additionally, the city's industries are polluting nearby Lake Victoria and the lake's invasion by water hyacinth (a leafy floating aquatic plant) is also ruining navigation and choking off important fisheries.

Traditional Housing

Most traditional houses in Uganda are of the round wattle-and-daub grass-thatched hut variety. There are some variations in traditional housing materials and construction techniques depending on what materials are available in the local environment and the lifestyles of the various ethnic groups. Moreover, the size of Uganda's traditional houses depends on individual and family space needs. For instance, some of the houses put up by traditional monarchies such as that of Buganda were quite large, for example, *Kabaka* Mutesa's house in Kampala. But for the most part, because Ugandans spend most of their time outdoors, houses tend to be small and sparsely furnished. Most houses have one or two rooms, with the inner room being used as a bedroom and the outer room serving as living room or kitchen/dining/living room in the case of poorer households. Wealthier households often have an adjoining house that serves as a kitchen. Outhouses, rather than indoor plumbing, are the main means of human waste disposal, and drinking water is fetched from nearby streams and wells. Most (80%) of the lighting is from smoky kerosene candles (known locally as tadooba) while firewood is the main cooking fuel for nearly all (91%) rural Ugandan households.

In traditional society, residences were separated by gender, with men and women living in separate huts. The male head of the family often lived in a separate hut surrounded by his wives' huts. There was also an older boys' hut, while girls and young children often shared a hut with their mother. These living arrangements are still prevalent in many rural areas of Uganda.

Urban Housing

The nature of urban housing in Uganda varies by age, use, and the ethnicity of the owners as well their economic resources. Uganda's oldest urban areas are roughly 100 years old. Thus, urban housing that spans this period, from the colonial to the very modern, is found in the country's cities, especially Entebbe, Kampala, and Jinja. European colonialists introduced modern architecture to Uganda, represented by early colonial buildings such as Kampala's Imperial Hotel and St. Paul's Cathedral on Namirembe Hill. Urban housing also varies by use, from residential, government, sacred, to commercial. Government and sacred housing looms large in Ugandan cities such as Kampala, where St. Paul's Cathedral on Namirembe Hill, Kibuli Mosque, the Hindu Temple, Parliament Building, and Makerere University campus are notable examples. Commercial housing dominates Ugandan cities' central business districts. Because of the high cost of land in urban downtown areas, buildings here tend to be high-rises made of durable materials such as steel, cement, and blocks.

Much of the diversity in Uganda's urban residential housing stems from the diversity of its residents' ethnicity and socioeconomic class. Urban Uganda's ethnic diversity, which includes Africans, Europeans, and Asians, is also reflected in the city's residential housing as each ethnicity seeks to express its architectural heritage. European architecture dominates urban housing in Uganda because Europeans are largely responsible for the establishment and development of the country's cities. This history also makes the country's cities somewhat alien to locals.

Urban housing also varies by economic class. In the hilly city of Kampala, for instance, the upper slopes are occupied by middle- and upper-class Ugandans, while the lower slopes and the valley bottoms are home to low-income people in high-density settlements. The middle- and upper-class houses are built of durable materials such as brick, stone, and cement and have red tile roofs and are generally located in well-planned neighborhoods that have low population density. Housing in the poor areas is haphazardly laid out and made of poor-quality materials.

In general, most (59%) urban residences in Uganda are made of permanent materials such as brick and cement, 17 percent have mud and pole walls, 82 percent have iron sheet roofs, 12 percent have thatch roofs, and 29 percent have rammed earth floors. Most of these residences are lit by electricity (39%) and kerosene candles (33%); rely on charcoal (67%) and firewood (22%) for cooking; and have access to safe drinking water (93%). Slightly more than 2 percent of the residences lack access to convenient toilet facilities.

5

Cuisine and Traditional Dress

CUISINE

Uganda's cuisine varies by ecological zone and ethnic group. The country produces a wide variety of food crops (especially in the more agriculturally favorable south, west and central regions) including plantains and bananas (*matooke*), maize/corn, rice, sweet potatoes, yams, groundnuts/peanuts, pumpkins, beans, cowpeas, and various green vegetables, and fruit. These staples are prepared in diverse ways to suit the tastes of the various ethnic groups.

Uganda's agricultural Bantu groups such as the Baganda, Basoga, Banyankole, Batoro, Banyoro, and Bakiga have traditionally dominated the production of these crops. Many of these farming groups have in the past supplemented their diet with meat from wildlife and domesticated animals such as chicken, goats, sheep, and cattle. These subsistence practices still persist save for the significant decline of wildlife hunting because of reduced wildlife habitats as a result of population increase.

In the drier northern parts of the country, the major food crops include ground cassava, millet, sorghum, and simsim. This region is also home to the country's Nilotic and Nilo-Hamitic groups such as the Acholi, Alur, Sebei, Karimojong, Iteso, and Langi. Many of these groups are agriculturalists, except for the Karimojong herdsmen who have for ages subsisted on cattle meat, milk, and blood and have often exchanged them for millet and other grains from the surrounding agricultural groups. Many of the Nilotic and Nilo-Hamitic groups have for centuries supplemented their food supplies with meat from fish and wildlife, although the latter's importance has declined over time.

With more than 30 ethnic groups, Uganda has no national dish, although *matooke,* a mashed green banana or plantain meal that is often eaten with groundnut/peanut sauce or, on rare occasions, *luwombo* (chicken, goat, or beef stew), can be considered because it is popular among many indigenous Ugandans, especially the majority Bantu groups in the southern part of the country.[1] To prepare a *matooke* dish, green bananas/plantains are peeled and boiled until they are fully cooked and then mashed. Groundnut sauce is made by boiling a mixture of mashed nuts, chopped onions and tomatoes, and salt in water.

Besides the *matooke* dish, other typical meals that generally follow the starch and meat/protein pattern include *posho/ugali/nsima* (stiff corn porridge similar to Italian polenta), served with beans or meat sauce and washed down with banana beer (*marwa* or *pombe*) or water; fried cassava, sliced sweet potatoes, and pea sauce; and *matooke* or *posho* with fried or stewed fish. Most Ugandans also relish *nsenene* (green grasshoppers available during the rainy season) and white ants or termites. Cornmeal (i.e., *posho, ugali,* or *nsima*) is mostly consumed in the country's urban areas because it is cheaper than *matooke* and is a good substitute staple food for Ugandans who grew up on

Most of Uganda's staple foods are readily available in the country's markets. This market specializes in Irish potatoes and meat (background shacks). Courtesy of Earl P. Scott.

millet or cassava. Most schools in the country also feed corn to their students. Schools often serve corn porridge (*uji,* prepared by boiling a mixture of corn flour, water, and sugar) for breakfast.

Although corn was introduced to East Africa by the Portuguese, it has over time become a popular staple food throughout Uganda and the rest of the East African region. In the drier northern parts of the country, sweet potato is quickly becoming one of the main staple crops in place of cassava and is likely to continue playing a greater role in the country's nutrition, food security, and economy. Uganda is already Africa's largest producer of sweet potatoes. The consumption of sweet potatoes varies seasonally, peaking during famine. Sweet potatoes are also a source of income and a cheap staple for the rural and urban poor.[2] Throughout the country, a variety of fruits, including bananas, pawpaw (papaya), watermelon, mangoes, passion fruit, and jack-fruit, is available and eaten at mealtime or as snacks throughout the day. Uganda's staple foods and fruits are sold in markets (e.g., Kampala's Nakasero and Owino) across the country.

Because of their broader ethnic diversity and higher incomes, Uganda's urban areas have a greater variety of dishes. Besides the traditional dishes already discussed, modern foodstuffs such as rice, wheat bread, *chapatti* (a flat, unleavened, round-shaped bread made of wheat flour, water, and salt) with meat stew, *sambusa* (a tasty meat or vegetable pie), and *mandazi* (a puffy donut) are popular. The best of Ugandan cuisine is on display in the cosmopolitan capital city of Kampala, where diverse restaurants offer local and European, Chinese, Indian, French, Italian, and Greek cuisine. Many of these foreign dishes are consumed by the city's nonindigenous population, tourists, and the local African elite.

Uganda has an abundant supply of fish from lakes Victoria, Kyoga, Edward, George, and Albert and from the Nile River.[3] Fish consumption is pronounced in areas around these lakes and rivers and in urban areas but very low in areas dominated by traditional cattle herdsmen, such as the Bahima and the Karimojong. Three of the most prized fishes in the country are mudfish, the gigantic Nile perch, and the much smaller but tastier tilapia. All three can be broiled, deep fried, or stewed and eaten with a variety of dishes, for example, *posho/ugali* (cornbread). Commercially produced crocodile meat is also beginning to be widely consumed.

Most Ugandans have three meals a day, with six or seven hours between meals. Most people seldom have snacks in between meals (save for widely available fruits) because of a high incidence of poverty and poor food processing, storage, and distribution. Poor Ugandan households often eat fewer than three meals a day. Breakfast usually lasts anywhere from sunrise to around 9 A.M., lunch is usually around noon, and dinner/supper lasts anytime from sunset until around 10 P.M. Although what is served for breakfast, lunch, and dinner varies by location, ethnicity, and income, most Ugandans' breakfast consists of a cup or two of maize (corn) porridge with or without bananas. The porridge is even tastier when mixed with milk. Coffee, tea, and bread are common items in well-off rural and urban households. Lunch usually consists of *matooke* (or some other starch base), boiled sweet potatoes and bean, groundnut, or meat sauce. Dinner usually features the same items as lunch, although wealthier households may have rice and meat stew for dinner.

Because of Uganda's social set-up, food preparation is primarily the responsibility of women and girls. Men are usually involved in food production but not preparation. Meal-time etiquette usually requires that men, especially older ones, be served first with choice and generous portions. Women and

Traditional Ugandan cooking pot and fireplace. Courtesy of Ken Goyer.

Firewood is Uganda's main cooking fuel. Courtesy of Ken Goyer.

children often eat afterward and, in many cases, separate from men. In religious households, saying grace precedes eating. In most cases, food is usually eaten by hand, with forks, spoons, and knives common in urban areas and when eating foreign foods such as rice.

In many rural Ugandan households, food is often cooked in traditional or modern pots over three-stone fireplaces. Wood, crop residues, and cow dung are the predominant cooking fuels in rural Uganda. Improved and fuel-efficient mud stoves with chimneys are becoming common in the Ugandan countryside. In urban areas, simple metal or ceramic-lined charcoal stoves are used for cooking. In wealthier urban households, electric and gas cookers are preferred, although charcoal stoves are usually kept as back-ups in case of power outages or cooking gas shortages. In much of the country, kerosene is used for illumination rather than for cooking. Food is seldom refrigerated because of a scarcity of affordable refrigerators and limited access to electric power.

Beverages

A wide variety of beverages is consumed in Uganda. Besides water, there are many local brews derived from staple foods such as bananas, maize, and millet. *Waragi,* or gin derived from banana or cassava beer, is perhaps the most popular beverage in the country. Both of the country's major breweries make and distribute variants of *Waragi.* Many of the globally popular soft drinks, for example, Pepsi, Fanta, Coke, and Sprite, are also widely available in Uganda, as are many fruit juices derived from the country's fruit bounty.

Mealtime beverages vary by age, occupation, and income. Wealthy Ugandans enjoy the widest variety of mealtime beverages. Water is a universal mealtime beverage for all ages and social classes. Milk, fruit juice, and soda are also popular among children, women, and men who are teetotalers. High-income professionals often have beer, wine, and malts during mealtimes. As in many other countries, alcoholism is one of the major social problems in Uganda.

Cuisine and Ceremonies

As in many other African societies, food and drink are an essential part of various social ceremonies such as marriage, naming ceremonies, funerals, and other rites of passage and celebrations. In traditional society, cuisine was also an essential part of worship as food and drink (especially beer) were used to appease the gods. However, this practice is declining because of the growing influence of Christianity and Islam and the attendant decline of traditional religions. In many Uganda communities, weddings are perhaps the most festive ceremonies, and families go to great lengths to serve good food. On such occasions, expensive delicacies such as bread, rice, meat stew, soda, and cake are served.

Internationalization of Ugandan Cuisine

Uganda's cuisine is becoming increasingly internationalized because of many factors including growing international travel by Ugandans, increased tourism, and Ugandans' rising access to international media which exposes them to foreign food commercials and recipes. The growing presence and influence of international food companies and distributors in the country, coupled with many Ugandans' rising incomes is promoting their growing consumption of foreign cuisine.

Uganda's growing numbers of foreign tourists, business people, and major international hotels (e.g., the Sheraton) are also aiding the consumption of foreign cuisine in the country. The country's rising level of urbanization also means that many more Ugandans are being exposed to foreign dishes that they then help to popularize in their rural areas of origin. The consumption of foreign dishes is also a common symbol of high social status in Uganda and is a major factor in the growing internationalization of the country's cuisine.

Equally important is that the political trauma that Uganda experienced in the 1960s through the 1980s, produced a large number of Ugandan exiles who not only helped to internationalize the cuisine of their various host countries by bringing in their native dishes; but have also been changing Uganda's food tastes as they return home following the end of war in most parts of the country since the mid-1980s. Moreover, some of the exiles chose to stay abroad and have recently been joined by many voluntary Ugandan migrants. Together, these two groups constitute the burgeoning Ugandan diaspora that is not only helping to connect Uganda to other countries, but is also aiding the internationalization of its cuisine.

TRADITIONAL DRESS

Traditional Ugandan dress was made from readily available materials such as tree leaves, grass, bark cloth, as well as livestock and wildlife skins.[4] Traditional dress varied by sex and ethnicity. Some ethnic groups, especially the sedentary Bantu groups, for example, the Baganda, had fairly elaborate attire. Women normally wore long bark clothes that extended from the armpits to the legs and were held in place by a waistband and were accompanied by beads and bangles. Similarly, men wore bark cloth with a knot over one shoulder, although their work attire often consisted of a simple waist wrap tucked between the legs. For both sexes, the garments usually consisted of either two pieces (an upper- and lower-body wrap) or one large knee-length piece that was wrapped around the chest under the armpits (in the case of women), or tucked under one armpit and tied in a knot over the opposite shoulder in the case of men. Nobles often accentuated this basic attire with hats and leopard-skin overcoats, these being part of the state regalia. Children did not wear any clothing until the onset of puberty, although girls were often adorned with colorful necklaces and earrings.

In many traditional Ugandan societies, personal adornments were widespread, though they varied by community and region and were most common and elaborate in the drier northern sections of the country—probably because of the ease of maintaining them in the drier climate. Some of the common personal adornments included tattoos, body marks, beads, earrings, nose and lip ornaments, bracelets, oil, ghee (clarified butter), headdresses, cow dung, and ochre body paintings. Tatoos and body marks were most common among the Bamba, Bahima (pastoral Banyankole), and Langi. Among the Langi, women were tattooed on the back and front while men were tattooed on the back only, and both sexes normally used oil or ghee as skin lotion.

The removal of some teeth, especially the two to six lower front ones, was also common in many societies (e.g., the Lugbara) and was a form of adornment, initiation rite, or medicinal practice. From a medical standpoint, the gap created by removing these teeth made it possible for very sick people to be sustained, as they could be fed with fluids. The Karimojong and other pastoral groups were the ones who most often used cow dung as a body lotion. Like the Maasai of Kenya, some Ugandan groups (e.g., the Lugbara) painted their bodies with ochre as part of their adornment and initiation. Among the Karimojong, men also wore animal-skin sandals. Some Ugandan groups wore little or no clothing. For instance, the Bambuti pygmoid peoples traditionally (and to some extent today) preferred to go naked.

In nearly all traditional Ugandan communities, there was special-function attire. Examples include that worn by dancers (e.g., grass skirts; fly whisks; elaborate headdresses consisting of hats adorned with beads, cowrie shells, and bird feathers; and ankle jingles or bells), warriors, shamans, traditional healers, and medicine men. Such attire was not only functional (e.g., that worn by musicians) but was also believed to possess certain magical powers that, for instance, helped traditional medicine men to function.

POPULAR MODERN DRESS TYPES

Popular modern dress came to Uganda with the advent of Christianity and colonialism. Embarrassed by what they considered to be scanty native dressing, European Christian missionaries set out to change that, starting with Buganda, where contact between Western and Ugandan culture commenced in the mid-1800s. The missionaries designed an ankle-length Victorian dress (*gomesi* or *busuti*) for women and a similarly long tunic for men. Over time, the *gomesi* has become a popular national dress, made of bright multicolored cloth with padded shoulders and an equally elaborate sash for tying it around the waist. More expensive variants of the *gomesi* are made of imported silk and have a sash with a bow in front. The dress is often worn with a wraparound tie-on cotton skirt or sarong (known locally as a *khanga* or *kikoi)* that has many other uses, including serving as an apron.[5] Because the *gomesi* can be heavy, it is now commonly worn on special occasions such as weddings, marriage betrothals, funeral ceremonies, national formal events, church functions, and audiences with dignitaries.[6] Formal shoes, headscarves, handbags, and watches are also worn. On such occasions, Ugandan men wear suits or long, white, floor-length tunics (known as *kanzu or boubou),* with long-sleeved jackets and shoes. Some *kanzus* are embroidered. Some men also wear hats. Businessmen wear suits

Kanzu and *Busuti*, Victorian floor-length men and women's dress styles are popular in Uganda. Men often wear *Kanzu* with dress coats while women wear elaborate sashes over Busuti or gomesi. Courtesy of Emmanuel Twesigye.

and ties. It is common for Christian grooms to wear suits and brides to wear Western-style wedding gowns.

In everyday life, Ugandan women usually wear dresses or blouses and knee-length skirts. It is not culturally acceptable for women to wear trousers, although they are becoming more common in major urban areas. Older women often wear headscarves. Similarly, men wear trousers or shorts with T-shirts, shirts, caps, sweaters, and jackets, while women wear knee-length dresses or skirts with long- or short-sleeved blouses. For casual formal wear, Ugandan men often wear *kampala jumpa,* a short embroidered shirt.[7] Schoolchildren are required to wear uniforms from primary through high school.

Adornments

The use of modern adornments in Uganda is now widespread. Women wear necklaces, bangles, hats, watches, earrings, rings, and hair weaves or nicely braided or combed hair to formal events such as weddings and church functions. Girls and poorer women usually wear their hair short. Popular men's adornments include watches, necklaces, and bangles.

Fashion

Ugandan fashion extends from the traditional to the modern. Traditional modes of dress are widespread in the less Westernized parts of the country such as the north, although even in the more developed parts of the country (e.g., Buganda), traditional dress (e.g., bark cloth) is worn on ceremonial occasions.

In the more Westernized parts of the country, Western fashion and consumption patterns predominate, especially among the urban elite who patronize the high-fashion shopping malls of the country such as Kampala's Shoprite. High-end American and European apparel and footwear products such as those by Nike, Adidas, Dunlop, and Reebok are popular among Uganda's affluent young people, thanks to the influence of international television, magazines, music videos, and global merchandise firms. Even among low- and

Second-hand clothes (e.g., this Pittsburg Steelers t-shirt) are cheap and popular in Uganda. Courtesy of Ken Goyer.

middle-income Ugandans, these items are popular because of the widespread availability of secondhand clothes and shoes from the United States and Europe. It is also common for Ugandans of all social classes to wear sports paraphernalia from popular U.S. and European teams.

Other important promoters of Western fashion in the country are large global corporations and the major tourist hotels, such as the Sheraton, that welcome hordes of American and European tourists clad in popular fashion items. Yet, in recent decades, locally tailored versions of Nigerian- and Congolese-style men's and women's clothes have become popular in Uganda.

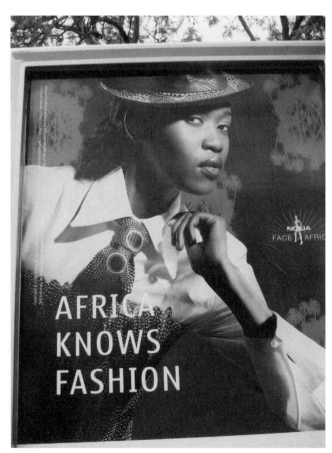

Sleek marketing by international companies such as cell phone giant Nokia help shape Ugandan fashion styles. Courtesy of Ken Goyer.

DRESS AND IDENTITY

Dress is one of the most important means of expressing individual, ethnic, religious, class, gender, age, and professional identity. Whereas individual dress preferences are a means of expressing ones personality; ethnic, class, gender, age, and professional dress preferences give individuals in the group a sense of belonging and help to distinguish them from other groups.

Although the relationship between dress and ethnic identity was most clearly defined during the precolonial period, Uganda's diverse ethnic preference for certain dress colors, styles, and adornments can still be a basis for distinguishing the country's ethnic groups.

The dress preferences of the various professions, religions and gender groups in modern Uganda are, perhaps, easiest to discern. For instance, members of the medical and security professions and primary and secondary school students wear uniforms while on duty and at school, respectively. Similarly, the country's traditional monarchs wear royal regalia during official functions while high-ranking government and business executives usually dress in suits or *Kanzu* to work. Likewise, Ugandan Muslim women wear veils or *Hijab* while the men usually wear turbans, long white robs, hats, and scull caps. Most Ugandan women also wear dresses, skirts and blouses, and in some cases, trousers. Overall, most Ugandans wear age appropriate modern attire although traditional dress is still common in the less modern parts of the country.

6

Gender Roles, Marriage, and Family

Marriage and family are any society's most important social institutions because they ensure social reproduction, that is, birth and nurture of offspring to become responsible members of society. Thus, Ugandans highly esteem the role of marriage and family in the perpetuation of their society. As in many parts of the world, marriage precedes family formation in Uganda.

Ugandan society has cultural rules that determine the gender identity, expression, and role of its members. To appreciate Ugandan social organization, one must therefore understand the role that gender plays in determining one's place in society, as males and females have specific roles that contribute to the formation of a unique Ugandan culture. Because Uganda is a patriarchal society, males have more access to the country's socioeconomic resources and privileges than do females.

LINEAGE

Lineage is an integral part of individual or clan identity in Uganda. Around the world, there are four main ways of tracing one's descent or lineage: patrilineal descent (through the father), matrilineal descent (through the mother), bilineal or duolineal descent (through both parents), and bilateral descent (through both paternal and maternal grandparents). Ugandan society is patriarchal, and there is virtually no matrilineal, bilineal/duolineal, or bilateral community in the country.

Besides contributing to the determination of individual identity, lineage plays a critical role in many Ugandan communities' property inheritance customs as well as in their clan-based social system. Essentially, clans are large extended family units that trace their lineage to a single ancestral patriarch. Clan members regard each other as close relatives regardless of the size of the clan. Consequently, intraclan marriages are discouraged because they are considered to be incestuous.

Good social standing in the clan often supersedes one's standing in the family because many Ugandan societies are communally organized, with individual triumphs, tribulations, and malfeasance readily shared or attributed to whole clans. Because of this, one of the most severe forms of punishment in many Ugandan societies is rejection by the clan, as this makes one a nonentity. So entrenched is the clan system that among the Baganda, for instance, children take clan last names rather than those of their fathers. As a consequence, it is easy to tell one's clan from one's name but not one's father. Because of the importance of the clan, ignorance of one's clan ancestry and history is damaging to one's social standing and sense of belonging.[1]

MARRIAGE

Marriage is traditionally one of the most important social customs in Uganda. Because many Ugandan ethnic groups are communal, marriage has been a central means of uniting families, lineages, and clans. Consequently, the extended families of both the bride and groom have historically played an important role in ensuring the survival of marriages. Older and experienced clan members are especially relied on to solve marital conflicts, and their judgments are binding (e.g., among Bakiga). As a result, divorce is generally rare in many traditional Ugandan marriages, although some communities, for example, the Baganda and Bakiga, have historically had high divorce rates.

In many Ugandan communities, marriage confers on both men and women high social status. For instance, the Baganda have historically considered unmarried men and women to be incomplete and have accorded them little respect. Traditionally, polygamous men were more highly esteemed than those in monogamous marriages. The number of wives a man could have was limited only by his ability to pay bride wealth and support them. Because of Buganda's low bride wealth, favorable climate, and fertile soils, Baganda men found it easy to be polygamous.[2] Changes in these material conditions have steadily undermined the practice of polygamy in Buganda.

Marriage in modern Uganda has undergone profound changes because of socioeconomic and cultural changes. Rising urbanization and the accompanying decline of traditional culture and changing gender roles and socioeconomic conditions have all led to significant increases in monogamous marriages. Population growth and increased dispersion and intermingling of people from various communities in the country owing to changing opportunities in the modern economy have made it difficult for traditional societies to enforce many marriage taboos, such as the ban on intraclan marriage. Moreover, intertribal marriages that were culturally unpopular in many communities are beginning to be more widespread. Western courtship and marriage practices are also becoming common, especially in the urban areas. Nevertheless, factors such as ethnicity, religion, occupation, parental consent, and social class are important considerations in courtship and marriage in modern Uganda.

Divorce is also becoming more common and is frequently caused by infidelity on the part of the wife or neglect and/or physical abuse by the husband. Divorce because of a husband's infidelity is rare in Uganda, as the patriarchal society frowns more on female than on male infidelity. However, the country's growing Christianization and Westernization is beginning to put equal weight on male and female infidelity.

Marriage Forms

Monogamous and polygamous heterosexual unions are the main forms of marriage in Uganda. Polygyny, the practice of men having more than one wife at a time, is the most common form of polygamy in the country. Polyandry, which is when a woman has more than one husband, is taboo and nonexistent in Uganda. Thus, polygamy is synonymous with polygyny in Uganda.

Polygyny was more widespread in traditional Ugandan society for many reasons. First, it gave traditional society a way of dealing with the normal excess of females over males. Because society placed a high value on family, lifelong singleness was simply not an option for either males or females. Society also placed a premium on children (especially males) because of their importance in the social support system, especially in old age—female children had not been as valued because they join other families on marriage. Given the importance of children, childless marriages are considered incomplete or cursed and barren couples go to great medical lengths to conceive. Failing this, they consult traditional medicine men and diviners in order to overcome cases of barrenness due to witchcraft or ancestral curses. Because childlessness is often assumed to be the woman's fault, many women have in fact been divorced for their husbands' impotence.

Second, because Uganda is a patriarchal society, women do not inherit property, especially land, except in Buganda. Thus, women have traditionally been expected to marry, even to polygamous men, if only to secure land and livestock, which are important sources of livelihood in Uganda's agrarian society.

Third, many traditional Ugandan societies valued large families. In fact, a man's prestige often depended on the number of wives and children that he had. Given the abundance of farming and grazing land, high infant mortality, a short average lifespan, and the low cost of living in many traditional Uganda societies, polygyny was encouraged and widespread. Among the Banyarwanda/Bafumbira, for instance, monogamy was seen as being akin to marrying one's mother.[3] Because of the general acceptance of polygyny, the number of wives that a man could have was limited only by his ability to support them, bridewealth obligations, and age.

Fourth, Islam, one of Uganda's major religions, permits men to marry up to four wives, so polygyny is common in the country's substantial Muslim community and recent attempts to ban the practice have naturally drawn opposition from them.[4]

Overall polygynous marriages have been in decline as Uganda has modernized and as the material and cultural conditions that supported it have eroded. Moreover, such unions are increasingly frowned upon because of their higher incidence of poverty owing to rising costs of living as well as the prevalence of friction arising out of jealousy among the wives. The practice is also increasingly seen as a major contributor to the country's HIV/AIDS epidemic because one infected partner eventually spreads it to others.[5]

Marriage Types

Marriages in Uganda can be either traditional, religious (Christian, Islamic etc.), or civil. Traditional marriages adhere to the customs of indigenous Ugandan societies. Religious marriages follow the customs and rituals of the various religions in Uganda, while civil marriages are based on Uganda's civil law. Whereas the country's modernization is increasingly undermining traditional marriages, religious and civil marriages are thriving, especially in urban areas. Traditional marriages remain dominant in rural areas.

Traditional Marriages

Marriage customs among Uganda's ethnic communities have traditionally varied widely, with the most discernible differences occurring between the broad Bantu, Nilotic, Nilo-Hamitic, and Sudanic people groups (see Chapter 1). For instance, wedding arrangements in most Bantu groups tend to be brief and less ritualistic compared with those of the Nilotes. However, in all cases, family formation begins with courtship, payment of dowry or bride wealth, and then marriage. Traditionally, most marriages were arranged by parents, intermediaries, or close clan members. But over time there has been a growing tendency for boys to find their own mates before seeking parental consent for marriage.

Although courtship practices in traditional Ugandan societies vary widely, courtship is generally initiated by either the boy or the would-be couple's parents. It is customary for boys to approach girls, and not the other way round. In traditional society, courtship was closely supervised by family and clan members to avoid premarital pregnancy. Among the Bakonjo-Bamba, Bakiga, and the Banyarwanda/Bafumbira, virginity was so valued that premarital pregnancy was punishable by the girl's death, usually by abandonment in a deserted forest. There is no indication that the boy responsible for the girl's pregnancy was subject to a similar sentence.

Other communities (e.g., the Karimojong) permitted premarital sex as long as pregnancy was avoided. But in the event of such pregnancy, the Karimojong forced the offending couple to get married and imposed a hefty 30-cow fine on the boy. Many other communities imposed lesser fines but generally practiced the forced marriage custom. Although this custom remains common in many Ugandan communities, it is in decline because of society's growing modernization and acceptance of children born out of wedlock. Moreover, forced marriages are undesirable in cases of premarital pregnancy resulting from rape by strangers and criminals, especially in the war-torn and lawless north. Nevertheless, marriage prospects for premarital mothers are low, and poverty rates among these women are generally high throughout the country.

During courtship, great care is usually taken to gather background information about the prospective bride or groom's family. Ugandans usually try to avoid marrying from or into families with a history of laziness, witchcraft, gluttony, drunkenness, barrenness, and other unacceptable social behaviors or traits. Traditional Ugandan families especially value hard-working and responsible spouses, as "love" is defined as the young person's ability to fulfill socially defined gender roles. Marriage among close kin members is discouraged, more strictly so among the Karimojong and the Banyarwanda/Bafumbira. The latter believed that such marriages render offspring weak and vulnerable to spiritual attacks. Without the benefit of modern genetic science, this has been an effective way of preventing the genetic diseases frequently observed among the offspring of close relatives. Prevention of close kin unions has also been a way of preventing incest.

Christian and Muslim Marriages

Christian marriages are conducted in church by priests or pastors using state-issued marriage certificates. The ceremony usually comes after the satisfaction of customary dowry requirements—this being one of the elements of African culture that has been incorporated into local Christian practice. Christian marriages are monogamous and are prevalent in areas most influenced by the various Christian denominations of Uganda. Because Christianity was brought to Uganda by Europeans, Christian marriages in the country usually feature elements of European or Western weddings, for example, white wedding dresses for brides, flower girls, groomsmen, bridesmaids, maids of honor, and best men. Christian marriage ceremonies feature Western or Ugandan Christian music, receptions with local and Western cuisine, exhortations to the newlyweds, music, and dance. Such marriages are usually consummated on the wedding night, and honeymoons are common among wealthy urban Ugandans.

Muslim marriages are usually arranged by parents to ensure marital compatibility. But before marriage, the match has to be agreed to by the potential marriage partners, at which point the girl and the boy exchange engagement rings and the groom gives the bride dowry (*mahr*). According to Islamic culture, dowry is the property of the wife and cannot be taken from her even in divorce. Then the marriage ceremony takes place, usually a simple affair that does not necessarily require the presence of the bride as long as witnesses, usually her father and someone else, are present. During the ceremony, brides usually wear cherry-red wedding gowns and decorate their hands and feet with henna to enhance their beauty. The marriage ceremony is usually preceded by a meal, typically dinner. Then the imam (Islamic priest) or some other presiding official is invited to read the relevant sections of the Koran and oversee the signing of a mutually agreed-on contract and the exchange of marriage vows and to declare the couple legally married. Wedding rings are then exchanged, followed by sumptuous celebrations with plenteous food, and music and song. Muslim marriages, like their Christian counterparts, incorporate certain elements of local cultures. But unlike in Christianity, marriage is an obligatory religious duty in Islam.[6]

Muslim marriages can be polygamous because the Koran permits men to marry up to four wives as long as they are able to provide for them. This practice has recently forced Ugandan Muslims to protest the country's draft Domestic Relations Bill (DRB) because it seeks to outlaw polygamy, bride price, and cohabitation and to increase the legal age of consent to marriage to 18 rather than the customary onset of puberty for Muslims.[7]

Civil Marriages

Ugandan civil marriages are conducted by government officials (e.g., a district registrar) for those who are not religious or willing to undergo the drawn-out process of traditional or religious marriages. Interracial and interethnic couples facing opposition from their families also tend to resort to civil marriages. To a large measure, even religious marriages are civil marriages to the extent that the marriage certificates they issue come from the state.[8]

Cohabitation

Although not legally considered as a form of marriage in Uganda, cohabitation is becoming common in the country's urban areas. Though rare in traditional society, the breakdown of social customs engendered by modernization has contributed to the rise of cohabitation. High poverty levels that prevent many marriage-age people from meeting the up-front costs of marriages (e.g., dowry, weddings, and receptions) are also contributing to rising cohabitation, as is the desire for some people to try out marriage before committing to one another. Because of the growing number of cohabiting households, the proposed Domestic Relations Bill (DRB) has a provision to automatically convert 10-year or longer cohabitations into legal marriages.[9] This provision is apparently designed to protect women and children in such relationships.[10]

Bride Wealth

Bride wealth, bride price, or dowry, and other gifts are integral to marriage in Uganda. Among some communities such as the Bakonjo and Bamba, no marriage is recognized until a dowry is paid. Dowry serves as a traditional marriage seal besides compensating the girl's family for the loss of her labor—a significant loss in traditional agrarian societies. By custom, the most common dowry items are cows, goats, and digging implements—the tools are a symbolic replacement of the girl's lost labor and productivity.

Traditionally, the actual number of each dowry item varied widely among Uganda's societies, based on factors such as whether the girl is a virgin or a divorcée (e.g., among the Bakonjo-Bamba, Banyankole, Bakiga, Banyarwanda/ Bafumbira, and Basamia-Bagwe); the groom's socioeconomic status and titles (e.g., among the Basamia-Bagwe); family status, and clan or ethnic group. Thus, while dowry was generally low among the Baganda, it was substantial among the Batooro, usually consisting of 6 to 20 cows and a varying number of goats and hoes. Other communities, such as the Banyoro, did not traditionally view dowry as a precondition for marriage because of high divorce rates, marriage instability, and cohabitation. As a result, the Banyoro have a history of paying dowry after the marriage has gained some degree of stability.

Many of the societies that traditionally demanded high dowry for virgins also had stiff penalties for girls who became pregnant before marriage. For instance, among the Bakonjo-Bamba and Banyarwanda/Bafumbira, premarital pregnancy was punishable by death. The latter simply abandoned these unfortunate girls in the forest, where they died of starvation or attacks by wild animals. Conversely, although the Banyankole charged premium dowries for virgins, they imposed no capital punishment on girls who lost their virginity. Nevertheless, they required a nonvirgin bride to give her new husband a perforated coin or some other hollow object to alert him to her condition.

By custom, the amount of dowry paid for a bride also depended on how she got married. If she eloped (a practice known as *ukwijana* among the Banyarwanda/Bafumbira), often because of premarital pregnancy, she fetched a low dowry. But if she was forced into marriage (*gufata* or *gaturura*), she fetched a punitively high dowry. *Gufata* usually occurred when a boy, with the help of his friends, kidnapped a girl and took her to his home to be his wife. This usually occurred when the boy's marriage proposal was rejected by the girl's family for any reason or when a boy smitten by a girl was unable to afford the required dowry. Thus, although *gufata* normally called for exorbitant dowry, it still worked to the boy's advantage because the dowry was not necessarily all payable at once. Besides, *gufata* often forced the girl's family to accept the boy's marriage proposal or to lower their dowry demands, knowing that if their exorbitant demands broke the marriage, the girl would fetch even less dowry as a divorcée. In short, *gufata* put the girl's family in a no-win situation.

In many traditional Ugandan societies, divorce necessitated the return of the dowry. Usually, the communities that highly valued dowry were also the ones that insisted on the return of the dowry after divorce. To avoid this unpleasant prospect, both the groom and bride's nuclear and extended families and even clans worked hard to resolve marital conflicts. For this reason, divorce in many traditional Ugandan societies tended to be low. Nevertheless, the most common causes of divorce in Uganda were traditionally spousal barrenness, laziness, misunderstandings, drunkenness, ill treatment, adultery, gluttony, refusal or inability to offer sex, and other socially undesirable instances.

Uganda's changing socioeconomic conditions since colonialism have also left their imprint on the practice of dowry. Foremost is the end of some Ugandan communities' practice of killing girls for loss of virginity as the social norms and practices that enforced premarital chastity have declined as a result of growing Westernization of Ugandan society and increasing acceptance of premarital sex. However, other factors such as a woman's educational status, and hence her earning potential in the modern economy, have become more important considerations in dowry negotiations in contemporary Uganda. Second, because it is impractical for urban families to give or receive dowry in the form of livestock, cash or other modern material things have become a common substitute. Third, declining rural grazing lands and rising population densities are also increasingly limiting the size of many families' livestock herds, hence the rapid decline in the quantity of livestock given as dowry even in many rural Ugandan societies. It is, therefore, increasingly common for rural families to pay or receive dowry in the form of cash or a combination of cash and a symbolic number of livestock. But for Uganda's pastoral communities, for example, the Karimojong, livestock is still the preferred form of dowry.

Last, the country's modernization has begun to undermine the practice of dowry altogether, especially in urban areas. In fact, the country's Domestic Relations Bill seeks to outlaw dowry. However, given that this bill has been in development for the better part of Uganda's independence and has been repeatedly introduced and shelved because of opposition from various social groups, it may be awhile before dowry becomes illegal in the country.

MARRIAGE TRADITIONS

Uganda's marriage traditions begin with courtship, followed by payment of dowry, and then the wedding. This pattern underlies nearly all marriages in Uganda, whether traditional, religious, or civil. The only exception is those marriages that start through cohabitation.

Every Ugandan community has its own traditions, with some communities being more elaborate than others. As such, marriages in communities such as the Baganda that traditionally had short marriage ceremonies differ significantly from those of societies that have traditionally had elaborate ceremonies (e.g., the Karimojong). Nevertheless, among all Ugandan communities, the elegance of marriage ceremonies also depends on the prospective couple's socioeconomic status. Thus, marriage ceremonies are fairly reliable indicators of the groom and bride's socioeconomic status.

Although the broad pattern of courtship, dowry, and then marriage applies to most Ugandan communities, differences are discernible between the major people groups of Bantus, Nilotes, Nilo-Hamites, and Sudanics. The following Ganda (Baganda) and Karimojong marriage traditions illustrate Bantu and Nilo-Hamitic practices, respectively.

Bantu Marriage Traditions: The Case of the Baganda

Although the Ganda (Baganda) have long regarded marriage as a central aspect of life, their marriage ceremonies have traditionally been relatively simple (save for those of the *Kabaka*). In centuries past, the parents initiated marriage for their children by choosing spouses for them without so much as obtaining consent from the children. Over time, however, boys started choosing their own mates with the approval of parents, with due diligence to avoid courting relatives and people with undesirable family and social traits. After this, introductions and payment of dowry were made and then a marriage ceremony was conducted to hand over the girl. In this whole process, the girl's role amounted to no more than giving her consent. All these steps to marriage usually involved large social gatherings with eating, drinking, and dance. Before the formal introductions, the girl would be dressed by an aunt and the boy invited to see whether he liked her. If so, introductions, dowry, and the handover ceremony followed. Most Ugandan Bantu marriages traditionally followed this pattern, save for the Bakiga, who had a custom of secluding girls for a month for feeding (fattening) and training in the art of family management.

Nowadays, most Baganda boys identify the girls they would like to marry and proceed to court them, often with minimal parental involvement because much of the courtship takes place at school or urban workplaces or away from parents. Unlike in traditional society where courtship led to payment of dowry and then marriage, growing poverty is increasingly making it difficult for boys to pay a dowry and afford a marriage ceremony. Consequently, cohabitation is a growing feature of Baganda culture. Moreover, depending on one's values and socioeconomic status, modern Baganda have a choice between traditional, religious, and civil marriage. This is also true of many other Ugandans.

A typical traditional Ganda marriage (*Kwanjula*) ceremony lasts three to four hours and consists of the following steps:

- *Abatambuze Bali Ku Mulyango:* The bride's father's spokesman welcomes the groom and his party. Until so welcomed, the groom and his party are considered strangers or passersby.
- *Abagenyi Bayingidde:* After being welcomed, the groom and his party enter as guests.
- *Abagenyi Batudde—Abaana Balamusa:* If the bride has siblings, they are allowed to greet the groom and his party.
- *Abagenyi Banyonyola Ekibaleese:* The groom's spokesman explains the visitors' reason for coming (*Ensonga*).
- *Ekyaleese Abagenyi Kimanyibwa:* Because the groom's party does not come until "invited" by one of the bride's aunts, the aunt who gave the invitation "admits doing so after being exposed" (*Ssenga Ow'ensonga*). This "outing" is usually done in a lighthearted manner, as everybody at the gathering is privy to the reason for the meeting but feigns ignorance until the groom's spokesman declares their reason for coming and the aunt is "outed."
- *Abagenyi Baleeta Enjogeza:* The groom and his party serve the "conversation starter," usually a drink. The acceptance of the drink by the bride's father's party is a positive sign that they are willing to entertain subsequent negotiations.

- *Okw'ogera Ebikwaata Ku Mulenzi:* The groom's spokesman relates the groom's heritage and status, that is, his family background, ancestry, work ethic, and achievements. The groom's spokesman does his best to cast the groom in a good light, as dubious ancestry or reputation on the part of the groom is enough reason for the girl's family or clan to reject the proposed union.
- *Olukiiko Lulamusa:* The groom's party accepts greetings from the girl's uncles, aunts, and neighbors. To show respect, the women in the groom's party stoop or kneel as they are greeted.
- *Okw'ogera Ebikwaata Ku Muwala:* The bride's father's spokesman relates the bride's heritage and status, that is, her family background, ancestry, and achievements. As with the groom's spokesman, the bride's father's spokesman does his best to highlight the bride's good reputation, work ethic, ancestry, and achievements, as shortcomings in any of these areas can cause the groom's party to reject the bride.
- *Okusiima Ebirabo:* If satisfied with the bride's reputation (and they usually are, because by the time this ceremony takes place, the necessary background investigations would have been conducted to the satisfaction of the groom and his family), the groom's spokesman seeks permission show the groom's appreciation for the excellent job that the bride's parents, family, and clan have done in raising her. He then proceeds to give gifts to the bride's father, mother, brother (*muko*), paternal aunt (*Ssenga*), other aunts, grandparents, and others.
- *Okuyingira Mu Nju—Okulya Entaba Luganda:* The groom and his spokesman and two to three others enter the bride's family house for a brief meeting with the bride's uncles and aunts, and the groom is formally accepted as a son of the family. At this time, roasted coffee beans and drinks are shared to seal the kinship or brotherhood (*Oluganda*).
- *Okulya Ekijjulo:* Once the kinship is sealed, the conversation changes from formal to familial. The main feast is announced, and the groom eats with another group (excluding parents) inside the house.
- *Obusiimo, Empeta Ne Cake:* Then optional events such as picture taking, presentation of additional presents, exchange of engagement rings, and the cutting of a cake take place.
- *Okusibuula:* The groom and his party leave for home and come for the bride at the *Kasuze Katya* Ceremony.[11]

Nilo-Hamitic Marriage Traditions: The Case of the Karimojong

Among Uganda's Nilo-Hamitic groups, the Karimojong have had some of the most elaborate traditional marriage ceremonies. The process began with a boy's declaration of his intent to get married. This announcement traditionally required that the boy prove his maturity by single-handedly killing a lion or an elephant with a spear, and to report this achievement at an elders' meeting (*baraza*), featuring a bull feast (the communal feasting on a roasted bull) provided by the boy's father. After this, the boy was allowed to wear an ostrich feather and a leopard skin as signs of maturity. The father then instructed the boy to look for a girl and initiate sexual contact with her, provided premarital pregnancy was avoided, as this resulted in a hefty 30-goat fine for the boy. Thereafter, marriage and bride wealth negotiations between the two families commenced. The girl's parents then sent a delegation with the girl to the boy's family to fetch the dowry. On the way back, the girl's delegation was accompanied by a delegation from the boy's home. On arrival, the girl's mother welcomed the boy's group with a lit pipe that was enjoyed first by the elders in the group. Afterward, the boy's group returned to his home and on arrival, the boy removed the leopard skin and ostrich feather he had been wearing, but he did not sleep with his bride because sexual contact had already occurred during courtship.

On day two, the boy's mother took a calabash full of cooking butter to the girl's house and summoned her. She put a necklace and *emuria* grass on the girl, smeared butter all over her, except on her legs, removed the girl's ornaments, and dressed her in a goatskin and calfskin like a married woman. Then the bride and three other girls from her village (bridesmaids) fetched firewood for the boy's mother to complete the marriage. The groom then slept with his bride and continued to do so until a child was born. Then he built a separate hut for her and became eligible to marry again, with the number of wives he could have limited only by bride-wealth obligations and age.

The Karimojong allowed for divorce provided the dowry was returned. If a woman was childless at the time of divorce, she reverted to dressing as an unmarried girl. If she had a child or children, she kept her married woman's attire but was free to remarry. Although the Karimojong had a permissive attitude toward premarital sex, adultery was a serious offense punishable by the offending man's death at the hands of the woman's husband, or by repeated confiscation of all of his livestock until the aggrieved party believed that his honor had been restored. The seized property was usually shared among the aggrieved man's family.[12]

As with many Ugandan societies, the Karimojong have had to contend with modern forces that are changing, not only their traditional way of life, but their marriage customs as well. For instance, the age-old custom of proving maturity by killing a lion or an elephant is clearly impractical and illegal in modern Uganda because of the limited number of lions and elephants and the importance of these animals to the country's tourism industry. Thus, the ritual of killing lions and elephants has had to be replaced by other initiation ceremonies. Second, the practice of seizing another man's property for committing adultery with one's wife violates modern state laws, even though it is in line with tradition. Third, as Karimojong youngsters are increasingly educated, many are abandoning their community's traditional way of life and marriage customs. Fourth, the long civil war in northern Uganda and the attendant introduction of firearms into the area has displaced many and made life unbearable for the Karimojong and their neighbors. As a result, marriage traditions have had to adapt to the new reality. Lawlessness has especially made life dangerous for northern Uganda girls and women, who are under constant threat of abduction, rape, sexually transmitted diseases, unwanted pregnancies, and death.[13]

FAMILY AND GENDER ROLES

Ugandan families and societies have traditionally had distinct gender roles. In general, women are responsible for most of the domestic chores such as cleaning, food production and preparation, fetching water and firewood, care giving and child rearing. Even in the area of trading, women usually engage in activities that are related to or extensions of their domestic chores, such as basket weaving. Conversely, Ugandan men play smaller domestic roles. However, they function as breadwinners and owners of most of the country's productive resources, especially land, make most of the social and economic decisions of their families, and have traditionally been the main providers of shelter.

In many traditional societies, men contributed to household food security through animal husbandry, hunting, fishing, and, in some societies, working alongside women in agricultural food production. For instance, among the Kakwa, the men cleared, dug, and planted the fields, while the women removed the refuse from the fields, weeded, harvested, cleaned, and stored the harvest. Although the domestic chores of women have scarcely changed since precolonial times, men's roles have undergone significant change, and many now contribute to the family's socioeconomic well-being by contributing cash income from their modern-sector jobs.

Although there was more equity in the male-female division of labor in traditional Ugandan societies, significant inequality has developed since colonialism, resulting in a situation in which women now do most of the labor-intensive activities, such as food production and preparation. Moreover, women are disadvantaged in their access to education and productive resources (e.g., land, employment, and income) and are underrepresented in most Ugandan societies' decision making and governance.[14] Even at the family level, wives usually defer critical decisions to husbands, many of whom make decisions without consulting their wives.

Ugandan children play an important role in raising other children. Courtesy of Ken Goyer.

Many of the social conditions that disadvantage Ugandan women are culture-based. For instance, women's limited access to land is a result of their lack of land inheritance rights, because it is culturally assumed that women have access to land through their husbands. Thus, unmarried women (an increasing segment of the Ugandan population) usually find it difficult to access land, which, in an agrarian society such as Uganda, limits their ability to produce food. Even among married women, access to land is usually secondary, meaning that they lack the full rights to dispose of it if necessary. In fact, even among the Baganda who allow women to inherit land, it is daughters rather than wives who inherit land from their fathers—this is a way of keeping the land within the man's clan. In many Ugandan societies, the death

Ploughing with oxen is generally considered a man's work. Courtesy of Ken Goyer.

of a woman's husband can result in her ejection from family land by her husband's male relatives, unless she has adult sons.

In contemporary Ugandan society, men also enjoy more leisure than do women. In fact, many women's leisure usually amounts to involvement in less demanding work such as dish washing. On the other hand, men are free to visit friends and enjoy a drink or two with them, especially in the afternoons. Men have such leeway because they not only control most of the productive resources but are also traditionally considered "owners" of their wives and children and of the fruits of their labor. This is why men make most of the family financial decisions even when they are not directly involved in the production of family income.

Other aspects of Ugandan culture also work against women. For instance, because of the widespread cultural understanding that women become part of the families they marry into, their families of birth often shortchange them in the allocation of resources, such as education, early in life. When a family has to choose between educating a girl or a boy, the boy is usually given preference. As a result, Ugandan women are less educated than their male counterparts and are not as well represented in the formal workforce, hence their continued operation in the domestic sphere, thereby reinforcing their culturally prescribed domestic role.

SOCIALIZATION

Ugandan societies have traditionally aspired to socialize their children into functional members of society. The core elements of traditional socialization were cultural values such as discipline and respect for elders, morality, honesty, hard work, cooperation, spirituality, cultural taboos and totems, and clan relations and boundaries so as to avoid incestuous marriage relations. Antisocial activities such as theft, sorcery, and premarital pregnancy (where disallowed) were discouraged by harshly punishing offenders, often by death.

Gender roles were structured in such a way as to prepare children for successful family and adult lives. Although socialization took place throughout the growing-up years, matters pertaining to family life were usually taught during initiation ceremonies (e.g., circumcision) that marked the transition from childhood to adulthood. In most societies, circumcision and other initiation ceremonies were usually followed by marriage. Although still practiced in many modern Ugandan societies, the role of circumcision as an initiation ceremony has been severely eroded, supplanted by such things as school matriculation.

Traditionally, children were taught various vocational skills such as animal husbandry, farming, hunting, rainmaking, divination, and healing through apprenticeship, and as a result, these skills were hereditary. Both boys and girls were usually taught skills related to their gender roles. Thus, girls were taught basketry and pottery, while boys were trained as blacksmiths, diviners, and rainmakers. In some communities, skills such as pottery were taught to boys as well. Children learned their gender roles by working alongside their parents—girls by their mothers and sons by their fathers. In this way, blame for a maladjusted boy or girl was placed on the father or mother, respectively.

Grandparents played an equally important role in socializing children by teaching children, at evening fireside, stories that glorified desirable behaviors or moral traits and disparaged the undesirable ones. Grandparents were integral and effective socializing agents because they combined personal life experiences and heroics with the freedom to broach sensitive subjects such as sex. This multigenerational social set-up ensured a near-flawless socialization of children in traditional society.

Since colonialism, however, there have been many socioeconomic changes and population movements that have severely stressed this traditional system of socialization and made it difficult for many societies to cope. For instance, the role of families and clans in socialization has largely been taken over by schools where children spend most of their youth away from both parents and grandparents. The advent of the modern cash economy often forces one parent, especially the father, to spend considerable amounts of time away from the family, thereby further weakening the socialization process, especially that of boys. In some cases, parents and their children live in urban areas away from rural-based grandparents who seldom see and help socialize their grandchildren. Besides, many grandparents are also increasingly disconnected from their grandchildren by language barriers that are engendered by the modern school system. The increased separation of the children from the parents and grandparents is to a large degree responsible for the rapid increase in the number of maladjusted, unproductive, and lawless youth.

School socialization is not working as well as traditional socialization because it often teaches skills and behaviors that are irrelevant to local needs and relies on a limited number of adult role models. Thus, the school system creates an environment where students socialize each other in ways that are not necessarily beneficial to society. The system is also fraught with cases of sexual exploitation of girls by teachers and older boys, with nearly half of the sexually active primary school girls being forced to have sexual intercourse.[15] Moreover, many students' growing access to global information mediums, especially the Internet, is also complicating the country's socialization efforts because most parents and teachers are unfamiliar with the technology and are, therefore, unable to give their children and students direction in its proper use. The result is a society that is being flooded with many foreign cultural ideas (e.g., pornography) that are not necessarily good for it and that is undergoing rapid cultural change without the benefit of time to reflect on its direction.

SOCIAL CHANGE

The seeds of drastic social change in Uganda were planted during colonialism with its attendant introduction of alien values, work ethics, languages, government structures, religions, and other socioeconomic systems to Uganda. These changes have profoundly affected all facets of Ugandan society, including its gender roles and institutions of marriage and the family.

The continued weakening of indigenous cultures is a major challenge to Ugandan society. As the new values take hold, nontraditional gender roles, marriage, and family practices are becoming common. In the area of family, for instance, female-headed single-parent households that were traditionally rare are becoming commonplace in many parts of the country, especially in urban areas. Economic changes are also forcing many married rural men to leave their wives behind and seek wage employment in urban areas where, contrary to traditional gender roles, they have to fetch water and firewood, prepare their own meals, wash their clothes, and clean their houses. Moreover, this extended male absence is creating room for the wives who are left behind to take on traditional male responsibilities such as making major financial decisions.

Because of long spousal separation, behaviors such as adultery are also on the increase. In urban areas, for instance, many men with wives in rural areas are increasingly finding comfort in the arms of prostitutes, thereby aiding the rapid growth of commercial sex and sexually transmitted diseases, both of which were rare in traditional Ugandan societies.

The development of the modern prison system and its extended seclusion of men and women (contrary to traditional social practice) and the growing tourism industry have also given rise to gay sexual behavior that was rare or unheard of in traditional Ugandan society. Although the behavior is also becoming common in the country's single-gender boarding secondary schools and major urban areas, gay marriages are banned in Uganda.[16]

Similarly, cohabitation is becoming a common domestic arrangement. Although present in some traditional Ugandan societies, it has virtually extended its reach to all communities, especially those in urban areas. Moreover, the popular traditional practice of wife inheritance (i.e., inheritance of a deceased man's wife by one of his kinsmen) is being weakened by the growing power of women over their destinies and the economic burdens that such a practice engenders in modern-day Uganda. Moreover, wife-inheritance in contemporary Uganda can be fatal because many men die from HIV/AIDS and often unknowingly infect their wives.

7

Social Customs and Lifestyle

Uganda's rich culture embodies many local, regional, and national social customs and lifestyles that vary based on ethnicity, religion, occupation, income, and educational levels. This variety of customs and lifestyles is caused by the interaction of internal/local and external customs and traditions, resulting in the abandonment of some social customs and lifestyles, the modification of others, and the creation of new ones in the light of new information. For instance, the social custom of female genital cutting (circumcision) in some Ugandan communities is in decline because of pressure from local and international activists.

Ugandan social life generally revolves around the community, although individualism is beginning to take root, especially in urban areas, as Western social and cultural influences and the development of the modern capitalist economy affect the country. Ugandans highly value communal events and gatherings such as weddings because they are enjoyable and fulfilling, and participation in such events is central to the preservation of one's social standing. This communal orientation is rooted in traditional Ugandan culture.

Although modern communications and transport are increasingly available, Ugandans prefer to discuss important matters face-to-face. Ugandan culture is largely oral, so people prefer the rich interaction possible in face-to-face conversations. Additionally, because of the country's low literacy levels, oral communication in local languages facilitates interaction between all classes of Ugandans. Proverbs, idioms, riddles, and stories are frequently used to enrich and enliven oral communication besides demonstrating one's mastery of the language.

Social Relations

As in many African societies, interpersonal relations in Uganda are governed by generosity, friendship, honesty, hospitality, good moral behavior, and respect for elders, with the oldest members of society, the rich, and those in positions of authority accorded the highest levels of respect. Respect is conveyed in many ways, for example, by kneeling or bowing slightly when greeting an elder.

Greetings and salutations are a central part of Ugandan life. Although these vary by community, when people first meet for social or business engagements, they usually greet or salute one another and inquire about each other's health and that of their families. Whereas the appropriate form of verbal greeting varies with the time of day, social occasion, and the social or professional rank of the addressee or greeter, a general greeting is as follows:

> Person 1: Hello, How are you? (*Oli otya?* [in Luganda])
>
> Person 2: I'm fine, thanks, or I am well (*Gyendi* or *bulungi* [in Luganda]). How are you?
>
> Person 1: I'm fine, thanks. How is your family?
>
> Person 2: They are fine, thanks (if unwell, person 2 usually states so here). How is your family?

The preceding conversation is usually accompanied with a handshake or a hug, especially when greeting someone of the same gender. Handshakes between men and woman may be inappropriate in some situations. In many parts of Uganda, females and children kneel or bow when greeting or serving men, in-laws, guests, and community leaders. The use of professional, political, or other titles of reverence is common when greeting social dignitaries such as leaders and elders.[1] It is generally not acceptable for younger people to address their elders by their first names as though they are age mates. Instead, it is normal to precede the elder's last name with his or her professional, political, or marital title, for example, Dr., Honorable, Mrs., Mr., Ms., or any other acceptable salutation. Children usually address their parents as "mom" or "dad" rather than by name. With the growth of Kiswahili (Swahili) language use in Uganda, Swahili greetings are also popular. A typical Kiswahili greeting is as follows:

> Person 1: *Jambo* ("Hello")
>
> Person 2: *Jambo sana* ("I'm fine, thanks," or "I am well")
>
> Person 1: *Habari yako* ("How are you doing?")
>
> Person 2: *Njema* ("I'm fine, thanks")

The Banyoro have some of the most elaborate greeting customs in modern Uganda. They use various pet names (*empaako*)—*Abwoli, Adyeri, Araali, Akiiki, Atwoki, Abooki, Apuuli, Bala, Acaali, Ateenyi, Amooti,* and sometimes *Okali*—to greet one another. When relatives formally greet each other, the elder invites the younger to sit on his or her lap. Among the Babiito subclan, young people greet elders by touching their forehead and chin with their right-hand fingers. Depending on the occasion, greetings are then followed by servings of chewable coffee berries and smoking tobacco.

The Banyoro also have had special greetings for the *Omukama* or king, who usually sat at well-publicized places at particular times of the day to facilitate visits by his subjects. Known as *okukurata,* this process required adherence to certain procedures that varied by gender, the use of respectful language usually in the third-person singular, and the use of the right greeting from the more than 20 different kingly addresses for different times of the day. Because the king was not expected to give a verbal response to greetings by common men, he seldom did. However, he often answered women's greetings verbally. Women usually knelt when greeting the king.[2]

Many Ugandan societies have rules that govern male-female relations. To begin with, there is a gender division of labor that enables males and females to play their daily roles without much interaction between the sexes, more so in rural areas. As a result, most close friendships are with members of the same gender. Close cross-gender friendships outside of romantic involvement tend to be few. Public displays of romance and discussions of sex are generally unacceptable, although efforts to combat the country's high HIV/AIDS epidemic have recently managed to open up public discussions of sex. At social events, men and women sit separately, even when participating in the same functions, for example, church services. In urban areas, however, restrictions on cross-gender interactions are either fewer or breaking down.[3]

Throughout Uganda, women are generally subservient to men, more so in rural areas. Men occupy most leadership positions, make most of the critical family decisions, and whenever meals are prepared, usually by women and girls, men are served first and with choice portions. In many communities, the role of women amounts to no more than bearing and raising children, producing and preparing food, and taking care of the family.[4] In general, Ugandan women bear the brunt of the country's harsh living conditions because they have limited access to education and productive resources such as land, lack independence and decision-making autonomy, are underpaid for their long hours of work, and generally lack control of their lives.[5, 6] Because polygamy is socially acceptable, it is common in many parts of Uganda. Although Ugandan husbands are expected to provide financial support for their wives and children, their social responsibilities to parents and peers frequently override those of their own nuclear families. Because Uganda is a communal society, the term *family* often means extended family.

Social interaction is also age-based. Traditionally, people were initiated into age-groups that went through life's subsequent stages together. Although traditional initiation and socialization systems are increasingly being replaced by modern ones, especially the school system, age-based interaction is still important in Ugandan society.

It is traditionally taboo to engage in public displays of affection, but Western cultural influences among Ugandan urban youth are eroding this custom. As a result, public hand-holding and kissing between boys and girls are becoming more common. Moreover, sexy Western dress such as miniskirts and tight jeans are also becoming fashionable among urban youth.

Ugandans generally have a less urgent sense of time than do Westerners. Because Ugandans, like many other Africans, subscribe to the notion of "African Standard Time," it is not unusual for events slated for a particular time, say 10 A.M., to begin several minutes or sometimes hours late. Respect for time is generally highest among Ugandans who operate in the urban formal work environment, although conditions such as bad weather and poor transportation frequently make this difficult. More traditional or rural Ugandans generally tend to wrap time around their various activities, taking as much time as necessary to finish a chore or a discussion. Thus, in certain instances, it can be offensive to interrupt the flow of social events or discussions in the interest of time.

CEREMONIES

Ugandans have many ceremonies that celebrate their communities' or country's history, important annual events, life events (birth, initiation to adulthood, marriage, and death), and spiritual matters.[7] Most of these ceremonies include food as well as spontaneous music and dance. Over time, many of these ceremonies, especially those that pertain to initiation rites such as circumcision, have undergone profound change as the country has modernized.

Although most Ugandans are reserved, they are festive when it comes to important social ceremonies such as marriage, child naming, death and burial, circumcision ceremonies (where practiced), rainmaking, worship, and, increasingly nowadays, college and university graduations. The most festive of these are marriage and other initiation ceremonies that mark important social transitions. Unlike graduations, which are limited to the elite, marriage and other social initiation ceremonies are all-inclusive.

Marriage is, perhaps, the most important ceremony in modern Uganda because it is a universal social foundation. Unlike some initiation ceremonies that are in danger of extinction, marriage has kept up with the times, despite the social and cultural disruptions of British colonialism and the subsequent modernization and Westernization of the country. Moreover, even the introduction of Christianity and Islam, and the attendant decline of traditional religions, has not diminished the importance of marriage. Rather, it has only changed the way marriages are celebrated. Essentially, these world religions have replaced traditional marriage ceremonies with their own.

Initiation Ceremonies

Initiation ceremonies were a central feature of traditional Ugandan societies and are to some degree still important even now. Whereas these ceremonies varied from community to community, they marked the passage from childhood to adulthood or entry into certain social, family, or spiritual groups. Examples include the outdated tradition of Karimojong boys single-handedly killing a lion or an elephant to prove their manhood and readiness for marriage; the circumcision of boys (and in some cases girls) to mark the transition from childhood to adulthood among the Bakonjo and Bamba, Bagisu, Sabiny, and Sebei; blood brotherhood ceremonies among the Batooro and Banyankore that united two unrelated people into bonds, obliging them to relate and support each other as biological brothers; and *Mukeli Gagi,* ritual marriages that initiated some Alur women's husbands into certain spiritual/religious cults. All these initiation ceremonies usually included training in the rights and responsibilities of the initiates.[8]

Uganda's rapid cultural change as a result of modernization is either undermining or transforming many of these traditional initiation ceremonies. For instance, the role of circumcision as a rite of passage from childhood to adulthood among the Bakonjo and Bamba, Bagisu, Sabiny, and Sebei is being transformed, and, in some cases, is being displaced by passage through the formal school system. Moreover, growing opposition to female circumcision by Western agencies and their Ugandan representatives has nearly wiped out the practice or transformed it. Among the Sabiny and Sebei, for instance, initiation ceremonies that traditionally included women's genital cutting have been changed to exclude this practice.[9] Thus, although the spirit of the initiation ceremonies has been retained, they are increasingly marked with dance, singing, and the exchange of gifts.[10]

Because the Bagisu have, perhaps, the most elaborate boy initiation practices in Uganda, their circumcision ceremonies deserve a closer look. The origin of Bagisu circumcision is unclear. But there are several competing explanations, one of which is that it improves a man's sexual prowess. The Bagisu circumcise 12- to 15-year-old boys once every two years. Before the mandatory ceremony, adolescent boys are given *ityanyi* herbs to arouse their interest in the painful ritual. For three days before the ceremony, the initiates are required to walk and dance around the villages, with their heads sprinkled with cassava flour and painted with a certain yeast paste. As they dance, sisters and other relatives accompany the initiates. The ceremonies also feature the famous *Imbalu* dancers, whose *Runyege* dance is especially memorable.

On the day of the event, the initiates are gathered in a semicircle and circumcised in turn by a traditional surgeon and his assistant. While the assistant extends the foreskin of the penis, the surgeon swiftly and deftly cuts it off and rounds off the operation by cutting a specific muscle below the penis and removing another penis layer that could grow into a foreskin. Traditionally, the procedure took place in secluded areas where only the initiates and the surgeons were permitted, but nowadays the entire community is allowed to witness the whole process. Initiates are expected to demonstrate bravery, courage, and endurance during the process.

After the surgical procedure, the initiate sits on a stool and a cloth is wrapped around his waist. He is then led to his father's house and made to walk around it before entering to be fed for three days—the initiate is not allowed to eat with his own hands. After the three days, the surgeon comes and performs the washing-of-the-initiates'-hands ritual, which officially ushers him into manhood, makes him eligible to marry, and allows him to eat with his hands. As he is ushered into manhood, the initiate is tutored on the rights and duties of manhood, the importance of being productive (especially in agriculture), and proper social conduct. After this, the initiate is allowed to heal, with the speed of healing believed to depend on the number of goats slaughtered at his circumcision ceremony—a belief that is probably meant to promote the initiate's family's generosity during this important ceremony.

After all fellow initiates are healed, they participate in the *Iremba* ritual that is witnessed by the entire village, and, nowadays, government officials. Traditionally, *Iremba* required new initiates to have sex with girls of their choice. The girls were expected to comply, lest, according to tradition, they become barren. The sex component of *Iremba* was instituted in earlier days when the main purpose in life was procreation. As Bagisu society has become more sophisticated, this custom has become less common.

According to Bagisu custom, a boy becomes a true *Mugisu* after circumcision. Uncircumcised men are degradingly referred to as *Musinde* and are often sought out and forcefully and scornfully circumcised. On the other hand, Bagisu boys or men who are willingly circumcised are endearingly referred to as *Musani*.[11]

Although circumcision endures among the Bagisu and other Ugandan communities, modernity is increasingly undermining its importance, especially in communities that traditionally circumcised both boys and girls but are increasingly under international pressure to end female circumcision. Furthermore, circumcision as a social initiation ceremony is being negated or undermined by the growing circumcision/initiation of immature boys who are in no position to appreciate the significance of the ceremony (in contrast to the traditional practice of circumcising adolescent boys who were ready to enter adulthood) and the growing inappropriateness of many aspects of the social training that accompanied traditional circumcision as Ugandans grapple with the need to prepare children for modern society. Moreover, in recent decades, the practice of circumcision has been attacked for aiding the spread of HIV/AIDS in the country because the traditional surgeons who perform it do not sterilize their knives properly. To protect public health, Ugandan President Yoweri Museveni has recently recommended that the operations be done by qualified doctors.[12] Although it is not clear whether the relevant communities will heed the president's call, it may be timely because male circumcision, when properly performed, has been shown to lower men's risk of contracting HIV/AIDS and to lower male-to-female HIV transmission through sexual intercourse.[13]

The decline of traditional initiation ceremonies has implications for Ugandan society. Because children were traditionally initiated into adulthood in age-sets that went through life together, initiation ceremonies such as circumcision contributed to social cohesion. Thus, the decline of these customs and the absence of suitable replacements may be undermining social cohesion in many communities and may be a reflection of the country's cultural crisis as its traditional social and cultural institutions are being eroded or replaced by Western cultural practices that do not necessarily fit the needs of Ugandan society. As a result, Ugandan youth are especially in danger of naively embracing inappropriate aspects of Western culture while ignoring many useful aspects of local Ugandan culture. To give its youth a cohesive cultural foundation on which to build their lives, Uganda may have to develop new initiation rites or try to modernize existing ones. The process may very well create a new hybrid culture that combines useful aspects of Ugandan and Western culture.

Child Naming Ceremonies

Traditional Ugandan communities have varying child naming ceremonies that are here exemplified by Baganda, Banyankole, Bagisu, Bagwere, and Banyoro practices. After giving birth, a Ganda mother remained in confinement until the baby's umbilical cord dried. After about two weeks, she had customary ritual sex with her husband to ensure the health of the baby. The baby was then named on the same day.[14]

On the other hand, the Banyoro named their children in the third or fourth month, depending on whether the baby was a boy or girl. Besides the individual name, the child also got one of the *mpaako* names (used for greetings) from its father, mother, grandparents, or other relatives. The given names usually memorialized the child's features; the circumstances of the child's birth; the parents' state of mind at the time of the child's birth or naming; and the constant death, sorrow, and poverty that prevailed in traditional Bunyore society and is still common today because of the scarcity of adequate medical facilities in Uganda. Thus, names such as *Tubuhwaire, Buletwenda, Bulimarwaki, Kabwijamu, Alijunaki,* and *Tibanagwa* relate to the high rate of maternal death and sorrow that accompanied childbirth; *Bikanga, Baligenda, Babyenda,* and *Bagamba* memorialized the parents' poverty at the child's birth; while *Itima, Tindyebwa, Nyendwoha, Nsekanabo, Ndyanabo,* and *Tibaijuka* pertain to the neighbors' malevolence at the time of the child's birth.

Other Ugandan communities such as the Banyankole named their children immediately after birth. The chosen name could be that of an ancestor or one that reflected the parents' experience or state of mind at the time of the child's birth, or the day or place of birth. Although the father, grandfather, or mother could all name the child, the father was usually given priority. Among the Bagwere, grandmothers or aunts named children.

The Bagisu had, perhaps, the most unusual child naming method in Uganda. The process commenced after the newborn cried continuously for, say, a day or night. This, according to tradition, triggered a visit from a dead ancestor (in a dream) who provided the name of the child, usually that of the departed ancestor.

Death and Burial Ceremonies

Traditional Ugandans had many death and burial ceremonies that are not as strictly adhered to today. The Baganda, who inordinately feared death, buried their dead after five days to ensure that the person was actually dead. Because female corpses were thought to rot faster than those of males, they were usually buried sooner—actually, the number days before burial and the length of mourning depended on gender prestige. The burial was followed by a month of mourning and *Okwabya Olumbe* (i.e., break up the disease or grief) funeral rights, at which a new heir or head of family was installed, if the husband died, and the spirit of the dead person was exorcised from the home. Once installed, the new heir was required to take care of those he inherited. *Okwabya Olumbe* was usually a festive ceremony attended by clan elders and many other people. It featured lots of food and drink, music, dance, and unrestrained sexual intercourse by attendees.

Banyoro death and burial ceremonies were more elaborate than those of the Baganda. The Banyoro viewed death as a fearful real being, although they also believed that sorcerers and ghosts could cause death. Whenever a household head died, older women in the household would prepare his body for burial by closing the eyes, trimming the fingernails, shaving the hair and beard, and washing it. The body was then wrapped in bark cloth and lay in state for one to two days, with its face exposed. Meanwhile the deceased's children were required to eat *ensigosigo,* a mixture of millet grains and simsim, placed in his right hand. Then these rites were performed before burial: the deceased's nephew would take the dead man's eating basket (*endiiro*), his bow, and the central pillar of his house and throw them in the middle of the compound (the removal of the central pillar made the deceased's house structure unstable and dangerous, so it was usually left unoccupied after its owner's burial); the cooking fire in the center of the house was put out and cooking in the house was banned for the first three days of mourning; a banana plant with fruit from the deceased's plantation was added to his pile of belongings in the middle of the compound; the deceased's nephew or son fetched water in a household water pot and broke it on the man's pile of belongings in the compound; the nephew or son then killed the man's cock to keep it from crowing; and the deceased's main bull was castrated to keep him from mating during the mourning period. Finally, the *Mugabuzi* ceremony, the killing and eating of the castrated bull, was conducted on the fourth day. During the mourning, it was permissible for women and children to wail loudly but not the men.

Banyoro burials were conducted in the morning or afternoon but not in the middle of the day to prevent the sun from shining directly into the open grave. Banyoro burial custom

- required that no weeping should take by the graveside,
- barred pregnant women from the graveside to prevent miscarriage,
- dictated that men be buried while lying on their right side and women on their left side, these also being the culturally recommended sleeping positions for men and women, respectively,
- required that the head be placed toward the east,
- barred anybody leaving the graveside until the burial was complete,
- required that the tools used to dig the grave be left at the graveside,
- required thorough washing of the grave diggers at the grave site to keep ritual pollution and soil from the grave from spreading to the rest of the compound and garden, where it was believed to cause disease, crop failure, and rot,
- required that a banana plant be buried if a grave was dug prematurely and the anticipated death (e.g., from sickness) did not occur,
- forbade leaving the grave unguarded to protect the grave-diggers and others from accidental death by falling into the open grave,

- required that funeral attendees deposit on the grave hair from the back and front of their heads,
- required that the grave be clearly marked with stones or some other marker to prevent others from building on it, as this would jeopardize family members' health and life,
- required that if a person died with grudges that the mouth and anus be stuffed with clay to prevent the ghost from haunting the begrudged individuals, and
- required that one of the grave diggers put soot on his hands and then squeeze a juicy plant and that the deceased's children drink the juice as it dripped from the grave digger's elbow.

Many Ugandan communities also had more elaborate burial ceremonies for chiefs and members of the royal family. Among the Baganda, for instance, the death of the *Kabaka* (king) set in motion a series of actions: the *Kabaka's Majaguzo* or drums were placed in safe custody and his *Gombolola* or sacred fire (that burned perpetually at the entrance of the palace) was extinguished, pending the appointment of a new *Kabaka* before being lit again—the kingdom was symbolically lifeless until a new *Kabaka* was enthroned and the royal fire rekindled. After this, the *Kabaka's* body was appropriately dressed and placed in the palace under the care of the chiefs of Bulemezi and Bugerere, whose respective titles were *Kangawo* and *Mugerere*. Before burial, the body was embalmed for six months, and the jawbone was removed, and a special shrine built for it because the Baganda believed that the spirit of a man remained with his jawbone. After the preliminary ceremonies, the *Kabaka* was buried with great honor at the Kasubi royal tombs. The Banyoro had similarly elaborate burials for their royalty.

Some Ugandan communities such as the Banyankore did not consider death to be a natural occurrence. As a result, most burials were preceded by consultations with witch doctors to ascertain the cause of death and to remove the ritual pollution caused by death in the community. Like the Baganda and Banyoro, the Banyankole had ceremonial burials for their royalty.

One of the Karimojong clans of northern Uganda did not bury their dead. Rather, the *Ng'inga'aricum* clan disposed of its dead in the open to be devoured by insects, ants, and wild animals. Among the Karimojong clans that buried their dead, a chief was usually buried in the middle of the *kraal,* while the wives and other family members were buried around the sides or near the *kraals* entrance.

Other notable burial customs among Uganda's peoples include Jopadhola customs that prohibited bathing less than three days after somebody's death; special burial rites among the Bagisu for the barren and for unmarried women that involved the practice of burying the dead with needles or grinding stones to keep the corpses "busy sewing or grinding" so as to keep them from answering

The *Kabakas* of Buganda had royal burial grounds. The Kasubi tombs shown here are one of Uganda's most popular tourist attractions. Courtesy of Ken Goyer.

the call of body hunters or witches; many communities' burial of their dead facing their supposed direction of origin, for instance, the Karimojong buried their dead with the head positioned in the north; special Basoga burial rites for household heads, childless men, married women, and the occasional burial of household heads in their huts; and Banyarwanda/Bafumbira and Banyankore's avoidance of farming or manual work during mourning to honor the deceased, console the deceased's family, and/or avoid curses.

Coronation Ceremonies

To facilitate understanding of coronation ceremonies in Uganda, it is important to briefly explore the current state of the country's monarchies. There are presently four to five traditional kingdoms in Uganda namely, Buganda, Bunyoro, Busoga, Toro, and the pending Ankole kingdom. Of these, the Buganda monarchy is, perhaps, the most influential because of its historical role in Uganda and proximity to the national capital Kampala.

Although Busoga is not one of Uganda's precolonial kingdoms, it was created by the British colonial authorities in 1906 (even though it collapsed soon after and was re-established in 1919) through the merger of the various kingdoms (some argue chiefdoms) of precolonial Busoga. This was done to facilitate indirect British rule of Busoga in a manner similar to the kingdoms of Buganda, Bunyoro-Kitara, Toro, and Ankole, which already had strong monarchies. The latter four kingdoms originated in the initial Bunyoro-Kitara kingdom that was founded by the Babiito dynasty in approximately 1200–1600 A.D. Babiito descendants are still the kings of Bunyoro-Kitara and Toro.

The Ankole kingdom, which like the other four was banned by President Obote in 1967, has not reconstituted itself since the passage of the 1993 law that restored the traditional monarchies. This is because of disagreements between the three Banyankore clans (that is, the Bahinda royal clan, Bahima pastoralists, and Bairu cultivators) over the hierarchical or caste-like occupational structure of the historical Ankole monarchy that largely benefited the *Omugabe* (King), the Bahinda, and the Bahima but at the expense of the Bairu. The Bairu have made substantial socioeconomic gains since Obote's abolition of traditional monarchies in 1967 and are fearful that their achievements would be lost if the Ankole monarchy, which they perceive to be unjust, is restored. To speed up the restoration of the Ankole monarchy, it might be necessary to abolish the clan hierarchy that is offensive to the Bairu or to exclude them entirely.

The restoration of the Ankole monarchy is also complicated by Yoweri Museveni, the Mnyankole (that is, from Ankole) president of Uganda, who is against the idea of Ankole kingship (*obugabe*). At the moment, John Patrick Barigye Rutashijuka Ntare VI is the *Omugabe* designate of Ankole.[15]

The reigning monarchs of Uganda's contemporary traditional kingdoms are: Prince Ronald Mutebi II, the twenty-sixth *Kabaka* (King) of Buganda; Oyo Nyimba Kabamba Iguru Rukidi IV, *Omukama* (King) of Toro; Prince Solomon Iguru, *Omukama* (King) of Bunyoro-Kitara; and Prince Henry Wako Muloki, the 3rd *Isebantu Kyabazinga* (President of the Council of Hereditary Chiefs) of Busoga.

Because the kingdoms of Buganda, Bunyoro, and Toro have a shared origin, their coronation ceremonies are somewhat similar and are invoked at the death of the reigning monarch. These ceremonies are exemplified here by the recent (September 13, 1994) enthronement of *Omukama* Oyo Nyimba Kabamba Iguru Rukidi IV of Toro, who at the age of three and a half years became the youngest reigning monarch in the world—his coronation at such a tender age echoes that of Daudi Chwa who in 1897 became the *Kabaka* of Buganda at the age of four years. The Toro monarchy was founded in 1830 by the secessionist Prince Kaboyo Kasunsunkwanzi Olimi I, the eldest son of the then king of the legendary Bunyoro-Kitara Empire.

A typical Toro coronation starts at 2:00 A.M. in the royal palace and lasts more than 13 hours. It consists of the following steps:

- The secret, nighttime, and men only coronation proceedings (the night rituals exclude women because their presence is thought to be a bad omen) begin soon after the king designate is awakened at 2:00 A.M. He then marches to the entrance of the royal palace, accompanied by a coterie of princes and princesses, and engages in mock battle with a rebel prince and his army. The soon-to-be king, with his superior fighting force, emerges victorious and is greeted by the sounding of the *Majaguzo,* the large traditional war drums that are a central part of the king's regalia. The mock battle signifies his willingness to lead the kingdom to war and to defend it at all costs and is a carryover from the precolonial period when the leaders of Uganda's traditional kingdoms led their troops to war.
- The king designate is led into the regalia room where the various symbols of office are stored upside-down as soon as the reigning king dies. In the regalia room, the head of coronation rituals *(Omusuga)* calls upon the gods to strike the soon-to-be King dead if he is not of royal lineage; which usually never happens since the kingship is hereditary. He then rings the royal bell.
- The soon-to-be king then proceeds to the main entrance of the royal palace and sounds a sacred Chwezi drum known as the *Nyalebe* and a ritual blessing involving the blood of a bull and a white hen is conducted—the Chwezi are a mysterious people who lived in the Toro area in the 1500s and are thought to be the spiritual ancestors of the Batooro.
- After these rituals that usually last until 4:00 A.M., the coronation is complete and is followed by thunderous drum beats and trumpet blasts that announce the new King's enthronement to waiting crowds of subjects and well-wishers who together respond with shouts of "welcome the greatest of men" *(Tusemerve Okukurora, Rukirabasaija)* and "long live your highness" *(haugiriza agutambae).*
- At dawn, the King enters the palace ceremoniously and undergoes another ritual blessing in which he sits on the lap of a virgin girl (women are allowed to participate in the ceremony at this stage because it is no longer dark) and is served a royal meal of millet bread. He is then made to lie on his side for a while without turning in order to signify his ability and willingness to faithfully discharge his duties and stick to his decisions.
- He is then presented with an ancient copper spear and leather shield with which he swears to defend his territory and subjects.

Omukama Oyo Nyimba's 1994 coronation also included rituals that indicated the Toro monarchy's adaptation to contemporary religious and political conditions. For instance, since most Toro monarchs and those of other Ugandan traditional kingdoms have been Anglican Christians—a clear sign of the denomination's political hegemony in Uganda since the colonial era—the newly-crowned King also attended church services at the nearby St. John's Anglican Cathedral, flanked by Ugandan President Yoweri Museveni and other central government leaders, kingdom officials, foreign ambassadors, and other dignitaries, and was once again crowned King of Toro by Bishop Eustance Kamanyire and presented with a Bible by Catholic Bishop Paul Kalanda.

Afterwards, the King returned to his palace and led a procession of highly honored men of Toro (*Abajwarakondo*) in inspecting the royal kraal, that is, a stockaded traditional Toro village with a livestock enclosure. On this occasion, the *Abajwarakondo* included president Yoweri Museveni who was included, despite being a Mnyankole (i.e., from Ankore), because he wields the executive powers that precolonial and colonial Toro kings once had and is, therefore, critical to the continued wellbeing of the kingdom that his government helped to restore in 1993.

Although the Toro monarchy has been in existence for nearly two centuries, its long-term viability is uncertain because it is located in an earthquake-prone region that has already forced the kingdom to build an expensive earthquake-proof palace. Moreover, the kingdom has suffered many unexpected losses of members of the royal family.[16]

But even more critical to the continued wellbeing of the Toro monarchy, and that of the other traditional kingdoms in Uganda, is their loss of influence since the beginning of the colonial era. This decline is the result of several factors. First, the British colonial authorities co-opted Buganda and other traditional kingdoms and transformed them into exploitative institutions that soon lost much of their social legitimacy and support. The colonial authorities aggravated the situation by imposing monarchies on parts of the country (e.g., Busoga) that had no precolonial system of centralized government. These "colonial kingdoms," especially Busoga, were both unwieldy and unpopular locally.

Second is the growing doubt about the place of traditional kingdoms in modern Uganda given the country's rapid modernization and the attendant weakening of the ethnic nationalism that undergirded these institutions in precolonial Uganda; a growing national identity especially among the many Ugandan ethnic groups that have no monarchic history and; the large number of Ugandans who grew up without traditional kingdom identity in the 1967–93 period because these institutions were banned. Moreover, these institutions' recent restoration as cultural but apolitical entities is a major obstacle to their growth and influence. In an attempt to ensure their future in modern Uganda, the kingdoms have been busy liaising with comparable institutions from around the world. However, it is unclear at the moment whether or not they will succeed in reclaiming their historical role in Ugandan society.

Rainmaking Ceremonies

Because Uganda's traditional communities were agriculturalists or pastoralists, their life was dependent on the receipt of timely and sufficient amounts of rainfall. Thus, droughts were a serious matter that many communities attributed to angry ancestors or gods who had to be appeased by sacrifices and offerings. The Bakiga and Karimojong are some of the Ugandan communities that had rainmaking ceremonies. Among the pastoral Karimojong, this rainmaking ceremony is known as *akirriket*. Whenever a severe drought hit, a delegation of two or three elders would present the medicine man (*Emurron*) a calabash full of milk and implore him to make rain. The *Emurron* would then ask the delegation to find him a black bull before setting a date for the rainmaking ceremony.

On the day, community elders assembled at a prearranged place and sat in a semicircle around the bull. A fire was then lit near the opening of the semicircle near the assembly of ordinary men. Grass was then spread near the bull in front of the elders and a man was asked to spear and kill the bull on the grass. For this high honor, the man recompensed the bull's owner with a heifer. The bull was then roasted. But before it was distributed and eaten, the *Emurron* took center stage, and with his back to the elders, he planted his spear upright in the ground, and then called for rain to come, which usually happened immediately or within days. After this, the feasting began, with the *Emurron* and the group of elders each getting the bull's roasted hind leg. The rest of the meat was then distributed to the elders by two helpers. After the elders had eaten, they shared the rest with the whole assembly, thereby bringing the ceremony to a close.

FESTIVALS

There are few nationally recognized festivals in Uganda, but there are many minor festivals throughout the country such as those that celebrate harvests, the arts, and literacy. Examples of national festivals include the annual National Book Week festival, the primary and secondary school National Drama Festivals, and Amakula Film Festival. Besides events at local libraries, the book festival features large local and foreign book exhibitions in Kampala. The national drama festivals showcase the best teams from local and regional competitions. The Amakula Film Festival is recent and is designed to promote cinema in Uganda.[17] Another promising national cultural festival is the Omuvango Festival, which has been held in the lakeside city of Jinja since 1996, and is designed to showcase Uganda's cultural heritage to a wider community and to help preserve Ugandan village culture by recognizing it. The festival, which is jointly organized by Nile Beat Artists and the Jinja

Municipal Council, features more than 60 cultural performing groups from around the country. The festival focuses on exposing authentic Ugandan village culture to international visitors who seldom venture into the villages and often have an inaccurate image of traditional Ugandan culture.[18]

NATIONAL AND RELIGIOUS HOLIDAYS

Uganda has 10 main national and religious holidays. These are New Year's Day (January 1), International Women's Day (March 8), Good Friday, Easter Monday, Labor Day (May 1), Martyrs' Day (June 3), Independence Day (October 9), Liberation Day (January 26), National Heroes' Day (June 9), Christmas (December 25), and Boxing Day (December 26). All Ugandans celebrate Independence, Liberation, National Heroes', and Labor Day. The majority Christian population celebrates Christmas, Easter, Martyrs' Day, and Boxing Day. Muslims celebrate *Eid al Adha* and *Eid al Fitr. Eid al Adha,* or Feast of Sacrifice, commemorates Abraham's willingness to sacrifice his son Ishmael at the command of Allah—the Jewish and Christian version of the story states that God asked Abraham to sacrifice Isaac rather than Ishmael. The feast reenacts Abraham's obedience by sacrificing a cow or a ram, one-third of which is eaten by the sacrificing family and the rest is donated to the poor. *Eid al Fitr* marks the end of Ramadan, the Muslim month of fasting.

Holidays with fixed dates are New Year's Day (January 1), International Women's Day (March 8), Labor Day (May 1), Martyrs' Day (June 3), National Heroes' Day (June 9), Independence Day (October 9), Christmas (December 25), and Boxing Day (December 26). Those with variable dates are the Christian holidays of Easter (Good Friday through Easter Monday) and Ascension Day, and the Muslim holidays of *Eid al Adha* and *Eid al Fitr,* which are based on the annual lunar calendar that varies slightly from year to year.

Church tradition mandates the celebration of Easter, the holiday that marks the death, burial, and resurrection of Jesus, between March 22 and April 25. Ascension Day, which celebrates the ascension of Jesus to heaven, occurs 40 days after Easter and is usually celebrated on Thursday.

Christmas is Uganda's most important annual ceremony. On Christmas, Ugandans of all stripes exchange the greeting: *Mukulike Okutuuka Ku Mazaalibwa,* as they congratulate each other for making it to yet another Christmas season. The celebration of Christmas in Uganda begins as early as the first week of December with the exchange of gifts such as Christmas cards and new clothes. Giant Christmas trees are lit in major cities and well-attended Christmas caroling, musicals, and dramas are organized in well-decorated churches. Christmas celebration services are popular and well attended because they draw people who seldom attend church.

On Christmas and the day before, Ugandans prepare sumptuous meals to be shared with family and friends. The meals are usually washed down with generous amounts of soda, beer, and wine. The resulting drunkenness and rowdiness often lead to numerous brawls, drunken driving accidents, and deaths. Many Christmas parties go on until the wee hours of the morning.

Independence Day marks Uganda's freedom from British colonial rule in 1962 and is the most important political holiday in the country. Independence Day celebrations usually feature patriotic speeches by the president and local government leaders, armed forces' parades, displays, flyovers, and performances by various school choirs and traditional dance troupes.

AMUSEMENT AND SPORTS

As elsewhere, amusement and sports are central features of Uganda's leisure life. Besides their leisure and entertainment value, amusement and sports events are important social gatherings. Key among Ugandan leisure activities are sports, cinema, drama, comedy, dance, various traditional games, for example, *Mweso,* a board game that is popular throughout Uganda, and beer drinking.

Sports

Uganda is a sporting nation. The most popular sports are soccer, boxing, athletics, basketball, cricket, golf, motor sport, rugby, tennis, volleyball, and camping.[19] Soccer is by far the most popular organized sport. Uganda has a competitive Premier Soccer League that features teams such as Kampala City Council, Express, Horizon, Sports Club Villa, Scoul, Rock Star, and Black Rhino. Although Ugandan radio and television has often broadcast games by these teams, declining soccer standards in the country owing to corruption, the exodus of top players to lucrative foreign leagues, and poor management have cost the local league fans. Many Ugandan soccer lovers are now avid followers of foreign soccer leagues, especially the English Premier League that is beamed in by satellite. Arsenal, Chelsea, Liverpool, and Manchester United are some of the most popular British teams in Uganda.[20] Ugandan soccer standards may need to improve soon if support for local soccer clubs is to increase.

Besides the national league clubs, there are numerous regional and local soccer clubs in the country. The school system, from primary to university, has its own soccer teams that compete against each other during the school year. These competitions culminate in national championships, with the secondary school championships being the most competitive and popular.

Some of Uganda's legendary soccer players include Phillip Omondi, Magid Musisi, David Otti, Godfrey Kateregga, and Paul Hasule. Although these players are nationally and regionally renowned, they mostly have led ordinary lives because the Ugandan soccer league is poorly financed by government and private companies. Poverty prevents most Ugandans from attending ticketed soccer games, thereby contributing to the players' low pay.

Another important aspect of Ugandan soccer is the national team, the Crested Cranes, which is drawn from the leading players of the country's Premier League clubs. The Crested Cranes are a regional soccer power and have participated in the continental Confederation of African Football (CAF) competitions that are used to pick teams to represent Africa in the World Cup. Although Uganda has not participated in the World Cup, the country's teams have won various East and Central African soccer championships. In 2005, the Federation of International Football Associations (FIFA) ranked Uganda 27th in Africa soccer rankings and 115th in the world.

The exodus of Uganda's top soccer players to more lucrative European, North American, and South American soccer leagues has contributed to the decline of soccer standards in the country. Although the search for greener pastures is beneficial to the players concerned, it has a downside in that the players are often unavailable to play for the national team because of schedule conflicts. For Uganda to retain its best players, its economy might have to improve enough to enable the country to improve its players' salaries.[21]

Golf is a popular sport in Uganda and is played mostly by the local business and political elite, tourists, and expatriates. The country has many golf clubs, the most notable being Entebbe, Kampala, and Garuga Golf Clubs. Other elite sports and facilities are rugby and tennis (Lugogo Club), swimming (Sheraton Hotel, Silver Springs Hotel, and Windsor Lake Victoria Hotel), flying lessons (Kampala Aeroclub), boat riding (Speke Marina Riding Stables), and jogging (Hash Hound Harriers).

Uganda has also produced top players in other sports, including Sam Walusimbi (cricket), Sam Sali (motor rallying), Aggrey Awori (4 × 100m) and Davis Kamoga (400m), Mary Musoke (table tennis), John Oduke (tennis), Dorcus Izinkuru (3000-meter steeplechase), and Leo Rwabogo, Uganda's first-ever winner of an Olympic boxing medal (bronze) at the 1968 Mexico games.[22]

Cinema

Although cinema is one of Uganda's elite entertainments, it is slowly becoming popular among the masses, especially in large cities such as Kampala and Jinja. Most of the country's top cinemas are concentrated in Kampala, including National Theatre, Plaza Theater, Ndere Center, Cineplex Garden City,

Cooper Theatre, and Makerere University. There are also numerous video halls throughout Kampala and the country. The growing popularity of cinema is the result of concerted marketing efforts such as the Amakula Kampala International Film Festival that was inaugurated in 2004 to inspire a culture of film in Uganda and East Africa. The festival annually screens films in all of Kampala's cinemas and most video halls. It also operates a mobile cinema unit that performs spontaneous movie screenings in various outdoor venues throughout the city.[23] The growing popularity of cinema in Uganda is evident in the growing number of video rental shops in the major cities.

Beauty Contests

Beauty contests are fast becoming an integral part of Uganda's popular culture and entertainment. Some of the country's beauty contests include Miss Uganda, Miss Kyambogo University, and Miss HIV-Stigma Free. Miss Uganda was launched in 2001 by Sylvia Owori and has become the most successful beauty pageant in the country. The pageant, whose theme is beauty with a purpose, is designed to "enhance the image, pride and dignity of the Ugandan woman."[24] The Miss HIV-Stigma Free seeks to lessen the stigma of HIV-AIDS in a country where the prevalence of the disease is high.[25]

Despite the growing popularity of beauty contests, the Ugandan government has threatened to ban them for corrupting the morals of young people, violating various religious teachings, and promoting nudity, pornography, and prostitution.[26] This situation arises because winners of Uganda's beauty contests do not make a lot of money and can be lured into prostitution and pornography.[27]

Comedy

Comedy is one of the forms of entertainment that is deeply rooted in Ugandan culture. But unlike in traditional society, comedy in contemporary Uganda is becoming increasingly commercialized and professionalized to serve the changing needs of society. Despite these developments, few Ugandans can afford to attend professional comedy shows. As a result, professional comedy is largely the preserve of the elite. Among Uganda's leading contemporary comedians are Kato Lubwama and Hajji Ashraf Semogerere.[28]

TRADITIONALISTS VERSUS MODERNISTS

Contemporary Ugandan culture is neither strictly traditionalist nor modern but is a complex mix of the two. In fact, the country's cultural situation is best visualized as continuum with traditionalists on the left and modernists on the right, with those in the middle having a near-equal mix of traditional and modern values. Traditionalists are those who adhere as much as possible to the values (e.g., respect for elders, communalism) of the various traditional Ugandan societies. Conversely, modernists are those whose outlook in life is informed largely by European or Western values such as individualism. The amount of modernity and traditionalism in Uganda varies greatly between urban and rural areas.

Uganda's rural people generally lead more traditional lives because of the higher degree of cultural homogeneity and low impact of Westernization in these areas. Such people view themselves as true Ugandans and are often skeptical of the values and lifestyles of their urban counterparts. Most Ugandans currently live in rural areas, so it is more likely than not that there are more traditionalists in the country, although their degree of traditionalism varies widely. Thus, even in rural areas, there are some modernists who have the income and material goods (e.g., television, cars) that go with such a lifestyle.

On the other hand, most urban Ugandans have a modern outlook in life, this being the product of their generally higher levels of education, income, and access to local and foreign media outlets such as newspapers and television. Nevertheless, because of Uganda's high levels of rural-to-urban migration, there are many urban dwellers whose outlook in life is fairly traditional. As the old adage goes, it is easier to take a person out of a rural area than to take the rural area out of him or her.

Many other Ugandans are neither traditionalists nor modernists. Rather, they pick and choose the most beneficial aspects of traditional and modern culture. Other Ugandans, for example, the circular migrants who frequent their rural and urban abodes, can best be described as "cultural chameleons" who change their values and behavior based on the surroundings. Thus, they adopt modern values when in urban areas and traditionalist values when in rural areas.

PASTORALISM, FARMING, AND VILLAGES

Pastoralism is still practiced to varying extents among the Karimojong, Sebei, Kumam, and Iteso of eastern and northeast Uganda, and the Banyankore of southwestern Uganda. There are many other Ugandan groups (e.g., the Langi) that were traditionally pastoral but were forced to abandon that lifestyle because of external influences or loss of land and livestock to other groups or disease. Even among the Karimojong, Sebei, Kumam, and Iteso, pastoralism is slowly waning because of the growing influence of modernity, economic transformation, introduction of new religions such as

Christianity, and decreasing grazing lands for their livestock. Moreover, the advent of the cash-based economy means that the value of cattle as a measure of wealth has been diminished. The introduction of modern education in pastoral communities also means that the younger generations are losing their connection to this way of life and are therefore abandoning it.

Pastoralism in modern Uganda is a pale shadow of its traditional counterpart whereby herders moved from place to place in search of pasture and water and lacked modern veterinary services that are slowly being introduced to improve the quality and survival of the livestock. Traditional pastoralism was also a relatively peaceful affair compared with the current situation where a long-running civil war threatens the lives of Ugandan pastoralists, and heavily armed cross-border cattle raids between the Karimojong of Uganda and the Turkana of Kenya have heightened the danger to both people and livestock. Moreover, increasing shortages of grazing lands and water caused by increasing human and animal populations are an added source of stress, not to mention new conflicts between pastoralists and agriculturalists over crop damage by livestock. In short, all these pressures on pastoralists are endangering their lifestyle, forcing many of them into mixed farming or some form of ranching.

Because the vast majority of Uganda's population consists of agricultural Bantu groups such as the Baganda, Banyoro, and Batoolo, farming has traditionally been an important aspect of Ugandan life. In traditional society, farming primarily served as a source of food, with the little available surplus being exchanged for other items, for example, iron implements or bark cloth. Nowadays, farming is not just a food source but is also a major economic activity that is one of the mainstays of Uganda's economy. Many Ugandan farmers practice mixed farming, producing crops (e.g., coffee, tea, cotton, tobacco, sugar cane, bananas, plantains, beans, maize, rice, wheat, and various fruits, vegetables, spices, and essential oils) and keeping livestock such as cattle, sheep, goats, and chicken. Fish and wildlife are also important food supplements in some areas of the country.

Overall, most Ugandan farmers practice subsistence farming. Most of the agricultural production takes place in small family-owned or -leased plots and seldom uses modern farm machinery such as tractors, fertilizer, or commercially available seed because these are too expensive. Instead, farmers work the land in a labor-intensive manner, using simple hand implements such as hoes and machetes, and use part of the previous season's harvest for seed.

Although Uganda is one of the most food-secure countries in Africa, agricultural output per farmer is low and could be substantially increased. The country's high rural-urban migration is partly a reflection of the increasing difficulty of accessing agricultural land because of rapidly increasing rural populations and decreasing or stagnant agricultural output that is increasingly unable to sustain families.

Uganda's future food security requires many changes in the society: a shift from traditional subsistence systems to modern agricultural production systems, removing cultural and legal barriers to women's land ownership, improving food processing and preservation to stem waste, improving agricultural marketing and distribution systems, discarding traditional land inheritance and tenure systems that reduce land productivity through endless fragmentation as the land is passed on from generation to generation, and reducing the country's dependence on agriculture by developing other economic sectors such as industry. Irrigation farming is also a promising avenue of increasing agricultural production, given the country's abundance of fisheries, for example, the Nile River and lakes Victoria, Kyoga, Albert, and Edward.

At the moment, most of the country's commercial agriculture pertains to the production of cash crops (e.g., coffee, tea, cotton, tobacco, and sugar cane) and some food crops, especially wheat. Uganda's commercial agricultural sector is controlled by Asian elites and multinational corporations and is concentrated in areas around Jinja and western Uganda. Disproportionate Asian control of the country's commercial agriculture and business sector is a source of indigenous resentment toward them and was a key factor in Idi Amin's nationalization of their assets in the early 1970s.

Traditional village life, while widespread in rural areas, is rapidly changing as the influence of modernity is felt. Symbols of modernity, for example, television, radio, cell phones, roads, cars, bicycles, health facilities, schools, and shopping centers, are increasingly invading rural village life, making it difficult to draw the line between the urban and the rural in some parts of the country. The modernization of traditional village life is greatest near urban areas that have historically proven to be powerful modernizing agents. Conversely, traditional village life is most pronounced in the remote parts of the country.

Another factor in Uganda's fast-changing village life are the urban dwellers who frequent their villages of origin during holidays and pass on urban values and consumption habits to their rural family members. Moreover, their higher income and consumption tend to widen the relative local income and consumption gap and increase the aspirations of other villagers. Ultimately, this leads to more rural-to-urban migration and hastens the pace of local modernization as the number of change agents increases.

AGENCIES OF CHANGE: WESTERN VERSUS LOCAL

Ugandan society is in a state of constant cultural change. These changes have especially accelerated since the middle of the 1800s because of the introduction of Islam and Christianity, increased foreign trade with Arabs and later Europeans, British colonialism and Western education, the development of modern communications and transport systems, and globalization. These agents of change have led to the decline of local cultural values and their increasing replacement by foreign or hybrid cultural values that combine local and foreign elements. Among these five factors, the most fundamental are the introduction of Islam and Christianity and colonialism.

Ugandans had their own indigenous religious beliefs before the introduction of Islam and Christianity (see Chapter 2). However, Christianity and Islam have so successfully undermined indigenous religions that they have become a way of life for many Ugandans. As a result, it is now possible to tell whether one is a Christian or Muslim based on manner of worship, dress, marriage, cuisine, association, and even speech. For instance, Ugandan Muslims revere the Koran, have Muslim names (e.g., Mohammed), prefer Arabic dress, rice, *Halal* meat (i.e., slaughtered according to the manner prescribed by the Koran), avoid eating pork, and, where possible, communicate with Allah in Arabic. Many attend Muslim schools (*Madrasas*) and even university. Mbale Muslim University is the first Islamic university in Uganda and is one of the few positive legacies of president Idi Amin.

Conversely, Christians revere the Bible, attend Christian schools and often universities, prefer European-style dress, worship in Latin or English led by a pianist/organist, and have European names besides their traditional ones; some increasingly exhibit European eating and dining styles and mannerisms, for example, eating at a table using cutlery rather than bare hands.[29] Some local Christian elites even prefer European rather than local cuisine.

Despite the overwhelming dominance of Christianity and Islam, there are pockets of traditional religious holdouts throughout the country. Moreover, many Ugandans mix traditional religious beliefs with those of Christianity or Islam.

British colonialism formally commenced in 1894 when Uganda was declared a British protectorate. By independence in 1962, the British had established in Uganda a British-style government, civil service, communications, transport, and educational system, capitalist economy, culture, and a defense system and had introduced and popularized English, which subsequently became the official language of the country after independence. Colonial Uganda traded almost exclusively with the United Kingdom at terms that favored the latter. This trade imbalance has not changed with Uganda's attainment of independence and may, in fact, be worsening because the country's mostly agricultural products have less value relative to British industrial and cultural products. Thus, Britain's dominance of Uganda continues unabated.

During the colonial era, the school system was effectively used to inculcate British culture in young Ugandans at the expense of local cultures. Many of the educated elites began to abandon their indigenous cultures in favor of British culture. This mental colonialism continues to afflict many Ugandans as evidenced, for instance, in the overwhelming popularity of English soccer in the country. This situation has not only undermined the development of local soccer by limiting its patronage and financial health but has also recently forced the Ugandan Premier League to schedule its matches in such as way as to avoid direct competition with the popular English soccer matches on television.

British colonialism also helped to shape Uganda's contemporary culture by setting in motion the country's globalization through trade and the development of modern communications and transport systems that now link Uganda to the rest of the world. Moreover, by introducing the English language in Uganda, the British inevitably linked the country with the global culture that is mostly transmitted in English by American and British media giants such as CNN and BBC. Although the transmission of culture is usually a two-way street, Uganda's weak global economic position puts it on the receiving end of global culture, which further helps to undermine local cultures.

Changing Economy and Values

Because major precolonial Ugandan communities (e.g., the Baganda) had capitalist economies, it was easier for the British to integrate the protectorate into their capitalist/market economy. This and the country's powerful indigenous monarchies led to the establishment of indirect colonial rule in Uganda and limited British settlement in the country—unlike in neighboring Kenya, where mass European settlement was encouraged to spearhead capitalist economic production, especially in agriculture. Besides leaving indigenous Ugandan administrative structures largely intact, the British early on encouraged local participation in the production of copper, cotton, and coffee. By independence, Uganda had, perhaps, the most developed indigenous entrepreneurial class and civil service in East Africa. These conditions enabled Uganda to take a leading role in the development of modern professional classes in the region. Moreover, as the home of Makerere University—once dubbed the Oxford/Harvard of Africa—more Ugandans gained access to university education than other East Africans.

Had Uganda's preindependence socioeconomic institutions remained intact, it would still be the beacon of development in the region. Instead, political turmoil engulfed Uganda from 1971 to 1986 and virtually wiped out its highly touted entrepreneurial class, civil service, and industrial development. Urban life became a nightmare. It was not until the restoration of political order by Museveni's National Resistance Movement in 1986 that the outlook began to brighten for Uganda. Since then, the country has been busy restoring its ruined socioeconomic institutions and structures in industry, education, defense, health care, business, government, and the civil service. This means that Uganda's economy is thriving once again, making it possible for many Ugandans to secure employment and to afford basic industrial consumer goods such as televisions, radios, cars, and some processed foods. In short, the country is witnessing the development of a cash-based mass consumer society that is centered on its growing urban areas.

These socioeconomic changes are bringing with them new social values such as individualism, demand for modern entertainment such as cinema, and a breakdown in traditional values. Modern lifestyles that require high levels of educational training, incomes, and consumption are increasingly displacing traditional lifestyles. As a result, traditional socialization systems are being replaced by the school system, whose skills are now more valued than those that were once acquired through traditional education. As the modern capitalist economy has taken root, the cost of living has increased and Ugandan society has been stratified into various economic classes, especially the haves and have-nots. To make ends meet, increasing numbers of urban Ugandans are being forced into slums and marginal economic activities such as crime, petty trade, and prostitution.[30]

Changing Political Culture

The advent of colonialism and the establishment of modern government structures have been accompanied by the decline of traditional political systems, for example, the Buganda, Bunyoro, Ankole, and Toro monarchies. Although many of these monarchies were restored in 1993, they lack the political power that they had in the precolonial and colonial era. For instance, the Buganda monarchy was so powerful that it played a key role in the governance of Uganda in the colonial period. The kingdom's power was such that at one time the British colonial authorities were compelled to send its head, the *Kabaka,* into exile in the United Kingdom.

After his return in 1955, the *Kabaka* played an important role in Uganda's independence negotiations with Britain. In 1963 he became the titular president and Head of State of Uganda under the terms of a power sharing arrangement with Prime Minister Milton Obote. But when they fell out and Buganda threatened to secede, Obote deposed him in 1966. He fled into exile in Britain where he later died. Obote then abolished the federalist independence constitution of 1962 and replaced it with a republican one in 1967 that, among other things, merged the offices of president and prime minister into a powerful executive presidency. This centralized power structure is largely intact, even though Museveni and his National Resistance Movement (NRM), since coming to power in 1986, has created a somewhat devolved administrative structure that consists of the village, parish, county, district, and a national presidency.[31]

Since independence, Uganda has been governed by a string of elected and dictatorial governments. Because of the country's centralized government structure since independence, ethnicity and religion have been factors in Uganda's political reality, with politicians using them to bolster their political power. For instance, while Milton Obote used his Langi kinsmen and other northerners to consolidate his power, Idi Amin, a Kakwa Muslim, was able to stay in power for close to a decade by relying on the support of Muslim Sudanese Nubian and Kakwa soldiers.[32] Similarly, Yoweri Museveni, Uganda's current president, has been accused of favoring fellow western Ugandans in government appointments. Additionally, Uganda's ongoing civil war, especially in the north, is partly rooted in many northerners' distrust of the Kampala government dominated by southerners and westerners.[33]

One of the major causes of political instability in Uganda has been the lack of genuine democratic government in the country. This situation has forced sections of the populace to air their grievances in socially disruptive ways, resulting in civil war. If greater social tranquility is to be achieved in Uganda, it will be necessary to institute more accommodating political systems.

8

Music, Dance, and Drama

Music and dance are integral aspects of everyday Ugandan life. There is music and dance for all occasions, for example, marriage, child naming, entertainment, work, and worship. Because Uganda's diverse cultural communities have their own music history and values, the country's music is quite diverse, even though it celebrates the same general human experiences such as birth, death, and marriage. In Ugandan culture, music accompanies everything from farm work to burials and entertainment for heads of state. Uganda's continuing cultural change feeds the ongoing evolution and renewal of its music.[1]

As with other socioeconomic areas of life, Uganda's music suffered severe damage during the reign of Idi Amin and Milton Obote, although the former loved music and often traveled around the country with dancers from the government's Heartbeat of Africa troupe.[2] The social turmoil of the reigns of Amin and Obote made it difficult for music artists to compose, perform freely, and earn a living from their work. Many musicians were thus forced into exile in Kenya and other countries. As a result, a substantial amount of Ugandan music was produced overseas in the 1970s and 1980s.

However, Museveni's rise to power and restoration of order since 1986 has put Uganda's music scene on a recovery path. One indication of this is the country's growing music export to surrounding countries. Moreover, many Ugandan musicians have become regional music icons, although their appeal is somewhat limited by the poor command of Kiswahili, East Africa's most popular regional language. Some of Uganda's leading contemporary musicians include Jose Chameleone, the Watoto Children's Choir, Medi Munabi, James Mutyabule, Richard Musana, Sheila Nvannungi, the late Philly Bongoley Lutaaya, Bebe Cool, Winnie Munyenga, Juliet Mugirya, Paul Kafeero, Dorothy Bukirwa, Juliana Kanyomozi, Omumbejja Sheila Nvannungi, and Mesach Semakula.[3]

Uganda's musical evolution spans three distinct time frames: precolonial, colonial, and postcolonial. The precolonial period was dominated by traditional music and instruments that were played within individual ethnic groups. There was limited music exchange between the groups. The colonial period, beginning in the latter 1800s, marked the beginning of modern music in Uganda, as European missionaries and colonizers brought with them new music cultures, instruments, and compositional techniques. Equally important is that Europeans initiated the commercialization of Ugandan music by introducing music recorders and players and by establishing radio stations that popularized recorded music and eventually led to the growth of markets and distribution systems for it. Although the postcolonial period has essentially expanded on the music trends initiated by colonialism, it is noteworthy that the country's increasing globalization, access to modern music technology and styles, population mobility, and incomes have all led to a sharp increase in the quantity and variety of recorded and live music available to Ugandans.

MUSICAL GENRES AND SINGING STYLES

Ugandan music can be broken down by historical foundation (traditional or modern or fusion), geographical origin (local or foreign), type (vocal or instrumental or both), performance (group/choir or solo/individual), structural form, repertoire, and functional use. This discussion of Ugandan music is mainly organized by geographical and historical origin and function.

Contemporary Ugandan music can be categorized as traditional, modern, or blended, that is, a fusion of traditional and modern music. Traditional music is most widespread in Uganda because it is indigenous to the country and easily passed on orally from generation to generation in local languages. The latter factor makes traditional music lyrics accessible even to those who lack formal schooling. Traditional music attends most social celebrations, festivals and ceremonies, and many modern artists have popular renditions of it.

Although Uganda is rapidly modernizing, it still retains its traditional music, that is, music by its people and for its people. More specifically, this is the "music that is still taught to, performed among, and embraced by rural-based ethnic groups" where most Ugandans live.[4] The music has many purposes. For instance, it plays a central role in funeral rites, communication, work, timekeeping (e.g., announcing the beginning of church services), therapy (e.g., alleviating sadness), regulating social behavior (e.g., songs praise socially acceptable behaviors and sanction unacceptable ones), education (e.g., teaching gender roles), and entertainment. The role of traditional music in Ugandan society depends on the social occasion or context. Thus, different occasions are marked by the use of specific music, dance, and instrument or ensemble. In Buganda, for instance, traditional wrestling matches and funerals are marked by *engalabi* (a single-headed cannonlike drum) drumming.

Traditional Ugandan music has many common characteristics: similar dance styles and steps, songs, and costumes; and a uniform use of the pentatonic or five-note scale, usually the first, second, third, fifth, and sixth tones of a diatonic scale. Nevertheless, the music exhibits rhythmic differences from one community to another and many other minor distinctions. For instance, traditional Baganda music is marked by its unique timbre (i.e., resonance or reverberation) of the *endingidi* (bowed lute or tube fiddle), significant reliance on drumming, and interlocking patterns of instruments that are presented in several interdependent but unique parts.[5] Two leading examples of Ugandan traditional musicians are the late Evaristo Muyinda and his student and successor Centurio Balikoowa.

Modern music, with a more recent history, is designed to appeal to the musical tastes of contemporary Ugandans, whose culture and lifestyles also inspire it. Conversely, blended music features aspects of traditional and modern music, for example, the rendition of traditional songs for contemporary audiences by various artists.

Ugandans enjoy music from various geographical sources. Although most of the music in the country is now homegrown, Ugandans also savor music from surrounding countries (e.g., Kenya, Tanzania, and the Democratic Republic of the Congo) because of shared historical, geographical, cultural, and linguistic links. European, American, and Caribbean music (e.g., jazz, reggae, pop, hip-hop, and classical) is also popular among many young people and educated Ugandans. Most of the foreign music comes to Uganda through commercial channels.

Whether the music is traditional or modern, local or foreign, vocal or instrumental or both; it is usually performed solo or by groups or choirs; and it has unique structural forms. Moreover, appropriate dance forms and instruments accompany each category of music.

Traditional Music Genres

The various functions of traditional Ugandan music are a convenient basis for categorizing the country's traditional music into classes that are not necessarily mutually exclusive. These categories include court music, entertainment and recreational music, work songs, ritual and worship music, festival music, funeral songs or dirges, music drama, and panegyric music.

Court Music

Court music has been performed for Uganda's traditional chiefs and monarchies since the precolonial era and is used to commemorate the monarchies' birthdays, coronation, war victories, and death, or to simply entertain members of the royal family.[6] The *Kabaka* of Buganda is one of the traditional Ugandan monarchies that extensively used court music until his and other traditional monarchies were abolished in 1967 by President Milton Obote. Buganda's court music was restarted when Uganda's traditional monarchies were restored in 1993 by the Museveni government, albeit with much less power and prestige.

Because of the Buganda kingdom's power and influence before, during, and after European colonialism, much is known about its court music, including its specific forms, instruments, and instrumentalists. It thus provides a fine exemplar of traditional Ugandan court music.

The most common Buganda court music instruments were drums, trumpets, flutes, xylophones, and harps. Although these instruments were widespread in the kingdom, those at the *Kabaka*'s court were more grandiose. Thus, while the common xylophone (*amadinda* or *entaala*) had 12 free keys, the *akadinda,* a large and exclusive version of the instrument for the *Kabaka*, had 22 keys. None of the palace drums were more impressive than the *majaguzo,* the *Kabaka*'s emblems of office. *Majaguzo* and other palace drums usually had names akin to people. Alternatively, the drums have been named after their functional role, part in various ensembles, or type.

The hierarchy of Buganda court musicians consisted of drummers, trumpeters, and flutists. But these may have been bested by the harpist (*Omulanga*), whose rare genius and trusted relationship with the *Kabaka* gave him the exclusive privilege of playing for the *Kabaka*'s wives and a widespread following in the kingdom. Examples of legendary Ganda royal court musicians include Albert Sempeke (currently based at the Uganda National Theatre and Cultural Center), Ludoviko Serwanga, Busulwa Katambula, Arthur Kayizzi, and Centurio Balikoowa (a teacher of traditional Ugandan music).[7]

The royal drums were made and played by drummers from the *Kawuula* and *Kimomomera* hereditary chieftainships. The royal trumpets (*amakondeere*) were made of elongated gourds and were played in five distinctive-tone instrument ensembles by trumpeters (*Ebisanja*) who lived in the *Kabaka*'s own trumpeters' village (*ekyalo ky'abakondeere*) and served at the palace in annual four- to six-week sessions. A five or six ragged flute (*endeere*) ensemble that accompanied a drum quartet was also part of the *Kabaka*'s repertoire of court music.[8]

Court music, as with other Baganda music, is dominated by antiphonal or responsive singing and chanting that is usually led by solo singers and accompanied by hand clapping. Because Luganda is a tonal language, the form of the responsive singing and chanting is determined by the tonal and accentual profile of the language. Particular attention is paid to the lyrics as these supersede every other song element. The song leaders have broad leeway in the use of the different tone levels.

Music for Entertainment and Recreation

In traditional Ugandan society, music is one of the main forms of entertainment and usually commences in the afternoon or evening after the day's work. In general, music at any nonsolemn social gathering, for example, weddings, also has an entertainment, recreational, and instructional value. Such music is prevalent at traditional beer parties and is designed to help people to relax and enjoy life. This music usually involves spontaneous audience participation through dance.

Work Songs

Many traditional Ugandan societies have songs that work parties sing for the purpose of synchronizing effort; entertainment; lessening the monotony of tedious and repetitive work, for example, farm tilling; exhortation—reminding laborers of the worth of their labor; and encouragement. Work songs usually differ by age, gender, profession, and from society to society. For instance, among the country's pastoral communities, cattle herders sing or whistle specific tunes when watering their herds.

Ritual and Worship Music

Ritual and worship music pertains to certain sacred rites or initiation ceremonies. For instance, invocations of the blessings and guidance of ancestors and gods require special music, dance, and instruments to produce the desired results. Among the Batooro, for instance, *Mandwa* cultists worship *Emandwa* by playing certain drum and trumpet (*etimbo*) tunes.

Similarly, initiation ceremonies are accompanied by special songs that are inappropriate for other social occasions. For instance, the renowned *Runyege* dance is performed by Imbalu dancers during Bagisu mass boy initiation ceremonies. In some Ugandan communities (e.g., the Bagwere), twins are welcomed to society by the *Eyonga* ritual dance.

Festival Music

Traditional ceremonies such as marriage, initiations, and coronations are accompanied by festive music. Wedding songs routinely praise the bride and the groom and also offer them advice on how to successfully conduct marriage. Initiation songs praise the initiates and also convey to them the rights and responsibilities of their new roles. Coronation songs glorify monarchs, chiefs, and other traditional leaders.

Funeral Songs or Dirges

Most funerals in Uganda feature dirges or funeral songs in praise of the deceased, the ancestors, or the gods. Many of the dirges mourn the loss of the deceased, implore the dead to go well and not come back to haunt the living, and encourage those left behind. Although funerals are usually somber occasions, they can be festive, especially when the deceased lived to old age or is an important person. Thus, celebrity and elderly funerals among the Bagwere are very festive.

Music Drama

These theatrical performances usually attend to various social ceremonies. Music dramas are also regularly produced and performed in the country's many theaters, especially the numerous open-air ones. In 1988, Willy Mukaabya composed *Kayanga,* a music drama that depicts controversial political, ethnic, and gender issues in contemporary Uganda.

Panegyric Music

Panegyric music refers to songs or chants in praise of the characteristics, achievements, and other qualities of individuals, families, clans, members of the royal family, regions, objects, or ethnic groups. In contemporary Uganda, such music is most common in the courts of the various traditional kingdoms, for example, Buganda.

The Future of Traditional Music and Dance in Modern Uganda

Uganda's modernization is a major challenge to the survival of its traditional music because it undermines the customs that keep this music alive. Even so, there are groups trying to the preserve Uganda's traditional music for future generations. During the early years of Amin's rule, the Theatre Limited music group studied and performed traditional Ugandan music from across the country. Suspicious of the group's popularity and intentions, Amin arrested several of its members and the rest went into exile in Sweden or elsewhere. Simultaneously, Amin enjoyed and supported the musical talents of the Heartbeat of Africa troupe whose repertoire included traditional Ugandan songs and dances. Currently, the Museveni government supports a similar group, the Ndere Troupe, which is named after the *endeere* or flute. Other examples of groups engaged in the preservation of traditional Ugandan music are Nanziga SDA Primary School, Annet Nanduja and the Planets, Aboluganda Kwagalana, Percussion Discussion Afrika, the Busoga Pride Cultural Group, and the Alliance Française's Beat That Drum concert.

Annet Nanduja and the Planets and Nanziga SDA Primary School kids' choir specialize in traditional Buganda songs and dance. Nanduja's two well-known albums *Etooke* and *Obufumbo Bwaleero* celebrate *matooke* (bananas), Buganda's traditional dish, and lament the environmental damage wrought by plastic bags.

Nanziga's most popular song is probably *Tuzzewo Ekitibwa Kya Buganda*. Clad in traditional bark cloth, the Nanziga kids' well-choreographed traditional dancing style and melodious singing, accompanied by modern instruments, is a mesmerizing performance. Although the song memorializes the glory, power, and conquests of the precolonial Buganda Kingdom, it also laments the loss of the kingdom's prestige as a result of colonial and postcolonial national government policies. It mourns the loss of Buganda's ancestral lands and seat of power to Kampala, the capital of Uganda. Even though the city is built on seven hills, including Mengo Hill (the traditional capital of Buganda Kingdom), and is completely surrounded by the Baganda people, it is officially not part of Buganda. The song suggests, therefore, that a new Buganda capital should be built and defended from outside encroachment at all costs. As would be expected, the song is not welcomed by the national government, which sees it as a call to Buganda's secession from Uganda.[9]

Aboluganda Kwagalana and Ndere Troupe specialize in cultural music from all over Uganda. Aboluganda Kwagalana is directed by Albert Sempeke, a Kiganda music specialist and instructor at the Uganda National Theatre and Cultural Center, who has been performing traditional Ugandan music since 1945, and was once a Buganda court musician. Besides its traditional folk music and dance performances at various public forums, for example, conferences, Aboluganda Kwagalana also composes traditional tunes for commercial product endorsements.

Ndere Troupe was formed in 1986 to promote and rekindle Ugandan pride in its traditional culture. The group is named after the traditional Ugandan music instrument, *endeere* (flute) because the instrument is universal, not just in Uganda, but worldwide. Ndere's repertoire consists of more than 40 authentic dances and songs that are accompanied by traditional instruments such as the *amadinda* (xylophone) and *endigidi* (tube fiddle). Their memorable dances include the Bakiga dance *Kizino*, the Acholi dance *Ding Ding*, and the Buganda Royal Court dance *Baakisimba*. The troupe, which has produced four music CDs, is currently led by Stephen Rwangyenzi.

Besides music, Ndere Troupe is actively engaged in development theater, which allows it to communicate modern development initiatives, for example, AIDS control, in culturally relevant ways. Its theatrical productions include *Munaku* (1988), *Ekirabo* (1991), and *Time Bomb* (1993). The group's success and Ugandan government largesse have enabled it to travel widely in countries such as Belgium, the Netherlands, Germany, Austria, Canada, and Kenya.[10]

Percussion Discussion Afrika's music is instrumental, and it primarily features drums and other percussion instruments.

The Busoga Pride Cultural Group (BPCG) is mainly concerned with the preservation of Kisoga music. Led by Nalongo Likudhe of Buwenge, Busoga, the group seeks to promote Kisoga folk songs through dances such as *Irongo*, *Nalufuka*, *Tamenha*, and *Amayebe*. But unlike many modern traditional music bands, the group lacks the financial backing to record its songs and dances because the urban-based, commercially oriented music promoters and recording studios see little value in promoting traditional music in rapidly modernizing Uganda. The lack of widespread commercial appeal is perhaps the greatest challenge to the preservation of traditional music in Uganda.

The Alliance Française organizes the Beat That Drum concert to showcase the country's cultural drumming and percussion heritage. This free event features groups from all cultural regions of the country. The most recent event was in November 2005 at the Uganda National Theatre and Culture Center.[11]

Modern Music Genres

Uganda's modern music is a medley of music from various historical foundations, geographical origins, structural forms, repertoires, and functional uses. The most important foreign influences on Ugandan music are the Congo, Kenya, Tanzania, the United States, Europe, and the Caribbean.

Whether vocal or instrumental, the country's music scene features various solo and group performances.

The modernization of Uganda's music scene began in the colonial period when Europeans introduced Ugandans to modern sound equipment, recording, and music composition and style. The advent of modern transport and communications also contributed to Ugandans' exposure to music from other areas, thereby contributing to the modernization of the country's music scene.

Christian missionaries were the first to introduce Ugandans to European-style music composition and instrumentation. The modernization of Ugandan music, which began in the church, was aided by significant missionary involvement in Ugandan education from the early colonial period. By the 1950s, Ugandan musicians such as Mbaki-Katana, Kyagambiddwa, Benedicto Mubangizi, and Ahmed Oduka were composing European-style music. For instance, Mbaki-Katana composed *Te Deum* to locally mark the coronation of Queen Elizabeth in 1953. Mubangizi's work includes a popular Ugandan Catholic church hymnal, while Oduka, who was director of the Uganda police band and had been trained at London's Royal Military School of Music, made significant contributions to the repertoire of the police band. These early musicians, especially Kyagambiddwa, Mubangizi, and Oduka, composed pieces that combined European and Ugandan music elements such as dance and instrumentation. Many contemporary Ugandan musicians have adopted this style of composition and have performed traditional songs in modern styles, using new instruments such as electric and bass guitars.

Uganda's first popular music bands were either Congolese or played music from the DRC, and to a lesser extent, music from Kenya, Europe, and the United States. Because Congolese musicians dominated these bands, they sang in *Lingala* and popularized their *Rumba* dance, which still continues to define Ugandan music. Congolese music maestros such as Tabu Ley and Franco also influenced generations of East African musicians, including Ugandans.

In the 1960s, Uganda's leading singers and bands included Charles Soglo, Fred Sonko, Bily Mbowa, Kawaliwa, Moses Katazza, Eli Wamala, Fred Masagazi, Freddie Kigozi, Orchestre Melo Success, the Kampala Six, and Equator Sound.[12] Many of these bands' recordings were made in Nairobi, Kenya, which has controlled East Africa's music recording industry since the colonial period.

In the 1970s, the development of the Ugandan music industry nose-dived with Amin's ascent to power. Although he liked music, Amin's rule made life very difficult for musicians. Nighttime curfews, insecurity, economic instability, and the fear of detention not only made life unbearable but also forced many into exile. Only a handful of major musicians, for example, Peterson Tusubira Mutebi and his Tames band, managed to perform throughout the tumultuous Amin years. Mutebi, who performed in several languages, including Swahili, Luganda, and Toro, produced a number of hits, for example, *Nyongera Ku Love,* and his career continued into the 1990s.

In the post-Amin era, the late Philly Bongole Lutaaya produced one of Uganda's first popular music albums, *Born in Africa,* while in exile in Sweden in the 1980s. Many of the musicians (e.g., bass guitarist Sammy Kasule and percussionist Gerald Nnaddibanga) and songs on the album are well known in the country. Before he became a victim of AIDS in 1989, Lutaaya helped to launch Uganda's successful anti-AIDS campaign with his album *Alone.* He was awarded a lifetime award at the 2004 Pearl of Africa (PAM) Music Awards gala.

The Big Five band, a Ugandan musicians' supergroup in Sweden, dominated the 1990s. In the same era, Geoffrey Oryema produced several successful albums. Oryema, whose parents, grandfather, and uncles were musicians and storytellers, started composing and playing the *nanga,* guitar, thumb piano, and flute early. Many of his compositions draw on his ancestors' rich folklore, Uganda's social and political turmoil, and his painful exile during the Amin years. His well-known works, for example, *Exile, Beat the Border, Spirit, Night to Night,* and *Makambo,* are sung in Acoli, Swahili, and English. His fan base extends throughout East Africa and beyond.

The early twenty-first-century music scene in Uganda is in full bloom with a large number of musicians, music groups, and music genres. Music promotion channels such as radio stations and television stations are also abundant. As a result, there are many successful Ugandan musicians, for example, Jose Chameleone, Sheila Nvannungi, and Bebe Cool. Another important recent development is the initiation of the Pearl of Africa Music (PAM) Awards to honor and celebrate the achievements of Ugandan musicians.

Kampala is the center of Uganda's modern music industry for two reasons: the city's growth into the country's cosmopolitan industrial, educational, political, social, and business center, and its strategic location on the main roads and railway thoroughfares from Kenya, the DRC, Rwanda, and Tanzania. This location has not only facilitated general population migration into the city but has also aided the inflow of musicians from various places—musicians who have played a key role in modernizing the city's and country's music. Moreover, the city's cosmopolitan population has traditionally facilitated the introduction of various music genres that have influenced Ugandan music.

Since the colonial era, Kampala's radio stations, nightclubs, and bars have broadcast foreign and modernized local music. Music from the Caribbean, Latin America, North America, and Europe has been especially popular since radio broadcasting debuted in the city (and country) in 1953.[13] Since the

1990s, the development of the local music scene has lessened the influence of DRC Lingala music in Uganda.

There are many modern music genres in Uganda. Some genres, including Christian, neoclassical, jazz, Afro-beat, hip-hop, cultural/folk, Kadongo-kamu, Takeu, reggae, R&B, contemporary, foreign, and patriotic, are discussed here.

Christian Music

Christian music has become widespread in Uganda since the introduction of Christianity in the country in the latter half of the nineteenth century. Because of the dominance of Christianity in Uganda, Christian music is one of the most pervasive music genres in the country.

One reason for the current upsurge in Christian music is the advent of danceable Christian songs such as *Koona endoongo*. Many of these songs blend Christian messages with hip-hop, rhythm and blues, contemporary, Afro pop or Afro-beat, or Latino dance styles that especially appeal to the young. The competition for Uganda's Christian music market is fierce and some of the Christian artists in the country are Chief Makabai, Juliet Mugirya, Harriet Magezi, Heaven Bound, Slooky Slook, Keith Ministries, Men in Christ, First Love, Alpha One Crew, ACT, Generation Boys, the Wogs, Saint CA, Daudy, Gertrude Ngama, and James Wood. Unlike the preceding musicians who have sought to modernize Uganda's Christian music, Gertrude Ngama sings traditional gospel music.[14] In 2004, Chief Makabai and Juliet Mugirya won Pearl of Africa Music (PAM) Best Gospel Single (*Nanunulwa*) and Best Gospel Artiste/Group awards, respectively.

High-energy contemporary worship music that uses modern instruments such as electric guitars, keyboards, and drums is also helping to popularize Christian music, as are the Christian radio stations (e.g., Power FM, Radio Maria Uganda, Impact FM, TOP-Tower of Praise) that have recently been set up with the liberalization of Ugandan media. Ugandan Christian music fans also have access to music from other countries, especially the United States.

No account of Uganda's Christian music scene would be complete without mention of the country's mass choirs, especially the Kansanga Miracle Centre Mass Choir, the All Saints 11 O'clock Choir, and the Kampala Pentecostal Church's Watoto Children's Choir. These three mass choirs are renowned for their fusion of African and Western elements to create powerful worship and praise music. Although all three have interesting histories, the Watoto Children's Choir drawn from the AIDS or war orphans that are supported by the Kampala Pentecostal Church is focused on here. The orphans are among the millions of children in Uganda who have had the tragic and life-altering experience of losing one or both parents to the AIDS virus or to war. Since 1994, the choir has regularly toured the world, performing its soulful blend of native African rhythms, contemporary gospel music, and ethnic dance. The choir's lively and riveting performances commence with the boom of the African drums. Then one by one the children enter the stage with radiant smiles and colorful Ugandan costumes. The performances are usually spiced with individual children's narrations of their somber experiences and new-found hope and aspirations that both sadden and inspire audiences. The choir has produced many popular CDs (e.g., *We Are the Children, Things Already Better,* and *Dancing in the House of the Lord*) and music videos and DVDs (e.g., *Live in Los Angeles* and *Ana Meremeta*).[15]

Uganda's Watoto Children's Choir consists mainly of HIV/AIDS orphans. The choir enables them to raise support for their education and upkeep. Courtesy of the author.

Neoclassical Music

Ugandans have been active composers of neoclassical music since missionaries introduced it to them in the colonial period. Many neoclassical Ugandan compositions blend European and Ugandan elements, a style that reflects the composers' Ugandan heritage and their compositional training in Europe and the United States. Because many of the early Ugandan neoclassical composers were trained by missionaries, their works tended to be church hymns. Contemporary composers have kept this tradition alive, although these works' African melodies, harmonies, polyrhythms, and other elements can be easily discerned.

One of Uganda's contemporary neoclassical composers is Justinian Tamusuza, whose first string quartet movement, *Mu Kkubo Ery' Omusaalaba (On the Way of the Cross),* in the *Pieces of Africa* recording by the Kronos Quartet topped the Classical and World Music Billboard Charts in 1992, leading to a global surge in the demand for his compositions. *Mu Kkubo Ery' Omusaalaba* emulates and brings to mind the Ugandan tube fiddle (*endigiti*) and xylophone (*akadinda*) and reproduces certain *Kiganda* musical elements.[16] Tamusuza's other major works include *Abaafa Luli* (composed for Woodwind Quintet in 1994), designed to be played on the flute, oboe, clarinet, horn, and bassoon; *Ekivvulu Ky' Endere* (An African Festivity for Flute, 1995), designed for the flute, viola, prepared harp, marimba and maracas; and *Abaana Bange Na-Ka-Lwa* (1996), played on the Bb soprano saxophone, electric guitar, and marimba.[17] Another renowned neoclassical composer is Solomon Mbaki-Katana, whose *Te Deum* was used to locally celebrate the coronation of Queen Elizabeth in 1953.

Jazz

Jazz is popular in Uganda, especially in the major urban areas. Although jazz brings to mind slow mellow music, in Uganda, it also refers to high-energy dance music. Currently, there are many jazz bands in various venues in the country, especially in Kampala (e.g., Millennium Band, Afrigo Band, Simba Sounds, and KADS Band).

Afro-beat

Afro-beat music is a fusion of African folk music and traditional or Ugandan-style pop music, African-style antiphonal or call-and-response singing, and other types of music. This music features modern instruments such as guitars and keyboards that are frequently accented with African drums and other traditional instruments.[18] One of Uganda's leading Afro-beat groups is East World, whose song, *Fodda,* won the 2004 PAM award for Best Afro Beat Single.[19]

Hip-hop

Hip-hop, or rap, the music genre pioneered by inner-city African Americans, is quite popular in Uganda, especially among the young people. Initially transmitted to Uganda through satellite television and later radio, this genre has now been energetically taken up by various Ugandan artists. Some of Uganda's leading hip-hop artists and examples of their songs are A 2 Zee ("Can I"), Hip-hop Allstars ("Mother Africa"), and Klear Kut ft Juliana ("All I Wanna Know").

A number of interesting trends are discernible in Ugandan hip-hop, especially the emergence of artistes who perform secular rap music in local and regional languages such as Luganda and Swahili or Kiswahili and those who produce gospel rap music in either local or regional languages. Examples of Luganda rap artistes and some of their best-known songs are Krayzie Native (*Tujababya*), Bataka Underground (*Eno Yensi*), Racomstarz (*Ebaluwa*) and De PPI (*Ekiro Mbaga*). Examples of Swahili/Kiswahili rap artists and some of their best-known songs are Maurice Kirya (*Binadamu*) and Msb Young ft Krukid (*Vako*). Gospel hip-hop artists and some of their songs include Generation Boys (*Sirina*), Alpha One Crew (*Dear God*), and Pure Souls ft St. CA (*Yesu Tawala*). Currently, Group-Obsessions is one of the best hip-hop groups in the country, having been voted the Best Hip-Hop Artiste at the 2004 PAM awards for its Best Hip-Hop Single, *Nod Yo Head.*[20]

Cultural/Folk Pop

Cultural/folk pop music is descended from or influenced by traditional folk music. Cultural pop, unlike traditional music, is usually performed by professional musicians and is spread commercially through channels such as radio stations, music studios, and record stores. Arguably, many modern Ugandan musicians are to varying degrees cultural pop performers because they are not only influenced by their cultural background but are also engaged in repackaging folk music and dance for modern Ugandan society. This usually involves the rendition of folk music using modern instruments and styles or the incorporation of traditional dances in contemporary music performances. Howz It is one of the best cultural pop groups in Uganda and was voted Best Folk Pop Artiste/Group in the 2004 PAM awards for their song "Nile Beat."

Kadongo-kamu

Kadongo-kamu is one of the most popular music genres in Uganda. The genre, which features narrative songs accompanied by nominal or infrequent drumming, originated in Kampala and is now centered in the city's Wandegeya area. *Kadongo-kamu* arose in Kampala out of the confluence of three main factors: (1) European colonialism and the attendant introduction of new (European) religion, music, culture, and musical instruments (guitars, pianos, Western drums and brass) that formed the basis of the modernization of Ugandan music; (2) the development of cosmopolitan Kampala, which served as a magnet of people, music, and musicians from all over Uganda and elsewhere; and (3) its use as a vehicle for Buganda nationalism in the 1940s and 1950s. Although Buganda nationalists were agitating for the restoration of the Buganda monarchy, cosmopolitan Kampala's location in Buganda territory forced *Kadongo-kamu* to become a hybrid musical style, containing elements of local Ganda culture as well as those of other cultures in the city.

Thus, although *Kadongo-kamu* is patterned after traditional Ganda music, it contains new elements as well. For instance, modern *Kadongo-kamu* guitar playing imitates traditional Ganda *ndongo* (lyre) playing; uses *baakisimba* drum rhythms on the bass guitar; gives prominence to the lyrics in a manner reminiscent of traditional Ganda music; and uses hidden language when addressing sensitive or potentially offensive subjects.[21]

The genre's seminal song is, perhaps, "Kayanda" by Willy Mukaabya of the Festak Guitar Singers. Said to allegorize current President Museveni's rise to power, the song also highlights Uganda's explosive gender, ethnic, and political situation. Fearful of government retribution, many radio stations in the country have shied away from playing it.[22]

There are many *Kadongo-kamu* performers but perhaps the most renowned is Bernard Kabanda. Paul Kafeero has also recently been voted Best *Kadongo-kamu* Artiste at the 2004 PAM awards for his Best *Kadongo-kamu* Single, "Swimming Pool."

Takeu

Takeu is a new regional popular music genre named after the first letters of *Ta*nzania, *Ke*nya and *U*ganda. *Takeu's* leading artists are Josè Chameleone, Ragga Dee, Rachael Magoola, and Bobi Wine. Of these, Josè Chameleone, is the most successful and has been ranked the country's leading musician for four years in a row. His song, *Jamila,* won the Song of the Year award at the 2004 PAM awards ceremony.[23]

Reggae

The influence of Caribbean music on Uganda has been significant since radio debuted in the country in the 1950s. Reggae music has especially blossomed since the 1970s and 1980s, when African reggae stars such as Alpha Blondy and Lucky Dube became continental superstars. There are currently many Ugandan reggae musicians groups, including Atomico, Bebe Cool, Bob King, Bobi Wine, Daniel Mutyaba, Fireman, Coco Banton, Mad Tiger, Mega Dee, Menton Summer, Others, Peter Miles, Raga Dee, Red Banton, Seba Mamba, Ssuuna, Thornbread, Tilmenshan, Toolman, Winston Mayanja, and Weatherman. Ragga Dee and Bebe Cool were voted Best Raggae Artiste/Group at the 2004 PAM awards.

Rhythm and Blues

R&B is another African American music influence on Uganda that predates rap or hip-hop music. Some of the best R&B musicians in Uganda today are Dorothy Bukirwa and Juliana Kanyomozi, both of whom were honored at the 2004 PAM awards for Best R&B Single and Best R&B Artiste, respectively. Others include Beatrix, Benon, Bush Baby, Buti Knight, Daudy, Evon, Hastla, Isaac Jazzin, Jaqee, Maurice Kirya, Michael Ross, Niky Nola, Qute, Sami-K, and Steve Jean.

Contemporary Ugandan Music

"Contemporary" is one of the broadest music genres in Uganda and may in fact include many of the other music genres already discussed. The genre can be either secular or sacred. Sacred contemporary music is associated with various religious organizations. Secular contemporary music, for general audience entertainment, is common in nightclubs.

The competition for the contemporary Ugandan music audience is intense, and it includes many musicians, for example, Bella, Blackman Uncle Rich, Chance Nalubega, Culture Man, Cyrus, Diamond Oscar, Enny Kayondo, Essence Kasozi, Fred Hunter, Halima, Hastla, King Nad, Jenkins Mukasa, Juliana Kanyomozi, Kabogoza, Kaweesa, Ken Wonder, King Faisal, Lemmy Cool, Lover Dee, Lake N, Luther T, Mariam Ndagire, Mr. Hush, Namu Lwanga, Omuana Isaacs, Opha, Philly Lutaaya, Prossy Kankunda, Puffman MC, Rachel Magoola, Ronald Mayinja, Roy Kapale, Sara Zawedde, Sarah Ndagire, Small Axe, Ssali Hytham, Sweet Kid, Sylvia, Tempra, Tony Senkebejje, Trishlaa, Weathaman, Winnie Muyenga, Voboyo, and Ziggy D., "Omumbejja"

Sheila Nvannungi and Mesach Semakula are currently top contemporary music performers, having been voted Best Female and Male Artiste of the Year, respectively, at the 2004 PAM awards.[24]

Foreign Music

Despite robust domestic music production, Ugandans still enjoy music from other countries, especially the Caribbean, United States, Kenya, the DRC, and Tanzania. Taarab, the Swahili/Arab/Muslim music, of coastal Kenya and Tanzania has also become popular among Uganda's Muslims.

Patriotic Music

Uganda's patriotic music includes the anthems of the traditional kingdoms (e.g., Buganda) and the country. A verse of the English and Luganda versions, respectively, of the Uganda national anthem (composed by George Wilberforce Kakoma and adopted in 1962) and the Buganda anthem are presented here.

Oh! Uganda, May God uphold thee	Ggwe Uganda! Dolunda Akunyweze
We lay our future in thy hand	Naawe otukulembere
United, free, for liberty	Tusse ekimunga tulimu
Together, We always stand.	Kisinde ky'emirembe
Oh! Uganda the land of freedom	Ggwe Uganda! Ensi eye'eddembe
Our love and labor we give	Wamma ka tukuweereze
And with neighbors all at our country's call	Nga (twa)galena nnyo ne bannaffe
In peace and friendship we'll live.	Baliranwa bo bonna
Oh! Uganda the land that feeds us	Ggwe Uganda atweyagaza
By sun and fertile soil grown	Lw'obugimu n'akasana
For our own dear land we'll always stand	Ffe abaana bo tunaataasanga
The Pearl of African's crown.	Ensi ebbona ly'Afrika

Buganda Kingdom Anthem (Ekitiibwa kya Buganda or the Pride of Buganda)

Composed by Reverend Polycarp Kakooza (Nte clan); Translated by Professor Emmanuel Twesigye.

From age to age	Okuva edda n'edda eryo lyonna
The Kingdom of Buganda	Lino eggwanga Buganda
Was ever famous	Nti lyamanyibwa nnyo eggwanga
Throughout the world	lyaffe
	Okwetoloola ensi yonna

Chorus

We rejoice indeed!	*Twesiimye nnyo!*
We rejoice indeed!	*Twesiimye nnyo!*
In our Buganda!	*Olwa Buganda yaffe!*
The pride of Buganda is ancient!	*Ekitiibwa kya Buganda kyava dda!*
We are its bearers!	*Naffe tukikuumenga!*

Our great ancestors	Abazira ennyo abatusooka
Fought well in the battle	Baalwana nnyo mu ntalo
For they were patriotic	Ne balyagala nnyo eggwanga lyaffe
Let us follow their example	Naffe tulyagalenga

Let us unite today	Ffe abaana ba leero ka tulwane
To advance Buganda	Okukuza Buganda
Remembering our forefathers	Nga tujjukira nnyo bajjajja baffe
Who died for our Land	Baafirira ensi yaffe

Let us sing great praises	Nze naayimba ntya ne sitenda
To our Great King	Ssaabasajja Kabaka
To reign over us all	Asaanira afuge Obuganda bwonna
Let us trust him	Naffe nga tumwesiga

O Good and Merciful God	Katonda omulungi ow'ekisa
Be our divine King	Otubeere Mukama
Bless us abundantly	Otubundugguleko emikisa gyo era
Preserve our nation	Bbaffe omukuumenga

To show proper respect to the *Kabaka* and Kingdom of Buganda, the entire anthem is never played when the *Kabaka* is absent; instead, only verses 1 and 4 and the chorus are sung.[25]

Leading Song Writers

Uganda has produced many leading song writers. Perhaps the most renowned is Okot p'Bitek, an Acholi, who wrote many songs (e.g., *Song of Lawino* and *Song of Ocol*), folklore, and satirical poems. Others include Justinian Tamusuza, the author of the string quartet *Mu kkubo Ery Omusaalaba* or *On the Way of the Cross;* the late Evaristo Muyinda, a great performer and teacher of traditional Ugandan music; and Centurio Balikoowa, the successor to Muyinda. As well, many of the contemporary musicians discussed write their own songs.

Music Galas

Many music galas in and outside Uganda feature Ugandan musicians and performers. These include the International Theatre Institute (ITI) awards, Pearl of Africa Music (PAM) awards, and the continental Kora Awards. Although the national PAM awards feature the largest number of Ugandans, the country's artists have also been honored at the ITI and Kora Awards. For instance, Meshach Semakula won Best African Contemporary Song of 2004 honors at the International Theatre Institute Gala, while gospel artist George Okudi won the Best Male Artist in gospel music from East Africa at the 2003 Kora Awards. Most of these gala awards are patterned after the Grammy Awards in the United States.

MUSICAL INSTRUMENTS

Ugandans have various instruments that accompany their singing. Plain instrumental music is traditionally uncommon in the country. Although many Ugandan communities share musical instruments, their features, function, tone, quality, timbre or resonance, and social value differs among communities. The ubiquitous nature of certain instruments such as drums is a reflection of the shared ancestry and history of many Ugandan communities.

Ugandan musical instruments fall into four internationally recognized categories, namely, drums, other percussive instruments, wind instruments, and string instruments. The uses of these instruments in Uganda are briefly described.

Drums

Drums are the king of musical instruments in Uganda (except among the Karamoja and Sebei) and are played at virtually all important social, spiritual, and political occasions, including the onset of war, coronation, death and burial ceremonies, marriage, and childbirth/childnaming ceremonies.[26] In Buganda, special drums known as *Majaguzo* are an important part of the *Kabaka*'s regalia.

Although all traditional Ugandan drums are made with leather strips or some other roping material used to attach animal skins to hollow wooden frames, the drums exhibit tremendous variety in sound, size, shape, and function. The sound variety depends on the thickness of the animal skin, the size of the wooden hollow used to make the drum, and the way it is played. Thin-skinned drums are played by hand, while the thick-skinned ones are played with sticks. Some drums are covered with skin on both ends; others have a skin cover on one end only. Lighter drums can be played while hanging from the neck or while held in the armpit. The heavier ones are usually set on the ground. Despite the advent of modern drums and drum-making technologies, traditionally made drums dominate Uganda's music scene because of their cultural relevance, cost, reliability, and ease of accessibility and maintenance.

Traditionally, drums have many uses in Uganda, including communication, coronation and other royal functions, worship, healing, spiritual exorcism, welcoming twins, and dance. Throughout Africa, drums are traditionally a major instrument of communication, whereby the kind of drum beat conveys specific messages, places of assembly, and the individual or communal response to the messages. Thus the drum beat for war differs from that for danger or for assembling people for work or various communal functions. Over time, though, the use of drums for communication purposes has been declining with the result that many Ugandans today cannot discern the message encoded in a drum beat.

Royal drums were an important aspect of traditional Ugandan monarchies (e.g., those of Buganda, Ankole, Bunyoro, and Toro); they were used to announce royal births, coronation, and deaths. As one of the key emblems of power, the royal drums had special names (e.g., *Majaguzo* in Buganda); they were made and tended by special craftsmen with hereditary offices; they were played by certain clan members or royal court musicians using special drumsticks (e.g., the bones of dead people in Buganda); they were specially decorated with beautiful beads and cowrie shells; and they were passed on at death from one *Kabaka* to the next.

Drums for the worship of ancestors or the gods, for healing, and exorcism of evil spirits along with the accompanying songs and dance have been con-

The drum is Uganda's most widespread music instrument. Courtesy of Emmanuel Twesigye.

sidered sacred and therefore only reserved for that purpose. Examples include Busoga's *Enswezi* and *Amayebe, Bul jok* of Lango, and *Lubale* drums of Buganda. These drums are accompanied by similarly named dances. In most cases, healing and spiritual exorcism happened when both healer and patient danced to the drum beat. Many Ugandan communities still use this form of healing because of the scarcity of modern hospitals or their inability to deal with certain traditional sicknesses.

In communities such as the Baganda, Basoga, and Iteso that honor the birth of twins, such an occurrence was greeted by ululations and the drum beat of the long and cylindrical *engalabi* (Buganda), *engaabe* (Busoga), or *emiidiri* (Iteso) drum. This was then followed by special community-specific dances that are increasingly rare.

Most dances in Uganda are coordinated by the drum. Thus, dance variations among Uganda's ethnic communities correspond to differences in drumming, for example, those between the *Amagunju* and *Tamenha Ibuga* dances of the Baganda and Basoga, respectively.

Percussive Instruments

Percussive instruments include logs, *amadinda* (xylophones), and rattles and shakers (*ensaasi*). Buganda's thumb pianos (*lukeme* or *okeme*) also belong in this category. These instruments can be temporary or permanent depending on what they are made from.

Wind Instruments

These are either hard- or soft-blown, depending on the amount of energy needed to play them. The one-holed long cow horn trumpets (e.g., *arupepe* in Teso) are primarily for communication. The long wooden and cow skin trumpets of Buganda, Bunyoro, and Toro (*amakondere*), West Nile (*agwara*), and Busoga (*amagwalla*) are royal instruments that are played in sets during the crowning, marriage, anniversary celebrations, and burials of kings or chiefs. Although the *arupepe* are usually played solo, the royal trumpets are often played melodiously in ensembles by themselves or with drums.

Soft-blown instruments are flutes made of small horns from goats and wild animals. Known variously as *omukari* (Ankole and Kigezi), *endere* (Buganda), *akalere* (Busoga) and *alamuru* (Teso), they are similarly made and used. Because they can also be made from a wide variety of temporary materials, they range from temporal children's toys to the highly durable ones made from small animal horns. Flutes consist of a blow-hole at the narrow end and four holes at the other end that are used to control their modulation. In Uganda, especially among the Banyankole, flute melodies are popular among dancers, cattle herders, and lovers. Flutes can be played solo, with drums, or in ensembles of various-sized flutes.

String Instruments

Single- or multi-stringed music instruments such as harps are about as widespread as drums. Examples of single-stringed instruments are the *endigire* or *endingidi*, *arigirigi* or *rigirigi*, which are so named because of the sound they produce. *Rigirigi* are usually played solo and are valued for their apparent ability to articulate words and mimic human speech.

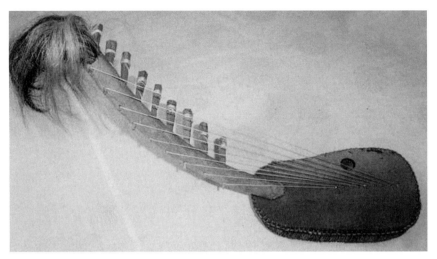

Ndigiti is one of Uganda's most common stringed instruments. Courtesy of Emmanuel Twesigye.

Examples of multi-stringed instruments are Buganda's *ennanga* and *entongoli* and the *adeudeu* of the Teso. As the Ugandan equivalents of guitars, these instruments accompany various kinds of songs for weddings, funerals, political ceremonies, and other celebrations.

DANCE AND ITS FUNCTIONS

Dance is one of the most widespread and integral parts of social life in Uganda. Dance serves various purposes such as entertainment and merriment. It celebrates childbirth, courtship and marriage, visits by relatives, and royal coronation and is an integral part of invocations to the gods for successful hunts and battles, funerals, and beer parties. Some dances, such as those that traditionally sought the ancestors' blessings for successful wars, are becoming extinct, given the decline of interethnic warfare in modern Uganda.

The most elaborate dances in Uganda are found among the more superstitious communities such as the Acholi and Bagisu. For example, eight major dances exist among the Acholi. These are

1. *Lalobaloba*—a drumless dual circle dance attached to no specific occasion. All dancers carry sticks. Men stay on the outer circle and move to the inner circle to secure women dance partners.

2. *Otiti*—a male-only dance that features dancers with shields and spears and shouting around a drumset on a pole in the center of the arena. *Otiti* usually transitions to *Lalobaloba* when the shields and spears are set aside.
3. *Bwola*—a dual-circle chief's dance. This most important dance is performed on the chief's orders and features male dancers with drums in the outer circle and drumless female dancers in the inner circle. The dance rhythm follows the drum beat and the motion of the male lead dancer and singer in the center. The lead singer and dancer is an important social figure whose traditional privileges included wearing a leopard skin.
4. *Myel awal*—a funeral dance in which male dancers carrying spears and shields perform the *Lalobaloba* while wailing women dance around the grave.
5. *Apiti*—a girls'-only song and dance that celebrates the mid-year rainy season. It is performed in a line and is never held when the rains fail.
6. *Ladongo*—a dance that celebrates successful hunts and is performed before returning hunters get to their homes. Men and women form two opposite lines and clap while jumping up and down. Traditionally, the Acholi were accomplished hunters with many types of hunting.[27] Over time, as the game habitat formerly occupied by the Acholi has declined or come under government control and as the community has modernized and become less dependent on wild game meat, the significance of the *Ladongo* dance has correspondingly declined.
7. *Myel wanga*—a dance held after marriage or at beer parties; it involves sitting male harp (*nanga*) players at the rear and women dancing *Apiti* in the front.
8. *Atira*—an armed-warrior dance held on the eve of battle. Besides dramatizing spear fighting, it psychologically prepared warriors for war and gave them a chance to sharpen and practice their war skills. *Atira* has long been a thing of the past.

Many other Ugandan communities had variations of the Acholi dances discussed. For instance, the Banyarwanda had a war dance that included various weapons and intimidating headgear. Depending on the occasion, traditional Ugandan dancers wore special dance attire to enhance their movements. Examples of these attires include sisal skirts (still widely used today), jingles, headbands and headdresses, feathers, shields, spears, rods or staffs, necklaces, bangles, and hats made of various materials. Heads were shaved in special patterns as well. Nowadays, most of the traditional dance attires are combined with modern clothing, or, in some cases, have been entirely discarded.

Similarly, the Iteso had various dances such as festive commemorations of the birth of twins; *akembe,* an away-from-home courtship dance for boys and girls; and dances for invoking ancestral spiritual intervention in various distressful circumstances. These invocations involved dancing to specific songs that would cause the ancestral spirits to possess and communicate their wishes through some of the participants.

The Banyarwanda/Bafumbira had elaborate wedding dances. The dances were performed in pairs, whether male-female or same sex. They involved women ululating while the men sang and rehearsed the community's memorable events. Many Banyarwanda/Bafumbira clans also had their own unique dances. For instance, Batutsi dances featured girls singing and dancing in pairs while men performed in a group of 10 or more.

DRAMA

Drama is one of the most developed forms of indigenous Ugandan entertainments. In the pre–radio and television era, drama, wrestling, song, dance, and storytelling were the main forms of entertainment. More important, they provided forums for the socialization of children, more so because traditional Ugandan culture has been orally and visually transmitted to the next generation. Although schools and the mass media now play an increasingly important role in the dissemination of Ugandan culture, the role of drama has not diminished because the society is still more oral than literate.

Ugandan drama falls into many categories, including dance/music drama, political plays, children's theater, cultural dances, folk songs, puppetry, acrobatics, community theater, and development theater. The country's drama productions focus on nearly all aspects of Ugandan life, including family life, death, marriage, the challenges of interethnic love and marriage, urban and rural life, corruption, as well as the country's HIV/AIDS and civil war challenges. Theater has been especially effective in helping Uganda to combat HIV/AIDS. Many development agencies in Uganda also use role-plays and theater to deal with various development issues, especially in rural areas where literacy levels, access to print and electronic media, and income are low.[28]

Founded in 1959, the imposing Uganda National Theatre and Culture Center (UNCC) in Kampala is Uganda's oldest and most prestigious drama/theater venue. It attracts some of the best plays and dramatists in the country, besides occasionally hosting visiting international theater groups. In the colonial period, the theater was reserved for whites and featured plays by the Indian-dominated Kampala Amateur Theatrics Society (KATS). The African Dramatic Society was the first indigenous Ugandan group to perform there in 1964. Since its founding, UNCC has been entrusted with the responsibility of promoting and preserving Uganda's cultural values.[29] There are other drama venues in the various universities, colleges, schools, and community centers around the country. Performances in rural areas are usually in the open and in native languages.

Uganda's dramatists come from many segments of society, including churches, primary and secondary schools, colleges, universities, and various professional and ethnic cultural groups. One of the country's leading church theater groups is the Kampala Pentecostal Church Drama Team that regularly stages spiritual plays at the UNCC. Some of their recent plays include *The Affectionate Foe* and *Logoma Is Searching* by Deborah Asiimwe.

Drama teams from the country's primary and secondary schools change frequently because of graduation and dropouts. Nevertheless, these teams compete annually for local and national drama honors at the Primary and Secondary School National Drama Festivals at the UNCC. Bweranyangi Girls' Senior Secondary School, Namagunga Girls' Secondary School, Tororo Girls' Secondary School, Gayaza Girls' High School, King's College Buddo, and Namiriango Boys' Secondary School have some of the leading drama companies in the country. College and university plays are held on various campuses around the country, although some are also performed at the UNCC. Kigezi College, Butobele, also has a notable government-built theater hall.[30]

There are many professional and recreational drama companies in the country, especially in Kampala. One of the most successful is the Kampala Amateur Dramatics Society (KADS). Although open to anyone interested in acting, directing, or helping with production, KADS is a membership organization that consists mostly of the capital's elite, especially members of the

The Uganda National Theatre and Culture Centre is the country's premier drama arts center. Courtesy of Earl P. Scott.

expatriate and diplomatic community. KADS usually puts on plays that are distinct, enjoyable, and accessible to the capital's diverse foreign and local audiences. It normally sponsors four productions a year: a play in March and October, a musical in the middle of the year, and a pantomime in December.[31] Most of KADS plays come from the United Kingdom. Some of its recent plays have included William Russell's 1983 musical *Blood Brothers* and Muriel Spark's 1961 novel *The Prime of Miss Jean Brodie*.[32] Other professional groups include Teamline (codirected by playwright Charles Mulekwa) and the Ebonies, who have recently performed their romantic dilemma, *Kalibbobo,* in which four women, including a beautiful white woman who is HIV/AIDS-positive, vie for the love of one man.[33]

Uganda has produced many playwrights, including Charles Mulekwa, Okot p'Bitek, John Ruganda, and Robert Serumaga. Other notable Ugandan playwrights and their works include Martyred Byron Kawadwa (*The Song of Wankoko),* Mercy Mirembe (*Lady, Will You Marry Me* and *The Corrupt Chief* or *The Chief of Shumankuzi*), Mary Karooro Okurut (*The Curse of the Sacred Cow),* and Deborah Asiimwe's *Logoma Is Searching.* Kawadwa, who was a leading playwright in the turbulent 1970s decade of the brutal Amin government, was killed for using his plays to criticize the regime. John Ruganda and Robert Serumaga are also credited with the development of Ugandan theater in the difficult 1970s and 1980s period, when many other playwrights, such as Okot p'Bitek, were in exile.[34]

Mulekwa is a leading contemporary playwright who has written 10 plays, mostly on Uganda's current social problems, including child defilement, conflict and war, HIV/AIDS, female genital mutilation, and other harmful cultural practices such as bride price or dowry. Two of Mulekwa's plays, *The Woman in Me* (1990) and *Nothing Against You* (1995), won the National Script Award in 1991 and the BBC African Performance Award in 1995, respectively. *The Woman in Me* is about a mother who insists on picking a spouse for her son. It critiques excessive parental control of children and many women's double character as adoring, caring, and loving mothers and mates and equally, as people who often use their influence to meet their selfish needs. *Nothing Against You* is a critique of the Ugandan cultural practice of bride price or dowry because it has become a burden that must be paid even after the death of one's wife.[35] The practice not only demeans women by making them objects that can be bought or sold, it also burdens young men of marriageable age, especially in Uganda's current difficult economic environment. Okot p'Bitek's play *White Teeth* (1989) also explores this issue. Mulekwa has also written *A Time of Fire* (1999) and *Between You and Me* and is the codirector of the drama group Teamline, on the committee of the

Kampala Amateur Dramatic Society, and an executive member of the National Theater Guild.

Ugandan theater currently faces many challenges. Foremost is that many Ugandan plays and dances are unscripted. This is partly because of the illiteracy of many traditional "playwrights" and the political turmoil of the 1970s and 1980s that made it risky to write plays, especially those that might have been construed as being critical of the Amin and Obote regimes. The unscripted nature of these plays and dances hinders their export to the global marketplace and constrains Uganda's contribution to the international theater scene. In turn, this inhibits global awareness of Ugandan playwrights and theater productions.

As well, many Ugandan plays and dances are grounded in specific ethnic settings and languages that are not necessarily accessible to outsiders. Although the country lacks a good *lingua franca,* these plays need to be translated into other major national languages (e.g., English) to make them accessible to larger audiences. Translation into English may also be considered as a way of opening the plays up to international audiences, even though it may be difficult to translate certain traditional or cultural concepts. Overall, the translations might help to increase the national and global visibility of Ugandan theater, besides enhancing its contribution to Uganda's social, cultural, and economic development.

Limited government funding for drama and other performing arts is another challenge because these are often seen as luxuries. Private funding is also frequently unavailable. A poor general population also means that there is a limited number of people who can afford to pay to watch theatrical performances. Most performers do not live on their theater earnings and have to moonlight to make ends meet. As result, most of the country's theatrical productions are of poor quality. In some cases, the performances also alienate customers for various reasons.[36]

There is also the challenge of creating performances that are socially and culturally relevant and yet progressive. This means that playwrights and performers cannot go too far ahead or lag behind their audience's aspirations, lest they alienate them and worsen their precarious position.[37]

Finally, although Uganda affords its performers reasonable freedom of operation, they are not completely free to create and perform any work of art that they please. Because there have been cases when Uganda's government has banned certain theatrical performances that it considers offensive, artists frequently have to censor themselves to avoid offending the authorities.[38]

Despite these and many other challenges, Ugandan theater is growing. Moreover, the growing strength of regional organizations such as the Eastern Africa Theatre Institute (EATI) that includes Ethiopia, Kenya, Uganda, and Tanzania is helping to coordinate theater activities in the region, create a forum for the exchange ideas among artists from the region, and give artists a chance to work jointly to solve their problems and improve their working environment.[39]

Glossary

Abajwarakondo   A group of highly honored men of Toro.

Adeudeu   Teso multi-stringed instrument.

Agwara   West Nile long wooden and cow skin trumpet.

Akadinda   Luganda for a large and exclusive xylophone for the Kabaka.

Akalere   Five or six ragged Basoga flute.

Akembe   Iteso away-from-home courtship dance for boys and girls.

Akirriket   Karimojong rainmaking ceremony.

Alamuru   Five or six ragged Teso flute.

Amadinda or entaala   Luganda for a xylophone.

Amagunju   Luganda dance.

Amagwalla   Basoga long wooden and cow skin trumpet.

Amakondeere   Buganda Kingdom's royal trumpets (also used in Bunyoro and Toro).

Amayebe   Lango sacred drum.

Apiti   Acholi girls' rainy season song and dance.

Arupepe   Teso cow horn trumpet.

Balubaale   Plural of *Lubaale* in traditional Ganda religion.

Baraza   Kiswahili/Swahili for "Council of Elders."

Bukule   One of Katonda's shrines in Kyaggwe, Buganda.

Bul jok   Lango sacred drum.

Bur   Acholi hunting trap that consists of a pit in the animal's path.

Buzu   One of Katonda's shrines in Kyaggwe, Buganda.

Bwola   Acholi dual-circle chief's dance.

Chapati/Chapatti   Popular East African/Indian flat bread.

Dwar arum   Acholi group dry season hunt.

Dwar obwo   Acholi group hunt using nets, spears, and dogs.

Ebisanja   Buganda Kingdom's royal trumpeters.

Eid al Adha   Islamic religious holiday.

Eid al Fitr   Islamic religious holiday that marks the end of Ramadan (month of fasting).

Emandwa   Deity of the Batooro Mandwa cultists.

Emiidiri   Ateso for a long cylindrical drum.

Empaako   Runyoro for pet name.

Emuria   Karimojong for a type of grass.

Emurron   Karimojong medicine man.

Endere   Five or six ragged flute.

Endiiro   Runyoro for a man's eating basket.

Endingidi   Luganda for a bowed lute or tube fiddle.

Engaabe   Lusoga for a long cylindrical drum.

Engalabi   Luganda for a long cylindrical drum.

Ennanga   Buganda multi-stringed instrument.

Ensaasi   Rattles and shakers similar to Latin American maraca (hollow-gourd rattle containing pebbles or beans).

Ensigosigo   Runyoro for a mixture of millet and simsim grains.

Enswezi   Basoga sacred drum.

Entongoli   Buganda multi-stringed instrument.

Etimbo   Religious drum and trumpet tunes of the Batooro Mandwa cultists.

Eyonga   Bagwere ritual dance that welcomes twins to society.

Gombolola   Sacred fire that burned perpetually at the entrance of the Kabaka of Buganda's palace and was part of his regalia.

Gomesi/Busuti   Ankle-length Victorian dress for women.

Gufata or gaturura   Forced into marriage among the Banyarwanda or Bafumbira.

Gyendi   Luganda for "I'm fine."

Habari yako   Kiswahili/Swahili for "How are you doing?"

Imam   Islamic priest.

Iremba   Bagisu coming-out ceremony for newly initiated boys.

Isebantu Kyabazinga   President of the Council of Heredity Chiefs of Busoga.

Ityanyi   Herb that Bagisu boys take to prepare themselves for circumcision.

Jambo sana   Kiswahili/Swahili for "I'm fine, thanks" or "I am well."

Jambo   Kiswahili/Swahili for "Hello."

Kabaka   Traditional title for the King of Buganda.

Kabarega   Traditional title for the King of Bunyoro.

Kadongo-kamu   Popular Ugandan music genre.

Kampala Jumpa   Short embroidered man's shirt.

Kangawo   Traditional title for one of the Baganda chiefs (of Bulemezi), who was responsible for the orderly succession of Kabaka.

Kanzu/Boubou   Floor-length men's tunic.

Kasozi k' mpala   Luganda for "Hill of Impala."

Kasuze Katya   Ganda bride handing-over ceremony.

Katonda   Supreme Being in traditional Ganda religion.

Kawuula   One of the Buganda Kingdom's hereditary chieftainships who made and played the royal drums.

Khanga/Kikoi   Women's wraparound tie-on cotton skirt or apron.

Kibuga   Traditional capital city of the Buganda Kingdom at Mengo Hill.

Kimomomera   One of the Buganda Kingdom's hereditary chieftainships who made and played the royal drums.

Kirange   Acholi onset of the rainy season hunt, in which the wildlife was driven into slightly flooded rivers and speared.

Kiswahili/Swahili   Common language spoken in East Africa.

Kraal   Enclosure for livestock or an indigenous village surrounded by a fence.

Kwanjula   Traditional Ganda/Baganda marriage.

Ladongo   Acholi successful hunters' welcome dance.

Lalobaloba   Acholi drumless dual circle dance.

Lubaale   Guardian saint in traditional Ganda religion (singular form of *Balubaale*).

Lubale   Baganda sacred drums.

Luganda   Language of the Ganda or Baganda people.

Lukeme or okeme   Baganda thumb piano(s).

Luwombo   Chicken, goat, or beef stew steamed in banana leaves.

Madrasa   Islamic school.

Mahr   Arabic for dowry, bride price, or bride wealth.

Majaguzo   Drums that are part of the Kabaka of Buganda's regalia.

Malaya   Kiswahili/Swahili for prostitute.

Mandazi   Popular East African puffy donut.

Mandwa   Katonda's priests in traditional Ganda religion.

Marwa   Beer.

Matooke   Luganda for plantains or bananas; the name of a popular dish in southern Uganda.

Mizimu   Spirits of departed ancestors in traditional Ganda religion.

Mugabazi   Runyoro ceremony marked by the eating of a dead man's bull as part of the funeral rites.

Mugerere   Traditional title for one of the Baganda chiefs (of Bugerere), who was responsible for the orderly succession of Kabaka.

Muko   Luganda for brother-in-law.

Musani   Circumcised Bagisu man.

Musinde   Uncircumcised Bagisu man.

Muwanga   Most powerful Lubaale in traditional Ganda religion.

Mweso   Ugandan board game.

Myel awal   Acholi funeral dance.

Myel wanga   Acholi marriage or beer party dance.

Namakwa   Katonda's shrine in Kyaggwe, Buganda.

Ng'inga'aricum   Karimojong clan of northern Uganda that did not bury its dead.

Njema   Kiswahili/Swahili for "I'm fine, thanks."

Njovu   Clans of Buganda.

Nsenene   Luganda for edible green grasshoppers.

Nyalebe   Sacred chewezi drum.

Obugabe   Ankole kingship.

Okia   Acholi rainy season single hunter/trapper hunt.

Okol Acholi hunting trap with a noose attached to a log of wood, used to catch small game.

Okukurata Public Runyoro king greeting ceremony.

Okwabya Olumbe Ganda funeral rights ceremony.

Oluganda Luganda for kinship or brotherhood.

Olyotya Luganda for "How are you?"

Omugabe Traditional title for the king of Ankole.

Omukama Runyoro for "king."

Omukari Five or six ragged flute in Ankole and Kigezi.

Omulanga Luganda for a harpist.

Omusauga Toro head of coronation rituals.

Otiti Acholi male-only dance that features dancers with shields and spears

Pombe Kiswahili/Swahili for beer.

Posho/Ugali/Nsima Thick porridge or corn cake eaten with stew (*Luwombo*).

Runyege Bagisu boy initiation dance.

Sambusa Popular East African meat/vegetable pie.

Ssenga Luganda for paternal aunt.

Tadooba Smoky kerosene candle.

Takeu Popular East African music genre named after *Ta*nzania, *Ke*nya, and *U*ganda.

Tamenha Ibuga Lusoga dance.

Tekke Acholi circular foot trap for small game.

Tong twok Acholi hunting trap for elephants that consists of a tree-suspended falling spear.

Uji Kiswahili/Swahili for porridge.

Ukwijana Elopment among the Banyarwanda or Bafumbira.

Waragi Gin derived from banana or cassava beer.

Yakan Cult religion in Uganda.

Notes

INTRODUCTION

1. Central Intelligence Agency, *The World Factbook,* 2005, http://www.cia.gov/cia/publications/factbook/geos/ug.html.

2. *Spectrum Guide to Uganda* (Nairobi, Kenya: Camerapix Publishers, 2004), 278–79. See also Country Studies, "Uganda," 2003–2005, http://countrystudies.us/uganda/ and United Methodist Church, General Board of Global Ministries, "Uganda: A Country Profile," February 16, 1999, http://gbgm-umc.org/africa/uganda/uprofile.html.

3. Richard Nzita and Mbaga-Niwampa, *Peoples and Cultures of Uganda* (Kampala: Fountain Publishers, 1997). See also Central Intelligence Agency, *The World Factbook,* 2005, and Country Studies, "Uganda."

4. Douglas Mpuga, "The Official Language Issue: A look at the Uganda Experience," paper presented at the African Language Research Project Summer Conference, Dunes Manor Hotel and Conference Center, Ocean City, Maryland, July 1–3, 2003, http://www.umes.edu/english/newalp/pdf/douglasmpuga.pdf.

5. Gitau Warigi, "The Relentless March of Kiswahili," *Daily Nation,* 2 October 2005, http://www.nationmedia.com/dailynation/. See also Rocha Chimera, *Kiswahili: Past, Present and Future Horizons* (Nairobi, Kenya: Nairobi University Press, 1998).

6. Republic of Uganda, Ministry of Education and Sports, "Primary Education Enrollment Flows since Inception of UPE in 1997," 2003, http://www.education.go.ug/. See also Patrick Kiirya, "Non-Formal Education in Uganda: Which Way?" Association for the Development of Education in Africa, 2002, http://www.adeanet.org/wgnfe/publications/symposium-Maputo-06-2002/NFEinUganda.doc.

7. A.B.K. Kasozi, Sam Katunguka, and Florence Nakayiwa, *The Proposed Strategic Plan for Higher Education 2003–2015,* Second Draft (Kampala: Ministry of Education and Sports, June 2003).

8. Emily Wax, "Underfunded and Overrun, 'Harvard of Africa' Struggles to Teach," *Washington Post,* October 29, 2005, A17. Available online at http://www.washingtonpost.com.

9. UNICEF, "Girls' Education in Uganda," 2003, http://www.unicef.org/girlseducation/files/Uganda_2003_(w.corrections).doc.

10. Uganda Bureau of Statistics, "2002 Population and Housing Census," 2005, http://www.ubos.org/.

11. Country Studies, "Uganda." See also Peter Nkedi-Kizza, Jacob Aniku, and Christina Gladwin, "Gender and Soil Fertility in Uganda: A Comparison of Soil Fertility Indicators for Women and Men's Agricultural Plots," *African Studies Quarterly* 6, no.1 (2002), http://web.africa.ufl.edu/asq/v6/v6i1a2.htm, and Uganda Export Promotion Board, "Uganda's Exports," 2001, http://www.ugandaexportsonline.com/exports.htm.

12. Uganda Export Promotion Board, "Uganda's Exports," 2001. http://www.ugandaexportsonline.com/exports.htm.

13. Uganda Bureau of Statistics, "Laborforce: Summary of Major Results of the 1997 Labour Force Pilot Survey," 1997, http://www.ubos.org/l_force2.html.

14. Uganda Home Pages, "Government of Uganda," 2003, http://www.government.go.ug/.

15. Library of Congress Country Studies, "Uganda: Early Political Systems," 1990, http://lcweb2.loc.gov/cgi-bin/query/r?frd/cstdy:@field(DOCID+ug0015).

16. Amii Omara-Otunnu, *Politics and the Military in Uganda, 1890–1985* (New York: St. Martin's Press, 1987).

17. Ibid.; Ogenga Otunnu, "Causes and Consequences of the War in Acholiland," Protracted Conflict, Elusive Peace: Initiatives to End the Violence in Northern Uganda, Accord, 2002, http://www.c-r.org/accord/uganda/accord11/index.shtml; Adam Seftel, *Uganda: The Bloodstained Pearl of Africa: And Its Struggle for Peace* (Lanseria, South Africa: A Bailey's African Photo Archives Production, 1994); Henry Kyemba, *A State of Blood: The Inside Story of Idi Amin* (New York: Ace Books, 1977; and Aili Mali Tripp, *Women & Politics in Uganda* (Madison: University of Wisconsin Press, 2000).

18. Besides Obote's need to use Amin and the army to win his political conflict with the *Kabaka,* the backdrop to Amin's hasty elevation was the 1964 mutiny of the African sections of the Uganda military over poor pay and lack of promotion. Although the mutiny was suppressed with the aid of British troops, Obote subsequently bought the army's loyalty by raising their salary and by swiftly promoting several African officers. Most notably, Idi Amin rose from major to colonel, brigadier, and major-general between 1964 and 1968 besides becoming army and air force chief of staff in 1966.

19. Nzita and Mbaga-Niwampa, *Peoples and Cultures of Uganda.*

RELIGION AND WORLDVIEW

1. John S. Mbiti, *Introduction to African Religion* (London: Heinemann Educational, 1975). See also John S. Mbiti, *African Religions and Philosophy* (Garden City, N.Y.: Anchor Books, 1970); Samuel Oluoch Imbo, *An Introduction to African Philosophy* (Lanham, Md.: Rowman and Littlefield, 1998).

2. Mario Ignacio Aguilar, "General Essay on the Religions of Sub-Saharan Africa," ELMAR (Electronic Media and Religions) Project Encyclopedia, 1998, http://philtar.ucsm.ac.uk/encyclopedia/sub/geness.html.

3. Uganda Bureau of Statistics, "2002 Population and Housing Census," 2005, http://www.ubos.org.

4. Lillian Ashcraft-Eason and L. Djisovi Ikukomi Eason, "Indigenous Religions and Philosophies," in *Contemporary Africa,* vol. 5, ed. Toyin Falola (Durham, N.C.: Carolina Academic Press, 2003), 553–83.

5. Chidi Denis Isizoh, "Christian Motivation for Dialogue with Followers of African Traditional Religion," 1999–2005, http://www.afrikaworld.net/afrel/motivation.html.

6. University of Pennsylvania, African Studies Center, "East Africa Living Encyclopedia," 2004, http://www.africa.upenn.edu/NEH/neh.html.

7. Mukasa E. Ssemakula, "Buganda's Indigenous Religion," http://www.buganda.com/eddiini.htm.

8. Aylward Shorter, *East African Societies* (Boston: Routledge & Kegan Paul, 1974), 84.

9. Ibid.

10. Ibid.

11. Country Studies, "Uganda," 2003–2005, http://countrystudies.us/uganda/. Elizabeth Isichei, *A History of Christianity in Africa: From Antiquity to the Present,* (Grand Rapids, Mich.: Eerdmans, 1995), 146.

12. Isichei, *History of Christianity.*

13. John A. Rowe, "Islam under Idi Amin: A Case of Déjà vu?" in *Uganda Now: Between Decay and Development,* ed. Holger Bernt Hansen and Michael Twaddle (London: Curry, 1988), 267–79.

14. The use of nonnative soldiers with different racial, ethnic, and religious backgrounds was a central feature of British colonial policy in Uganda and elsewhere because it guaranteed the loyalty of the military and made it difficult for them to form anti-British alliances with local people. Amii Omara-Otonnu, *Politics and the Military in Uganda, 1890–1985* (New York: St. Martin's Press, 1987), 14, 24.

15. Rowe, "Islam under Idi Amin."

16. Pagewise, "Stanley and Livingstone," 2002, http://de.essortment.com/davidlivingston_rhif.htm.

17. Isichei, *History of Christianity,* 145.

18. A. F. Mockler-Ferryman, "Christianity in Uganda," *Journal of the Royal African Society* 2, no. 7 (April 1903): 276–91.

19. Ibid., 279.

20. Isichei, *History of Christianity,* 145.

21. Mockler-Ferryman, "Christianity in Uganda," 276–89.

22. Ibid., 284.

23. Ali A. Mazrui, "Religious Strangers in Uganda: From Emin Pasha to Amin Dada," *African Affairs* 76, no. 302 (January 1977): 25.

24. Mockler-Ferryman, "Christianity in Uganda," 290.

25. U.S. State Department, Bureau of Democracy, Human Rights, and Labor, "International Religious Freedom Report 2002 (Uganda)," http://www.state.gov/g/drl/rls/irf/2002/13861.htm.

26. Country Studies, "Millenarian Religions," 2003–2005, http://countrystudies.us/uganda/32.htm.

27. Mazrui, "Religious Strangers," 24.

28. Dan Mudoola, "Religion and Politics in Uganda: The Case of Busoga, 1900–1962," *African Affairs* 77, no. 306 (January 1978): 23.

29. Mazrui, "Religious Strangers," 26–30.

30. David Gwyn, *Idi Amin: Death-Light of Africa* (Boston: Little, Brown, 1977), 11, 27, 111.

31. Ibid., 112.

32. U.S. State Department, "International Religious Freedom Report 2003," http://www.state.gov/g/drl/rls/irf/2003/23759.htm.

LITERATURE, FILM, AND MEDIA

1. Lillian Temu Osaki, "African Children's Literature," 2004, http://web.uflib.ufl.edu/cm/africana/children.htm.

2. Angela Nsimbi, "Document Rich African Heritage," *New Vision,* July 12, 2004, http://www.newvision.co.ug/.

3. Nana Wilson Tagoe, "Goodbye English," Connections: African Indigenous Language Publishing for Global Communities Conference at the Africa Centre, London, United Kingdom, 30 March 1999, http://www.africacentre.org.uk/connections.htm#Nana%20Wilson%20Tagoe.

4. Birthdates for the other female authors are unknown.

5. Brian Worsfold, "Literary Map of Africa: East Africa—Uganda," 2005, http://www.udl.es/usuaris/m0163949/uganda.htm. See also Goretti Kyomuhendo, "FEMRITE and the Politics of Literature in Uganda," *Feminist Africa,* no. 2, 2003, http://www.feministafrica.org/fa%202/2level.html.

6. Dan Reboussin, "Kimenye, Africana Collection," George A. Smathers Libraries, University of Florida, 1995–2004, http://web.uflib.ufl.edu/cm/africana/kimenye.htm, see also "Contemporary Africa Database: Barbara Kimenye—Ugandan Children's Writer and Short-story Writer," Africa Center, London, 2001–2004, http://people.africadatabase.org/en/person/15933.html.

7. African Books Collective. African Literature, http://www.africanbookscollective.com./

8. Michigan State University Press, "Select Book by Author," http://msupress.msu.edu/authorIndex.php.

9. G. A. Heron, introduction to the combined volume of Okot P'Bitek's *Song of Lawino & Song of Ocol* (London: Heinemann, 1984), 1–33, and "Contemporary Africa Database: Okot p'Bitek—Ugandan Poet, Novelist, and Social Anthropologist," Africa Center, London, 2002–2004, http://people.africadatabase.org/en/person/3359.html.

10. Sam Raditlhalo, "Interview: Taban Lo Liyong," 1997, http://www.ru.ac.za/institutes/isea/NewCoin/docs/97/i97june.htm.

11. "About Us," *New Vision,* 2004, http://www.newvision.co.ug/visioncorporate/.

12. Evelyn Kiapi Matsamura, "Red Pepper Sparks Controversy in Uganda," *Mail & Guardian,* October 11, 2005, http://www.mg.co.za/articlePage.aspx?articleid = 253391&area = /insight/insight_africa/.

13. Committee to Protect Journalists, "Attacks on the Press in 2002: Uganda," 2002, http://www.cpj.org/attacks02/africa02/uganda.html.

14. Ruth Ojiambo Ochieng, "Development of Community Media in Uganda" (paper presented at the Regional Seminar on the Promotion of Community Media in Africa, Kampala, Uganda, June 8, 1999), 8, http://www.isis.or.ug/downloads/1999_community.pdf.

15. World Bank, *World Development Report 1998/99: Knowledge for Development* (New York: Oxford University Press, 1999), 227.

16. Ochieng, "Development of Community Media in Uganda," 4.

17. Central Intelligence Agency, "Uganda," *The World Factbook,* 2004, http://www.cia.gov/cia/publications/factbook/geos/ug.html#Comm.

18. Monseignor Joseph Obunga (Secretary General, Uganda Episcopal Conference), interview by John L. Allen, Jr., *National Catholic Reporter,* 17 September 2004, http://ncronline.org/mainpage/specialdocuments/obunga.htm.

19. Ibid. See also Committee to Protect Journalists, "Attacks on the Press 2001: Africa 2001: Uganda," http://www.cpj.org/attacks01/africa01/uganda.html.

20. TVRadioWorld, "Uganda—Radio/TV Stations on the Internet," 2004, http://www.tvradioworld.com/region3/uga/Radio_TV_On_Internet.asp.

21. World Bank, *World Development Report 1998/99,* (1999), 227. See also Uganda Bureau of Statistics, "2002 Uganda Population and Housing Census," 2005, http://www.ubas.org.

22. World Bank, *World Bank Development Report 1998/99,* 195, 227.

23. Uganda Media Women Association, "101.7 Mama FM—Community Radio," 2001, http://interconnection.org/umwa/community_radio.html.

24. Ochieng, "Development of Community Media in Uganda," 8–9.

25. Uganda Media Women Association, "101.7 Mama FM—Community Radio."

26. Ntare Guma Mbaho Mwine, poster for the documentary film *Beware of Time,* http://www.bewareoftime.com/film.htm.

27. Deutsche Welle, "Cape to Cairo—11," December 16, 2003, http://www.dw-world.de/english/0,3367,3083_A_1062403,00.html. See also Amakula Kampala International Film Festival, "Story Lines," 2005, http://www.amakula.com/index.html.

Art and Architecture/Housing

1. Philip K. Kwesiga, "Art and Design in Makerere: Education through the Visual Imagery" (paper presented at ADEEA [Art, Design, Education Exchange with

Africa] seminar June 14–15, 2001, University of Art and Design, Helsinki, Finland), 11, http://arted.uiah.fi/adeea/adeea1.pdf.

2. "Lilian Nabulime," *The Art Room,* 2001, http://www.theartroom-sf.com/lilian.htm.

3. Philip K. Kwesiga, Catherine Gombe, and Kakuba Kapia, "Ugandan Indicators to Finnish Collaborators" (paper presented at ADEEA [Art, Design, Education Exchange with Africa] seminar June 14–15, 2001, University of Art and Design, Helsinki, Finland), 7, http://arted.uiah.fi/adeea/adeea1.pdf.

4. "Ugandan Art," *Guruve,* 2004, http://www.guruve.com/discover_/uganda.htm.

5. Kwesiga, "Art and Design in Makerere," 9.

6. "Ugandan Art," *Guruve.*

7. Ibid; Kwesiga, "Art and Design in Makerere," 10.

8. Sidney Littlefield Kasfir, *Contemporary African Art* (London: Thames & Hudson, 1999), 64–66.

9. Kwesiga, Gombe, and Kapia, "Ugandan Indicators."

10. Kwesiga, "Art and Design in Makerere"; "Ugandan Art," *Guruve;* Kasfir, *Contemporary African Art,* 151.

11. Kasfir, *Contemporary African Art,* 151.

12. Kwesiga, "Art and Design in Makerere," 9–10.

13. Catherine Gombe, "Indigenous Pottery as Economic Empowerment in Uganda," *Journal of Art and Design Education,* 21, no. 1 (February 2002): 44–51.

14. Kasfir, *Contemporary African Art,* 16.

15. Ibid., 130–32.

16. Kwesiga, "Art and Design in Makerere," 10; Kasfir, *Contemporary African Art,* 64–66, 130.

17. Kwesiga, "Art and Design in Makerere," 11.

18. Kasfir, *Contemporary African Art,* 151.

19. Fine Arts Center for East Africa, "George Kyeyune," 2004, http://www.theartroom-sf.com/gkyeyune.htm.

20. "Lilian Nabulime," *The Art Room.*

21. Ibid.

22. Fine Arts Center for East Africa, "Bruno Sserunkuuma," 2001, http://www.theartroom-sf.com/bruno.htm.

23. Kasfir, *Contemporary African Art,* 142–45.

24. Ibid., 66–67.

25. Fine Arts Center for East Africa, "Nuwa Nnyanzi," 2001, http://www.theartroom-sf.com/nuwannyanzi.htm.

26. Kwesiga, "Art and Design in Makerere," 11.

27. Fine Arts Center for East Africa, "Pilkington Ssengendo," 2001, http://www.theartroom-sf.com/ssengendo.htm.

28. Ibid.

29. Gombe, "Indigenous Pottery," 45–48.

30. Tom Sanya, "Ugandan Architecture through the Years," 2005, http://www.ugpulse.com/articles/daily/homepage.asp?ID=114.

31. Mark R. O. Olweny and Jacqueline Wadulo, "Searching for Identity: Architecture and Urbanism in Uganda" (paper presented at the Architecture and Identity Conference, Berlin, Germany, December 6–9, 2004), http://www.architecture-identity.de/conference_abstracts_olwenywadulo.htm.

32. Rita M. Byrnes, "The Society and Its Environment," in *Uganda: A Country Study,* ed. Rita M. Byrnes (Washington, D.C.: Library of Congress, 1992).

33. John R. Knight, William E. Herrin, and Arsene M. Balihuta, "Housing Prices and Maturing Real Estate Markets: Evidence from Uganda," *Journal of Real Estate Finance and Economics* 28, no. 1 (2004): 5–18.

34. Jacqueline Woodfork, "Cities and Architecture," in *African Cultures and Societies before 1885,* vol. 2, ed. Toyin Falola (Durham, N.C.: Carolina Academic Press, 2000).

35. Byrnes, "Society and Its Environment."

36. Knight, Herrin, and Balihuta, "Housing Prices."

37. Woodfork, "Cities and Architecture."

38. Byrnes, "Society and Its Environment."

39. Heike Berrend, *Alice Lakwena and the Holy Spirits: War in Northern Uganda, 1985–1997* (Athens: Ohio University Press, 1999), 16–17.

40. Uganda Bureau of Statistics, "2002 Population and Housing Census," 2005, http://www.ubos.org/.

41. "Facts about Kampala City," *Experience Africa,* 2004, http://www.experienceafrica.co.uk/H4.htm. See also V. P. Kirega-Gava, "Kampala—The Green City in the Sun," 2000, http://www.kampala1.com/kampala.html.

42. Paula Jean Davis, "On the Sexuality of 'Town Women' in Kampala," *Africa Today* 47, no. 3 (November 1, 2000): 29–60, 54.

43. Samuel Vivian Matagi, "Some Issues of Environmental Concern in Kampala, the Capital City of Uganda," *Environmental Monitoring and Assessment* 77, no. 2 (July 2002): 121–38.

44. Christie Gombay, "Eating and Meeting in Owino: Market Vendors, City Government, and the World Bank in Kampala, Uganda," in *Street-level Democracy: Political Settings at the Margins of Global Power,* ed. Jonathan Baker (Toronto: Between the Lines, 1999).

45. Daniel G. Maxwell, "Highest and Best Use? Access to Urban Land for Semi-Subsistence Food Production," *Land Use Policy* 13, no. 3 (June 1996): 181–95.

46. S. W. Lindsay, T. G. Egwang, F. Kabuye, T. Mutambo and G. K. Matwale, *Community-based Environmental Management Program for Malaria Control in Kampala and Jinja, Uganda,* Activity Report No. 140, Sponsored by the Office of Health, Infectious Diseases and Nutrition, Bureau for Global Health, U.S. Agency for International Development, Washington, D.C., September 2004.

47. Matagi, "Some Issues of Environmental Concern." See also F. B. Nsubuga, F. Kansiime, and J. Okot-Okumu, "Pollution of Protected Springs in Relation to High and Low Density Settlements in Kampala—Uganda," *Physics and Chemistry of the Earth* 29, no. 15–18 (2004): 1153–59.

48. Lindsay et al., *Community-based Environmental Management Program.*

49. Civil Aviation Authority, "History of Entebbe International Airport," 2001–2003, http://www.caa.co.ug/history.php.

50. "African Tropical Safaris, 2004: Entebbe—Gateway to Uganda," 2004, http://atskenya.com/ugtowns.asp?id=11&tow=Entebbe.

51. *Amicall,* July 14, 2003, http://www.amicaall.org/publications/profiles/jinja.pdf.

52. Lindsay et al., *Community-based Environmental Management Program.*

CUISINE AND TRADITIONAL DRESS

1. *Spectrum Guide to Uganda* (Nairobi, Kenya: Camerapix Publishers, 2004), 278–79.

2. G. J. Scott, J. Otieno, S. B. Ferris, A. K. Muganga, and L. Maldonado, "Sweetpotato in Ugandan Food Systems: Enhancing Food Security and Alleviating Poverty," CIP Program Report, 1997–98, http://www.cipotato.org/market/PgmRprts/pr97–98/40uganda.pdf. See also B. Odongo, R.O.M. Mwanga, C. Owori, C. Niringiye, F. Opio, P. Ewell, Berga Lemaga, G. Agwaro, L. Serunjogi, E. Abidin, J. Kikafunda, and R. Mayanja, "Development and Promotion of Orange-fleshed Sweetpotato to Reduce Vitamin A Deficiency in Uganda," 2002, http://www.cipotato.org/vitaa/Proceedings/VITAA-paper-Uganda-FINAL%20BY%20CDYER-8Apr2002.pdf.

3. C. T. Kirema-Mukasa and J. E. Reynolds, "Marketing and Consumption of Fish in Uganda," Food and Agriculture Organization of the United Nations, 1991, http://www.fao.org/documents/show_cdr.asp?url_file = /docrep/006/AD146E/AD146E01.htm.

4. Richard Nzita and Mbaga-Niwampa, *Peoples and Cultures of Uganda* (Kampala: Fountain Publishers, 1997).

5. Barry McWilliams, "Shopping in Uganda," 2002, http://www.eldrbarry.net/ug/ugshop.htm.

6. Charles Onyango-Obbo, "Janet [Museveni], [Sylvia] Nagginda, Miria [Obote]; Of Beauty, Fashion, Money," *Daily Monitor,* 3 November 1999, http://www.africanews.com/article335.html.

7. McWilliams, "Shopping in Uganda."

GENDER ROLES, MARRIAGE, AND FAMILY

1. Mukasa E. Ssemakula, "The Clans of Buganda," http://www.buganda.com/ebika.htm.

2. Richard Nzita and Mbaga-Niwampa, *Peoples and Cultures of Uganda* (Kampala: Fountain Publishers, 1997).

3. Ibid.

4. Evelyn Kiapi Matsamura, "Muslims Demand Changes in Bill on Women's Rights," Inter Press Service, April 7, 2005, http://www.ipsnews.net/interna.asp?idnews=28204.

5. Catherine Bond, "Uganda's Parliament to Re-examine Polygamy," 5 April 1998, http://www-cgi.cnn.com/WORLD/africa/9804/05/uganda.polygamy/.

6. Y. H. "Muslim Marriage," http://www.ngfl.ac.uk/re/muslimmarriage.html. See also B. R. Verma, *Muslim Marriage and Dissolution* (Allahabad: Law Book Co., 1971), 13–17.

7. Matsamura, "Muslims Demand Changes." See also Sue Alford, Nicole Cheetham, and Debra Hauser, "Science and Success in Developing Countries: Holistic Programs That Work to Prevent Teen Pregnancy, HIV and Sexually Transmitted Infections," *Advocates for Youth,* April 2005, http://www.advocatesforyouth.org/publications/sciencesuccess_developing.pdf.

8. Kituo Cha Katiba, "The Domestic Relations Bill 2003," East African Center for Constitutional Development, Faculty of Law, Makerere University, 2005, http://www.kituochakatiba.co.ug/dorebil.htm.

9. Ibid.

10. Vanessa von Struensee, "The Domestic Relations Bill in Uganda: Potentially Addressing Polygamy, Bride Price, Cohabitation, Marital Rape, Widow Inheritance and Female Genital Mutilation," July 2004, http://ssrn.com/abstract = 623501.

11. Omutaka Lawrence Matovu, "Ganda Marriage," GandaAncestry.com, http://www.gandaancestry.com/general/library.php.

12. Nzita and Mbaga-Niwampa, *Peoples and Cultures of Uganda.*

13. Justine Nannyonjo, "Conflicts, Poverty and Human Development in Northern Uganda," United Nations University, Research Paper No. 2005/47, August 2005, http://www.wider.unu.edu/publications/rps/rps2005/rp2005–47.pdf.

14. Augustus Nuwagaba, "Situation Analysis of Women in the Ugandan Political Economy," *Eastern Africa Social Science Research Review* 17, no. 1 (January 2001): 15–30, http://www.ossrea.net/eassrr/jan01/augustus.htm.

15. Advocates for Youth, "Sexual Abuse and Violence in Sub-Saharan Africa," 2001, http://www.advocatesforyouth.org/publications/factsheet/fssxabus.htm.

16. Stephen O. Murray, "Homosexuality in 'Traditional' Sub-Saharan Africa and Contemporary South Africa," February 14, 2005, http://semgai.free.fr/doc_et_pdf/africa_A4.pdf. See also Public Radio Exchange (PRX), "Homosexuality in Uganda," April 7, 2004, http://www.prx.org/pieces/1051; Dan Elwana, "Church Backs Museveni against Homosexuality," *Daily Nation,* November 14, 1999, http://www.nationmedia.com/; and Human Rights Watch, "Uganda: Same Sex Ban Deepens Repression," July 12, 2005, http://hrw.org/english/docs/2005/07/12/uganda11307.htm.

SOCIAL CUSTOMS AND LIFESTYLE

1. "Uganda," Food for the Hungry, 2003–2005, http://www.fh.org/uploads/images/1707/Uganda_2005.doc.

2. Richard Nzita and Mbaga-Niwampa, *Peoples and Cultures of Uganda* (Kampala: Fountain Publishers, 1997).

3. "Uganda," Food for the Hungry.

4. Ibid.

5. Augustus Nuwagaba, "Situation Analysis of Women in the Ugandan Political Economy," *Eastern Africa Social Science Research Review* 17, no. 1 (2001): 15–30, http://www.ossrea.net/eassrr/jan01/augustus.htm.

6. A.B.K. Kasozi, "Higher Education in Uganda: Problems of Cost and Access for Women and Other Disadvantaged Groups" (paper presented at the Women's Worlds 2002 Congress, Makerere University, Kampala, July 21–26, 2002), http://www.makerere.ac.ug/womenstudies/full%20papers/kasozi.htm.

7. "Uganda: The Country and the People—Bantu," Face Music, 2005, http://www.music.ch/face/inform/poeple_uganda.html.

8. Nzita and Mbaga-Niwampa, *Peoples and Cultures of Uganda.*

9. Aili Mali Tripp, "Women Emerging: A Tribute to Uganda Women's Movement," 2002, http://theartroom-sf.com/trippessay.htm.

10. Charlotte Metcalf, "Changing Ways in Uganda," *People & the Planet,* 2000, http://www.peopleandplanet.net/pdoc.php?id=310.

11. Nzita and Mbaga-Niwampa, *Peoples and Cultures of Uganda.*

12. Nathan Etengu, "Museveni Threatens to Ban Circumcision," *New Vision,* Kampala, Uganda, October 14, 2003, http://www.cirp.org/news/newvision10–14–03/.

13. Ronald H. Gray, Maria J. Wawer, Noah Kiwanuka, David Serwadda, Nelson K Sewankamboe, and Fred Wabwire, "Male Circumcision and HIV Acquisition and Transmission: Rakai, Uganda," *AIDS* 16, no. 5 (March 29, 2002): 809–10.

14. Nzita and Mbaga-Niwampa, *Peoples and Cultures of Uganda.*

15. MyUganda, "Monarchies—Ankole Kingdom," 1996–2006, http://myuganda.co.ug/monarchies/ankole.php.

16. Allen Mutono, "The Boy King," Safarimate, 1996–2005, http://www.safariweb.com/safarimate/boyking.htm.

17. "Amakula Kampala International Film Festival," Story Lines, 2005, http://www.amakula.com/index.html.

18. "Cultural Festival in Uganda," *Djembe,* no. 29 (July 1999), http://www.djembe.dk/no/29/15kn.html.

19. "Sports," myUganda, 2005, http://www.myuganda.co.ug/sports/index.php.

20. Evelyn Kiapi Matsamura, "The Home of English Football's Most Ardent Fans? Uganda," Inter Press Service, September 28, 2005, http://www.ipsnews.net/africa/nota.asp?idnews=30457.

21. Gertrude Kamuze, "Nation's Cup: Exodus of Stars Rocks Ugandan Soccer," *East African,* February 3, 2003, http://www.nationmedia.com/.

22. Mark Ssali, "Uganda's Hall of Fame: I Hear You Sekitto," *Daily Monitor,* 14 June 2005, http://www.monitor.co.ug/sports/spt06145.php. See also Simwogerere Kyazze, "Bike Crash: It Doesn't Pay to Be Cheapskate," October 30, 2005, http://www.nationmedia.com/.

23. "Amakula Kampala International Film Festival," Story Lines.

24. "Miss Uganda: Introduction," Miss Uganda Organization, 2005, http://www.missuganda.co.ug/press.php.

25. "Uganda Plans Beauty Pageant for Students with HIV," *New Vision,* May 31, 2005, http://www.aegis.com/news/nv/2005/NV050545.html.

26. Jack Boulware, "Pageants and Prostitution: Officials in Uganda Threaten to Ban Beauty Contests, Saying They Lead Contestants Astray," August 9, 2000, http://archive.salon.com/sex/world/2000/08/09/uganda/.

27. "Uganda Threatens to Ban Beauty Contests," *Namibian,* August 7, 2000, http://www.namibian.com.na/Netstories/2000/August/Africa/0097024EBB.html.

28. "Entertainment News," myUganda, 2005, http://www.myuganda.co.ug/sports/index.php.

29. Nzita and Mbaga-Niwampa, *Peoples and Cultures of Uganda.*

30. Joachim Buwembo, *How to Be a Ugandan* (Kampala: Fountain Publishers, 2002).

31. Adam Seftel, *Uganda: The Blood Stained Pearl of Africa: And Its Struggle for Peace* (Lanseria, South Africa: Bailey's African Photo Archives, 1994).

32. Henry Kyemba, *A State of Blood: The Inside Story of Idi Amin* (New York: Ace Books, 1977).

33. Aili Mali Tripp, *Women & Politics in Uganda* (Madison: University of Wisconsin Press, 2000), 57.

Music, Dance, and Drama

1. Ronnie Graham, *The World of African Music,* vol. 2 of *Stern's Guide to Contemporary African Music* (Chicago: Research Associates, 1992).

2. Henry Kyemba, *A State of Blood: The Inside Story of Idi Amin* (New York: Ace Books, 1977, 147).

3. "Clean Sweeps at PAM Awards," myUganda, 2004, http://www.myuganda.co.ug/entertain/details.php?unique=63.

4. Gregory Barz, *Music in East Africa: Experiencing Music, Expressing Culture* (New York: Oxford University Press, 2004), 76.

5. Ibid., 61–62, 102–6.

6. Uganda's traditional monarchies no longer wage war against their neighbors.

7. Joel Sembujo, "Sembujo Joel: Folklore from Uganda," http://bunjoe.8m.net/.

8. Peter Cooke, "Republic of Uganda," in *The New Grove Dictionary of Music and Musicians,* vol. 26, ed. Stanley Sadie (London: Macmillan, 2001).

9. MusicUganda, "Nanziga SDA Primary School Kids Moves the Nation," May 21, 2005, http://www.musicuganda.com/reviews/nanziga.htm.

10. Saint CA, "Zeroing in on Ndere Troupe," 2002–2004, http://www.musicuganda.com/groups/ndieretroupe.htm.

11. Uganda National Theatre and Cultural Centre, Beat That Drum Concert by Alliance Française, November 19, 2005, http://www.culturalcentre.or.ug/.

12. Graham, *World of African Music.*

13. Sylvia Nannyonga-Tamusuza, "Gender, Ethnicity and Politics in Kadongo-Kamu Music of Uganda: Analyzing the Song Kayanda," in *Playing with Identities in Contemporary Music in Africa,* ed. Mai Palmberg and Annemette Kirkegaard (Uppsala,

Finland: Nordiska Afrikainstitutet, in cooperation with the Sibelius Museum/ Department of Musicology, Abo Akademi University, 2002).

14. "Listen to Uganda Music," Music Uganda Ltd, 2002–2004, http://www. musicuganda.com/songs/index.htm.

15. Watoto Child Care Ministries, "The Choir," 2005, http://www.watoto.com. Also Kim Caruso, Country Director/International Tour Coordinator, Watoto Child Care Ministries United States, e-mail message to author, 16 August 2005.

16. Barz, *Music in East Africa,* 101–3. See also "Traditional African Music for Classical Musicians," Internationalopus, 2001, http://www.internationalopus.com/ Justinian_Tamasuza/.

17. "Traditional African Music for Classical Musicians," Internationalopus.

18. Eve Bender, "Psychiatrist Blends Music, Poetry to Change Society," *Psychiatric News* 40, no. 13 (July 1, 2005): 18, http://pn.psychiatryonline.org/cgi/content/ full/40/13/18.

19. "Clean Sweeps at PAM Awards," myUganda.

20. Ibid.

21. Nannyonga-Tamusuza, "Gender, Ethnicity and Politics."

22. Ibid.

23. Charles Otieno, "Chameleone's Royal Lifestyle," *Pulse, East African Standard,* 24 June 2005, http://www.eastandard.net/.

24. "Clean Sweeps at PAM Awards," myUganda.

25. "Buganda Anthem (Full Version)," GandaAncestry.com, 2005, http://www. gandaancestry.com/general/library.php.

26. Nannyonga-Tamusuza, "Gender, Ethnicity and Politics."

27. Examples include *line* hunting in the December dry season; *dwar arum* or group dry season hunting; *dwar obwo* or group hunting with nets, spears, and dogs; *kirange,* in which the wildlife was driven into slightly flooded rivers and speared during the onset of the rainy season; and *okia* or single hunter/trapper hunting during the peak of the rainy season. The size and sophistication of the traps used in *okia* hunting varied widely, depending on whether the hunter/trapper sought to catch a bird, small game, or an elephant. Some of the most common traps were *okol* (a noose attached to a log of wood), *tekke* (a circular foot trap), *bur* (a pit in the animal's path), and *tong twok* (the tree-suspended falling spear used to trap elephants).

28. Susan Battye, Mercy Mirembe Ntangaare, and Ian Allan, *Dance and Drama in Uganda: The Pearl of Africa,* 2005, e-book, http://www.hushvideos.com/SB-Afr. shtml.

29. Uganda National Theatre & Cultural Centre, "History and Mission of Uganda National Theatre & Cultural Centre," 2005, http://www.culturalcentre. or.ug/. See also Emmanuel Ssejjengo, "Uganda's Story at National Theatre" (commentary on *The Ebonies* play), *New Vision,* January 22, 2005, http://www.newvision. co.ug/.

30. Personal interviews with Mr. and Mrs. Emmanuel Twesigye, Delaware, Ohio, November 17, 2005. See also "Events," Uganda National Theatre and Cultural Centre, 2004. http://www.culturalcentre.or.ug/default.aspx

31. "Kampala Amateur Dramatics Society," 2005, http://kadsonline.org/.

32. Kalungi Kabuye, "Brodie: A Teacher with a Mission," *New Vision,* April 2, 2004, http://newvision.co.ug/D/9/38/350812. See also Charles Onyango-Obbo, "A Nation with Long Funerals and Plays Is Simply Doomed," *Daily Monitor,* May 22, 2002, http://www.africanews.com/article609.html.

33. Ssejjengo, "Uganda's Story at National Theatre."

34. Evelyn Kiapi Matsamura, "Inspired by Women (A Story about Ugandan Playwright Charles Mulekwa)," August 23, 2003, http://ipsnews.net/interna. asp?idnews=19719.

35. Ibid.

36. Abinet Getachew, "Art and Culture Are Sometimes Considered as Luxury Activities," Dramatool, November 1, 2004, http://www.dramatool.org/search/site/news/97. See also Onyango-Obbo, "A Nation with Long Funerals."

37. Richard Mziray, "Challenges Faces East African Artists," Dramatool, October 11, 2004, http://www.dramatool.org/search/site/news/85/.

38. Jeevan Vasagar, "Don't Mention the V-word: Uganda Bans Monologues," *Observer,* February 20, 2005, http://www.guardian.co.uk.

39. Getachew, "Art and Culture Are Sometimes Considered as Luxury Activities."

Bibliographic Essay

INTRODUCTION

For a general background on Uganda, see Rita M. Byrnes, ed., *Uganda: A Country Study* (Washington, D.C.: Library of Congress 1992); *Spectrum Guide to Uganda* (Nairobi, Kenya: Camerapix Publishers, 2004); David Gwyn, *Idi Amin: Death-Light of Africa* (Boston: Little, Brown, 1977); Holger Bernt Hansen and Michael Twaddle, eds., *Uganda Now: Between Decay and Development* (London: James Currey, 1995); Holger Bernt Hansen and Michael Twaddle, eds., *Developing Uganda* (London: James Currey, 1998); Henry Kyemba, *A State of Blood: The Inside Story of Idi Amin* (New York: Ace Books, 1977); Thomas Melady and Margaret Melady, *Idi Amin Dada: Hitler in Africa* (Kansas City, Kans.: Sheed Andrews and McMeel, 1977); Amii Omara-Otunnu, *Politics and the Military in Uganda, 1890–1985* (New York: St. Martin's Press, 1987); Ritva Reinikka and Paul Collier, eds., *Uganda's Recovery: The Role of Farms, Firms, and Government* (Kampala: Fountain Publishers, 2001); Adam Seftel, ed., *Uganda: The Blood Stained Pearl of Africa and Its Struggle for Peace* (Lanseria, South Africa: A Bailey's African Photo Archives, 1994); Odo Willscher and Wilhelm Eigener, *Uganda: The Cradle of the Nile* (Hamburg: H. Carly, 1964); Richard Nzita and Mbaga-Niwampa, *Peoples and Cultures of Uganda* (Kampala: Fountain Publishers, 1997); and Rocha Chimera, *Kiswahili: Past, Present and Future Horizons* (Nairobi, Kenya: Nairobi University Press, 1998).

RELIGION AND WORLDVIEW

See Elizabeth Isichei, *A History of Christianity in Africa: From Antiquity to the Present* (Grand Rapids, Mich.: Eerdmans, 1995); John S. Mbiti, *African Religions and Philosophy* (Garden City, N.Y.: Anchor Books, 1970); John S. Mbiti, *Introduction to African Religion* (London: Heinemann Educational, 1975); Samuel Oluoch Imbo, *An Introduction to African Philosophy* (Lanham, Md.: Rowman and Littlefield, 1998); Aylward Shorter, *East African Societies* (Boston: Routledge & Kegan Paul, 1974); A. F. Mockler-Ferryman, "Christianity in Uganda," *Journal of the Royal African Society* 2, no. 7 (April 1903): 276–91; Ali A. Mazrui, "Religious Strangers in Uganda: From Emin Pasha to Amin Dada," *African Affairs* 76, no. 302 (January 1977): 21–38; Dan Mudoola, "Religion and Politics in Uganda: The Case of Busoga, 1900–1962," *African Affairs* 77, no. 306 (January 1978): 22–35; U.S. State Department, "International Religious Freedom Report 2003," http://www.state.gov/g/drl/rls/irf/2003/23759.htm; Uganda Bureau of Statistics, "2002 Population and Housing Census," 2003, http://www.ubos.org; *Spectrum Guide to Uganda* (Nairobi, Kenya: Camerapix Publishers, 2004); Lillian Ashcraft-Eason and L. Djisovi Ikukomi Eason, "Indigenous Religions and Philosophies," in *Contemporary Africa,* vol. 5, ed. Toyin Falola (Durham, N.C.: Carolina Academic Press, 2003), 553–83.

LITERATURE, FILM, AND MEDIA

Authoritative sources on the Uganda's literature and media are few, but the following are useful sources: African Books Collective, "African Literature,"http://www.african bookscollective.com; Africa Centre, "Contemporary Africa Database," 2001–2004, http://people.africadatabase.org/en/person/15933.html. Some of Uganda's popular literature includes Mary Abago, *Sour Honey* (Kampala: Fountain Publishers, 1999); Aloysius Aloka, *Iteo Alive* (Kampala: Fountain Publishers, 2000); Regina Amollo, *A Season of Mirth* (Kampala: Femrite Publications, 1999); Henry Barlow, *Building the Nation and Other Poems* (Kampala: Fountain Publishers, 2000); Violet Barungi, *Cassandra* (Kampala: Femrite Publications, 1999); Violet Barungi, ed. *Words from a Granary: An Anthology of Short Stories by Ugandan Women Writers* (Kampala: Femrite Publications, 2001); Okot Benge and Alex Bangirana, eds., *Uganda Poetry Anthology 2000* (Kampala: Fountain Publishers, 2000); Austin Lwanga Bukenya, *Notes on East African Poetry* (Nairobi, Kenya: East African Educational Publishers, 1978); Joachim Buwembo, *How to Be a Ugandan* (Kampala: Fountain Publishers, 2002); Victor Byabamazima, *Shadows of Time* (Kampala: Fountain Publishers, 1999); Jane Kaberuka, *Silent Patience* (Kampala: Femrite Publications, 1999); J. K. Kagimu, *Tired!* (Kampala: Kamenyero Publishing, 1995); Julius Kaggwa, *From Juliet to Julius: In Search of My True Gender Identity* (Kampala: Fountain Publishers, 1997); Hope Keshubi, *Going Solo* (Kampala: Fountain Publishers, 2000); Susan N. Kiguli, *The African Saga* (Kampala: Femrite Publications, 1998); Rosemary Kyarimpa, *Echoes of Her Voice* (Kampala: MK Publishers, 1999); Goretti Kyomuhendo, *The First Daughter* (Kampala: Fountain Publishers, 1996); Mercy Mirembe Ntangaare, *Lady, Will You Marry Me* (Kampala: MPK Graphics, 2002); Taban lo Liyong, *Fixions & Other Stories* (London: Heinemann Educational, 1969); Taban lo Liyong, *Frantz Fanon's Uneven Ribs* (London: Heinemann Educational, 1971); Taban lo Liyong, *Another Nigger Dead* (London: Heinemann Educational, 1972); Taban lo Liyong, *The Cows of Shambat: Sudanese Poems* (Harare, Zimbabwe: Zimbabwe Publishing, 1992); Taban Lo Liyong, *Words That Melt a Mountain* (Nairobi, Kenya: East African Educational Publishers, 1996); Taban Lo Liyong, *Carrying Knowledge up a Palm Tree: Poetry* (Trenton, N.J.: Africa World Press, 1997); Julius Ocwinyo, *Fate of the Banished* (Kampala: Fountain Publishers, 1997); Mary Karooro Okurut and Violet Barungi, *A Woman's Voice: An Anthology of Short Stories by Ugandan Women* (Kampala: Femrite Publications, 1998); Mary Karooro Okurut, *Child of a Delegate* (Kampala: Monitor Publications, 1997); Mary Karooro Okurut, *The Curse of the Sacred Cow* (Kampala: Fountain Publishers, 1994); Mary Karooro Okurut, *Milking a Lioness & Other Stories* (Kampala: Monitor Publications, 1999); Christine Oryema-Lalobo, *No Hearts at Home* (Kampala: Femrite Publications, 1999); Okot p'Bitek, *White Teeth* (Kampala: East African Educational Publishers, 1989); David Rubadiri, ed., *Growing Up with Poetry: An Anthology for Secondary Schools* (Oxford, U.K.: Heinemann International Literature and Textbooks, 1989); Lilian Tindyebwa, *Recipe for Disaster* (Kampala: Fountain Publishers, 1995); Ugandan Women's Writers Association, ed., *Uganda Creative Writers Directory* (Oxford, U.K.: African Writers Collective, 2000); Ayeta Anne Wangusa, *Memoirs of a Mother* (Kamapala: Femrite Publications, 1998); Timothy Wangusa, *A Pattern of Dust: Selected Poems 1965–1990* (Kampala: Fountain Publishers, 2000); and Timothy Wangusa, *Upon This Mountain* (Oxford, U.K.: Heinemann Educational Publishers, 1989).

For media, refer to *Spectrum Guide to Uganda* (Nairobi, Kenya: Camerapix Publishers, 1997); World Bank, *World Development Report 1998/99: Knowledge for Development* (New York: Oxford University Press, 1999); Ruth Ojiambo Ochieng, "Development of Community Media in Uganda" (paper presented at the Regional Seminar on the Promotion of Community Media in Africa, Kampala, Uganda, June 8, 1999), http://www.isis.or.ug; Uganda Media Women Association, "101.7 MAMA FM—Community Radio," 2001, http://interconnection.org/umwa/community_radio.html; TVRadioWorld, "Uganda—Radio/TV Stations on the Internet," 2004, http://www.tvradioworld.com.

ART AND ARCHITECTURE/HOUSING

For Ugandan art, see Sidney Littlefield Kasfir, *Contemporary African Art* (London: Thames & Hudson, 1999); Catherine Gombe, "Indigenous Pottery as Economic Empowerment in Uganda," *Journal of Art and Design Education,* 21, no. 1 (February 2002): 44–51.

For architecture and housing, refer to Tom Sanya, "Ugandan Architecture through the Years," 2005, http://www.ugpulse.com; Mark R. O. Olweny and Jacqueline Wadulo, "Searching for Identity: Architecture and Urbanism in Uganda" (paper presented at Architecture and Identity Conference, Berlin, Germany, December 6–9, 2004), http://www.architecture-identity.de/conference_abstracts_olwenywadulo.htm; Rita M. Byrnes (1992).

Spectrum Guide to Uganda (Nairobi, Kenya: Camerapix Publishers, 1997); Jacqueline Woodfork, "Cities and Architecture," in *African Cultures and Societies before*

1885, vol. 2, ed. Toyin Falola (Durham, N.C.: Carolina Academic Press, 2000); John R. Knight, William E. Herrin, and Arsene M. Balihuta, "Housing Prices and Maturing Real Estate Markets: Evidence from Uganda," *Journal of Real Estate Finance and Economics* 28, no. 1 (2004): 5–18; Samuel Vivian Matagi, "Some Issues of Environmental Concern in Kampala, the Capital City of Uganda," *Environmental Monitoring and Assessment* 77, no. 2 (July 2002): 121–38; Daniel G. Maxwell, "Highest and Best Use? Access to Urban Land for Semi-Subsistence Food Production," *Land Use Policy* 13, no. 3 (June 1996): 181–95.

CUISINE AND TRADITIONAL DRESS

Spectrum Guide to Uganda (Nairobi, Kenya: Camerapix Publishers, 2004); G. J. Scott, J. Otieno, S. B. Ferris, A. K. Muganga, L. Maldonado, "Sweetpotato in Ugandan Food Systems: Enhancing Food Security and Alleviating Poverty," CIP Program Report, 1997–98, http://www.cipotato.org; B. Odongo, R.O.M. Mwanga, C. Owori, C. Niringiye, F. Opio, P. Ewell, Berga Lemaga, G. Agwaro, L. Serunjogi, E. Abidin, J. Kikafunda, and R. Mayanja, "Development and Promotion of Orange-fleshed Sweetpotato to Reduce Vitamin A Deficiency in Uganda," 2002, http://www.cipotato.org; C. T. Kirema-Mukasa and J. E. Reynolds, "Marketing and Consumption of Fish in Uganda," Food and Agriculture Organization of the United Nations, 1991, http://www.fao.org; Richard Nzita and Mbaga-Niwampa, *Peoples and Cultures of Uganda* (Kampala: Fountain Publishers, 1997); Barry McWilliams, "Shopping in Uganda," 2002, http://www.eldrbarry.net; Charles Onyango-Obbo, (1999), "Janet [Museveni], [Sylvia] Nagginda, Miria [Obote] Of Beauty, Fashion, Money," *Daily Monitor,* 3 November 1999, http://www.newvision.co.ug/.

GENDER ROLES, MARRIAGE, AND FAMILY

The best sources on this are Richard Nzita and Mbaga-Niwampa, *Peoples and Cultures of Uganda* (Kampala: Fountain Publishers, 1997) and Aili Mali Tripp, *Women & Politics in Uganda* (Madison: University of Wisconsin Press, 2000). Supplementary materials include Evelyn Kiapi Matsamura, "Muslims Demand Changes in Bill on Women's Rights," Inter Press Service, April 7, 2005, http://www.ipsnews.net; Catherine Bond, "Uganda's Parliament to Re-examine Polygamy," April 5, 1998, http://www-cgi.cnn.com/WORLD/africa/9804/05/uganda.polygamy/; Vanessa von Struensee, "The Domestic Relations Bill in Uganda: Potentially Addressing Polygamy, Bride Price, Cohabitation, Marital Rape, Widow Inheritance and Female Genital Mutilation," July 2004, http://ssrn.com/abstract=623501; Justine Nannyonjo, "Conflicts, Poverty and Human Development in Northern Uganda," United Nations University, Research Paper No. 2005/47, August 2005, http://www.wider.unu.edu/publications/; Augustus Nuwagaba, "Situation Analysis of Women in the Ugandan Political Economy," *Eastern Africa Social Science Research Review* 17, no. 1 (January 2001): 15–30, http://www.ossrea.net/eassrr/jan01/augustus.htm. See also Kituo

Cha Katiba, "The Domestic Relations Bill 2003," East African Center for Constitutional Development, Faculty of Law, Makerere University, 2005, http://www.kituo-chakatiba.co.ug/dorebil.htm; Stephen O. Murray, "Homosexuality in 'Traditional' Sub-Saharan Africa and Contemporary South Africa," February 14, 2005, http://semgai.free.fr/; Public Radio Exchange (PRX), "Homosexuality in Uganda," 2003–2005, http://www.prx.org/; Dan Elwana, "Church Backs Museveni against Homosexuality," *Daily Nation,* November 14, 1999, http://www.nationmedia.com; Human Rights Watch, "Uganda: Same Sex Ban Deepens Repression," July 12, 2005, http://hrw.org/.

SOCIAL CUSTOMS AND LIFESTYLE

The best source on this is Richard Nzita and Mbaga-Niwampa, *Peoples and Cultures of Uganda* (Kampala: Fountain Publishers, 1997) and Joachim Buwembo, *How to Be a Ugandan* (Kampala: Fountain Publishers, 2002). Other good sources include Aili Mali Tripp, *Women & Politics in Uganda* (Madison: University of Wisconsin Press, 2000); Augustus Nuwagaba, "Situation Analysis of Women in the Ugandan Political Economy," *Eastern Africa Social Science Research Review* 17, no. 1 (2001): 15–30, http://www.ossrea.net; A.B.K. Kasozi, "Higher Education in Uganda: Problems of Cost and Access for Women and Other Disadvantaged Groups" (paper presented at the Women's Worlds 2002 Congress, Makerere University, Kampala, Uganda, July 21–26, 2002), http://www.makerere.ac.ug/womenstudies/.

MUSIC, DANCE, AND DRAMA

Ronnie Graham, *The World of African Music,* vol. 2 of *Stern's Guide to Contemporary African Music* (Chicago: Research Associates, 1992); Gregory Barz, *Music in East Africa: Experiencing Music, Expressing Culture* (New York: Oxford University Press, 2004); Peter Cooke, "Republic of Uganda," in *The New Grove Dictionary of Music and Musicians,* vol. 26, ed. Stanley Sadie (London: Macmillan, 2001); Sylvia Nannyonga-Tamusuza, "Gender, Ethnicity and Politics in Kadongo-Kamu Music of Uganda: Analyzing the Song Kayanda," in *Playing with Identities in Contemporary Music in Africa,* ed. Mai Palmberg and Annemette Kirkegaard (Uppsala, Finland: Nordiska Afrikainstitutet in cooperation with the Sibelius Museum/Department of Musicology, Abo Akademi University, 2002). On dance and drama, see Susan Battye, Mercy Mirembe Ntangaare, and Ian Allan, *Dance and Drama in Uganda: The Pearl of Africa,* e-book, 2005, http://www.hushvideos.com/SB-Afr.shtml; Uganda National Theatre & Cultural Centre, "History and Mission of Uganda National Theatre & Cultural Centre," 2005, http://www.culturalcentre.or.ug; and Kampala Amateur Dramatics Society (KADS), 2005, http://kadsonline.org.

Index

About the Author

KEFA M. OTISO is Assistant Professor of Geography, Bowling Green State University, Bowling Green, Ohio.